THE SECRET HISTORY
OF MAGIC

THE

SECRET HISTORY OF

MAGIC

*The True Story
of the Deceptive Art*

PETER LAMONT &
JIM STEINMEYER

A TarcherPerigee Book

tarcherperigee

An imprint of Penguin Random House LLC
375 Hudson Street
New York, New York 10014

Illustration credits appear on page 355.

Most TarcherPerigee books are available at special quantity discounts for bulk
purchase for sales promotions, premiums, fund-raising, and educational needs.
Special books or book excerpts also can be created to fit specific needs. For details,
write: SpecialMarkets@penguinrandomhouse.com.

Library of Congress Cataloging-in-Publication Data

Names: Lamont, Peter, author. | Steinmeyer, Jim, 1958– author.
Title: The secret history of magic : the true story of the
deceptive art / Peter Lamont & Jim Steinmeyer.
Description: New York : TarcherPerigee, 2018. | Includes
bibliographical references and index. |
Identifiers: LCCN 2018002632 (print) | LCCN 2018005903
(ebook) | ISBN 9781524704452 (ebook) | ISBN 9780143130635 (hardback)
Subjects: LCSH: Magic tricks—History. | BISAC:
PERFORMING ARTS / Theater / Stagecraft.
Classification: LCC GV1543 (ebook) | LCC GV1543
.L36 2018 (print) | DDC 793.8—dc23
LC record available at https://lccn.loc.gov/2018002632

Printed in the United States of America
1   3   5   7   9   10   8   6   4   2

Book design by Katy Riegel

To Professor Eddie Dawes,
a true historian of the deceptive art.

CONTENTS

Preface   ix

CHAPTER 1: Origin Myths   1

CHAPTER 2: False Accusations   19

CHAPTER 3: Disenchantment   44

CHAPTER 4: Second Sight   70

CHAPTER 5: Separate Spheres   93

CHAPTER 6: The Confessions   119

CHAPTER 7: The Unmasking   150

CHAPTER 8: The Golden Age   186

CHAPTER 9: Variety   214

CHAPTER 10: Thought Transmissions   239

CHAPTER 11: Before Your Eyes   272

CHAPTER 12: The Real Secrets of Magic   303

CONTENTS

Acknowledgments   320

Notes   321

Index   346

List of Illustrations   355

About the Authors   357

PREFACE

WE ARE GOING to reveal some secrets. We are going to tell you the story of magic and explain what really happened. We wish to correct a few mistakes, but we also wish to tell a better story: a story that explains what magic has been, what it is, and why it matters.

However, there are many things that we are not going to tell you. We are not going to tell you about many of the conjurors who have been discussed by other historians. There are several conjurors who deserve a mention, no doubt, but they do not get one here. There are also a few centuries that we fail to discuss, and far too many countries. We have done what a magic audience does: we have focused on what seems important to us, and we have ignored what else is going on. We have done what historians do: we have told a particular story, not the whole story, about the past.

We do explain how some tricks were done, but competent magicians need not worry. The reason they need not worry, as it happens, is part of the story. It is one of the reasons why magic has survived. However, we have revealed some secrets because unless you have some sense of how magic works, you simply cannot understand what magic has been, what it is, and why it matters.

In any case, as you shall discover, the secrets of magic are not what you imagine them to be.

CHAPTER 1

ORIGIN MYTHS

A LONG TIME AGO, in ancient Egypt, there was a magician whose name was Djedi.[1] On one particular day, Djedi was summoned to appear before the Pharaoh. So he went to the palace and stood before the Pharaoh. And he performed a miraculous feat with a goose.

He severed the head of the goose from its body. He placed the head of the goose on one side of the great hall and the body of the goose on the other side of the hall. He then uttered some magic words, and the body of the goose stood up. It began to walk toward its own head. The head and the body became reconnected, and the goose stood up and cackled at the Pharaoh. Djedi then proceeded to do the same thing with a long-legged bird. Then with an ox.

"This," according to the historian of magic Sidney Clarke, "is the earliest conjuring performance of which any record has come down to us."[2] Clarke wrote that in the 1920s, and since then, historians of magic have agreed. For almost a century, they (no, we, because we are historians of magic, too) have claimed that the first recorded magic trick was the decapitation and resurrection of a goose.[3]

In fact, the story is a myth. It appears in the Westcar Papyrus, which was discovered in the 1820s. The story is one of a series of five tales that describe miraculous deeds. Djedi himself is described in mythical terms: it is said that he is 110 years old and is able to consume five hundred loaves of bread, half an ox, and one hundred jugs of beer. He also promises to make it rain and predicts the birth of future kings. Beyond this romantic tale, there is little reason to believe that Djedi even existed.

*The Westcar Papyrus. For almost a century, standard histories
have cited the fable of Djedi as the earliest record of a magic trick.*

Nevertheless, if you read a standard history of magic, this is how it begins. Historians are not trying to deceive you. This is not an attempt to conceal reality in order to create an illusion. Historians of magic, in certain respects, have been more like a magic audience. Sometimes we have not looked closely enough, or we have looked in the wrong place. Too often, we have listened to what magicians have claimed and believed too easily what we have been told. As a result, in the story of magic, things are not always as they appear to be. If you want to know what really happened, then you need to distinguish between myth and reality.

When you take a closer look, behind the unbelievable tales, you discover the more extraordinary truth. The real history of magic is a story of people from humble roots who traveled the world, made and lost fortunes, and deceived kings and queens. In order to survive, they concealed many secrets; yet they revealed some, and they stole others. They exposed the methods of mediums and psychics, and they pilfered those of rivals. They engaged in deception, exposure, and betrayal in an ongoing quest to make impossible things happen. And they managed to survive in a modern world of wonders by providing us with a unique kind of wonder.

First, however, we must begin the story, and we cannot begin with the antics of Djedi. After all, *this* story is fact, not fiction. So the first thing we must do is find a beginning, and if it is not Djedi, then where to start? As it happens, there has long been an alternative. The Westcar Papyrus was not translated for decades, until the end of the nineteenth century. By then, however, histories of magic had already appeared, such as Thomas Frost's *The Lives of the Conjurors*, which was published in 1876. Knowing nothing of Djedi and his resilient goose, Frost had to begin with a different trick. How, then, according to Frost, did the story of magic begin?

$\circlearrowleft$

A LONG TIME AGO, in ancient Egypt, there were two men whose names were Moses and Aaron. On one particular day, they were summoned to appear before the Pharaoh. So they went to the palace and stood before the Pharaoh. And they performed a miraculous feat with a stick.

Aaron cast his rod to the ground, and it transformed into a serpent. So the Pharaoh summoned his local magicians, and they performed a similar feat. Aaron proceeded to turn the waters of the Nile into blood, and then he made a plague of frogs appear. And, according to the book of Exodus, the Egyptian magicians did the same.

At the end of the nineteenth century, before the Westcar Papyrus was translated, we thought that the first recorded magic trick was a rod that transformed into a serpent. Thomas Frost did not explain how it was done, though he believed that it required "a high degree of skill."[4] However, Henry Ridgely Evans, who wrote the next history of magic, suggested a theory. The rod, he reckoned, was not really a rod but a hypnotized serpent, stiff as a pole, which awoke from its trance when it hit the ground.[5] This, they reckoned, was the first recorded magic trick, but Aaron was not the first magician. It was the Egyptian magicians, who did the same afterward, who were given credit for the first illusion. Aaron's version did not count, because it was considered a genuine miracle.

If you want to understand the history of magic, then you need to separate the wheat from the chaff. However, as this story reveals, this is not so easy. Of course, you must consider the reliability of the sources, but people interpret these differently. In the case of the Westcar Papyrus, for example, you merely need to take a closer look to see that it is a series of fables. However, in the case of the Bible, many people believe that it is true. Thus, what some regard as fiction, others believe to be real. Indeed, when the early histories of magic were being written, this was the standard view. It was believed that Moses and Aaron could perform miracles, but as heathens, the Egyptian magicians could not. Hence the conclusion that they resorted to trickery.

This made sense at the time, though it now seems a rather odd conclusion. But we always interpret the past in a way that fits with our present assumptions. We do this now, we did it then, and we did it long before. A few centuries earlier, for example, early modern folk took a different view. Like the Victorians, they believed in miracles, but most of them also believed in witchcraft. So when they discussed the book of Exodus, they considered other options. In the sixteenth and seventeenth centuries, demonologists were eager to stress the dangers of witchcraft. In order to convince folk that witchcraft was real, they appealed to what everyone then regarded as the most reliable source: the Bible. In short, if witchcraft was in the Bible, then witchcraft must be real. And, according to the demonologists, the first case of witchcraft was when the Egyptian magicians managed to duplicate the miracles of Aaron.

However, while most early modern folk believed that witchcraft was real, some were skeptical. These skeptics saw innocent people being persecuted, subjected to torture and sometimes death, and they tried to persuade the majority that witchcraft was a delusion. But they did not question the accuracy of the Bible, so they had to provide an explanation for how the Egyptian magicians did what they did. Their strategy was to make the case that these were merely magic tricks. In an attempt to make this more convincing, some suggested how the tricks were done.

According to one skeptic, Thomas Ady, the first feat was accomplished by using "slight of hand to throw down an artificial Serpent instead of his staffe."[6] Another skeptic, John Webster, added a few more details. He claimed that the fake snake was made of "painted linen, perfectly resembling a serpent, with Eyes and all." And, to make it seem more lifelike, "with the wiar . . . he maketh it to move." How, we might wonder, did he manage to duplicate the other miracles of Aaron? "As for the changing water into blood, and the producing of Frogs," Webster continued, "they were so easy to be done after the same manner, that they need not any particular explication."[7]

Now, you might be forgiven for thinking that this explanation sounds rather vague. That is certainly what demonologists such as Joseph Glanvill thought. Glanvill pointed out a basic flaw in the theory. He wondered how "those jugglers should know what signs Moses and Aaron would shew, and accordingly furnish themselves with counterfeit Serpents, Blood and Frogs . . . or had they those always in their pockets? If not, it was great luck for them that Moses and Aaron should shew those very miracles."[8] His point, of course, was intended to prove that the

Egyptian magicians had relied on witchcraft. Nevertheless, it is a very good point.

Over the centuries, then, we have argued about various kinds of magic. We have interpreted evidence in different ways, based on different assumptions about what magic is and whether it is real. There have been times when it was normal to believe in witchcraft or in the miracles of a particular god. We continue to believe in a variety of psychic and supernatural phenomena. Some of us, on the other hand, would say that we do not believe in any kind of magic. But we believe in the existence of unseen things, of places unvisited, and of goals not yet reached. We believe in phenomena that are unobservable, such as gravity and democracy. We can see things fall and people vote and so can believe in invisible powers. We believe in such things because we assume that they exist, in some sense, beyond our vision.

We do not see such things as magical, of course, because they seem so ordinary. They are part of our daily experience, and so we take them for granted. But we also take other things for granted, such as mobile phones and air travel, which our ancestors would have regarded as impossible. Few of us truly understand how such things work, though we find them unremarkable. In other words, our ideas about what is possible and what is not have changed. And yet, as they have changed over the centuries and we have become harder to impress, magicians have continued to astonish us with magic tricks. The story of magic is a story of how, no matter what we take for granted, we can always be astonished.

First, however, we must begin the story, and we cannot begin with the antics of Djedi or with the miracle stories of Exodus. These were clearly not magic tricks, so they are not the earliest recorded magic tricks. As we shall see, the earliest references to what are clearly magic tricks do not appear until later. Meanwhile, we still need an origin story before we can begin. Origin stories are fundamental to understanding what we are talking about. Origin stories are, in fact, forms of definition. By describing how we began, they tell us something about who we are. The story of Genesis tells us that we are part of God's creation. The story of evolution tells us that we are part of the natural world. The story of how we came to be is a definition of who we are.

History, in general, is a form of definition. We tell stories about the past in order to understand the present. We tell stories about our ancestors in order to understand ourselves. The stories we tell, and the ones we prefer, define us in particular ways. They provide us with traditions that we can embrace, which shape how we see ourselves. And when we begin a history of something at a particular point, we are saying that this is when it began. Whatever happened earlier was something else; if not, then we would have begun at an earlier point. So choosing a beginning is important, because it should tell us something about the subject at hand. With this in mind, here is a new origin myth, though it may sound rather familiar. It is no truer than the story from the book of Exodus, though it is a little earlier. More important, it is a form of definition, which tells us something about what magic is.

○

IN THE BEGINNING, God created the heavens and the earth. And the earth was without form. Then He made light appear, and He saw that it was good. And it was indeed good, because now He could see that the earth was without form. And so He decided to improve things. He separated the land from the seas, and the day from the night, and He created vegetation and a variety of beasts. And He saw that it was good, and it was indeed good. But nobody else could see how good it looked, and so He created the first audience. But here's the thing: Adam and Eve did not express the slightest sense of wonder. Indeed, throughout the book of Genesis, there is not a single expression of wonder.

This is a better origin myth for magic, because it tells us something about the experience of magic. In the beginning, like the characters in Genesis, we live in a world of constant wonders. As infants, we experience the world as chaos because we do not understand the rules. Before we can experience magical things, we first need to understand that they should not happen. This is why young infants are not impressed by magic tricks, because they do not yet understand, for example, that objects are not supposed to appear and disappear. We have to learn the rules of what is possible before we can understand what is impossible. We need to form a worldview that rules out certain events before we can marvel at what should not happen. Until then, we live in a world in which anything is possible, but nothing is extraordinary.

The experience of magic depends on beliefs about what is possible and what is not. The problem for magicians throughout history has been that the limits of possibility have changed. Over the centuries, we have encountered a series of extraordinary technological developments. We have discovered the power of steam and electricity. We have been given the telephone, the television, and cinema. We are now surrounded by automobiles and airplanes, and we depend on computers and the internet. Our world has become full of technological wonders that our ancestors would have viewed as magical. Today, we take them for granted. Meanwhile, as all of this has been happening, magicians have had to find new ways to astonish us. Otherwise, they could not have survived.

This is the story of how they succeeded. This is the story of how they reminded us not to take extraordinary things for granted.

◯

THE ORIGINS OF MAGIC are long, long ago. The roots of deception are deeper. Deception, after all, is natural. The chameleon mimics its surroundings and seems to disappear. The stick insect transforms into a twig, and the cricket into a leaf. The bird feigns a broken wing and misdirects the predator from the nest. The opossum plays dead. The dog hides when it hears the bath running and pretends not to hear its master's voice. Deception is a matter of survival.

We humans can deceive before we can walk. As infants, we cry and pretend to be hurt in order to get attention. We can mislead with our eyes, before we can speak, and as soon as we can speak, we can lie. We deny what we did to avoid punishment and pretend to be sick to get off school. The older we get, the better we get, and the better we get at justifying it. We lie to spare the feelings of others, to make them feel better, or so we tell ourselves. We lie for the greater good, we claim. We deceive others, and we kid ourselves.

In short, deception comes easy. We deceive in order to survive, to get what we want, and to avoid what we'd rather avoid. And we know that others deceive us. We can spot a lie, when it is accompanied by a suspicious look or a clumsy delivery. We are wary of sales pitches and ideological sermons, and of any stranger who promises something but seems to be after something else. We know perfectly well that we can be deceived, and yet we are frequently deceived. We swallow the lie and believe the hype. We know well that others deceive us, but still we are prone to deception. This is because, in that moment, we do not realize that we are being deceived.

But magic is different. It is a unique form of deception, in which we know that we are being deceived, but still we are deceived. In such conditions, the liar, the snake oil salesman, and the con artist would fail. Their deceptions depend on a lack of suspicion. The magician, however, is known to deceive and yet has to succeed in spite of this. Animals and infants may deceive, and adults do so frequently. But only magicians explain that they will deceive you, and then live up to their word. So, while the origins of deception may be in our evolutionary past and our earliest years of development, the story of magic is different. It is a story about humans who deceived humans who knew that they were being deceived.

The true origins of the magic trick are a mystery, but perhaps that is appropriate. It allows us to try to guess, in hindsight, how this extraordinary thing might have happened. Perhaps it was invented in the Neolithic Age, while someone was casually playing with a stone. Perhaps, as it was being passed from hand to hand, it was unknowingly dropped. Perhaps, when its absence was suddenly noticed, this minor act of clumsiness was transformed into a moment of astonishment. Perhaps, having figured out what had happened, this accidental pioneer of wonder decided to show it to someone else. And so, without a wand to wave, the first magician appeared. Perhaps, but what the first trick was, and who performed it, remains a mystery.

There are references to various kinds of magic in ancient Egypt, India, and China, but we cannot be sure that these belong here, in a story about humans who deceived humans who knew that they were being deceived. We thought we had found magic tricks in ancient Egypt, but as we have seen, we were wrong about that. There would have been performers of magic tricks then, and perhaps they even served as inspiration for stories about decapitated geese or rods that changed into serpents. But, at present, we have no reliable evidence of this.[9] There are also some who trace the origins of conjuring to shamans.[10] And there is certainly evidence of shamans, in different cultures, using trickery in various ways. However, we do not know when they started doing this.

Once we get to ancient Greece, however, we are on more solid ground. Plato (c. 428–348 BCE) refers to magic tricks in *The Republic*, comparing them to other kinds of illusions. He observed how "the same objects look bent and straight when seen in and out of water . . . and every kind of deception like this is clearly present in our soul. So illusionist painting, by exploiting our natural shortcoming, is nothing short of wizardry, likewise conjuring and many other such tricks."[11] Precisely what these tricks were, however, Plato does not mention.

In the first century, Seneca the Younger refers to a particular trick: the "cup and dice." The cup and dice was an early version of the "cups and balls," which is still performed today. Seneca, as it happens, was not particularly impressed. As far as he was concerned, a magic trick was a trivial diversion, much like the arguments of sophists. The sophists, of course, were famous for paradoxes, such as:

That what you have not lost, you have.
You have not lost horns, therefore you have horns.

Seneca dismissed these "tricky word-plays" as "sophistries" and a waste of time. He sneered, "The man who is asked whether he has horns on his head is not such a fool as to feel for them on his forehead, nor again so silly or dense that you can persuade him by means of argumentation. . . . Such quibbles are just as harmlessly deceptive as the juggler's cup and dice, in which it is the very trickery that pleases me. But show me how the trick is done, and I have lost my interest therein." As far as Seneca was concerned, "Not to know them does no harm and mastering them does no good."[12]

Seneca might have thought that paradoxes and magic tricks were trivial, but others would have disagreed. After all, Plato's teacher, Socrates, had been rather fond of paradoxes. In a famous dialogue with Theaetetus, he had provided a few examples. The apparent contradictions caused Theaetetus to be amazed, until his head began to swim, and he wanted to figure out what was going on. This sense of wonder, according to

Socrates, is where philosophy begins. And, according to Socrates, the paradox is a source of wonder.

These early references to magic tricks are rather like origin myths, because they also tell us something about the nature of magic. On the one hand, the magic trick is trivial, because it is merely an illusion. On the other hand, it is far from trivial, because it is a source of wonder. This has been an ongoing theme throughout the history of magic. Some have dismissed magic as a trivial diversion, because it is not real. But the point of magic is not that it is real; the point is that it creates an effect. And the effect of magic is this: something happens that cannot happen. This is a paradox and a source of wonder.

This is the purpose of magic: to astonish us. We think we know what is going on. We think we know what is possible. But the magician shows us that we do not really know what is going on and that the impossible is possible. We know, of course, that it is an illusion, but that is not the point. The point is that as we watch a magic trick, we experience the impossible happening. We know that the event is not real, but in that moment, the experience is real. In one sense, magic is not real, but in another sense, it is. It provides a real experience of astonishment by showing us something that we know is an illusion yet still seems genuinely impossible. Magic has survived, since ancient times, by providing this experience.

Here, for example, is the first detailed description of a conjuring performance. It is from a man called Napeus, who went to the theater and saw a remarkable thing:

> I can tell you that one thing I saw made me almost speechless with astonishment. A man came forward, and, setting down a three-legged table, placed three little cups on it. Then under these cups he hid some little round white pebbles, such as we find on the banks of rapid streams. At one moment he

would hide them under each cup; and at another moment (I don't know how) he would show them all under a single cup; and then again he would make them entirely disappear from under the cups and exhibit them between his lips. Then he would swallow them and, drawing forward the spectators who stood near him, he would take one pebble from a man's nose, another from a man's ear, and the third from a man's head, and after picking them up he would make them disappear from sight again.[13]

Now, as it happens, like the story of Djedi, this is a work of fiction. The author is the third-century Greek writer Alciphron, and it appears in one of his epistles. These were fictitious letters written to portray the character of different classes of people. In this case, the character is Napeus, who is described as a simple rustic. However, even though the letter is fiction, it is clearly based on a genuine performance. It is, like the earlier reference to the cup and dice, an early version of the cups and balls. In other words, the story and the character of Napeus are fictional, but the trick itself is genuine. In one sense, it is not real. In another sense, it is real.

Like many fictions, the story contains some truth. The character of Napeus, a simple rustic, is made almost speechless with astonishment. He does not know how it is done, but he understands that it depends on sleight of hand. At the end of the story, Napeus concludes that the performer is "a very nimble-fingered gentleman!" Even the character of a simple rustic, then, is portrayed as someone who understands this: he is watching a trick. Like Plato, who described magic tricks as an illusion, and Seneca, who described them as trickery, ancient folk could understand that magic tricks were simply tricks. Elsewhere, Plato had also compared the conjuror to the sophist, whose arguments are illusions, based on deception.[14] In a similar way, Sextus Empiricus (c. 160–210 CE) compared magic tricks to deceptive rhetoric: he pointed out that in both cases, we "know that they are deceiving us, even if we do not know how they are deceiving us."[15]

Later, Augustine wrote about magic tricks. He also wrote at length about other kinds of magic, distinguishing true miracles from demonic magic. He was subsequently credited with having performed a few miracles of his own. However, he was quite capable of recognizing trickery for what it was, and so, it seems, were others at the time. Augustine describes how people "watch carefully and pay close attention to the conjurer, who freely acknowledges that he uses nothing but trickery; and if they are duped, because they cannot delight in their own knowledge, they delight in the knowledge of the one who has duped them."[16] From Plato to Augustine, we get the same picture of performers who were honest about their use of trickery and of audiences who were aware that they were being tricked.

Now, you might wonder why this point is being spelled out so clearly. After all, this is hardly a paradox: our ancestors understood that a trick was a trick. The reason for making this clear is that, centuries later, a myth was invented. When the first histories of conjuring appeared in the late nineteenth century, they told a different story. According to the historians Thomas Frost and Henry Ridgely Evans, our ancient ancestors were gullible types who could not distinguish illusion from reality. According to them, in ancient times, magic was used "to dupe the ignorant masses" and to make "their minds subject to priestly influence."[17] In fact, for Frost and Evans, the story of premodern magic was one long tale of gullibility. In the Middle Ages, magic was used "to gull a susceptible public."[18] As for the early modern period, this was "a much less enlightened age," when "many, even among the educated and better informed, regarded as real what the least educated spectator of the present day would know to be illusory."[19] In short, the story of magic, according to Frost and Evans, was this: before we became modern, we believed that magic was real.

There is a reason why this story was told, and why it continued to be told. It is another example of how history can be used to define who we are. We have compared ourselves to our gullible ancestors and have seen ourselves as smarter than them. We have defined our modern selves as rational by describing a primitive, irrational past. However, as is often the case in the history of magic, things are not as they appear to be. As we have seen, according to the evidence, our premodern ancestors were not so gullible. Nevertheless, historians of magic created this illusion. So how did they do it? How did they manage to give the impression that our ancestors believed that magic tricks were real?

Trickery in a Greek temple, a quite different kind of deception.

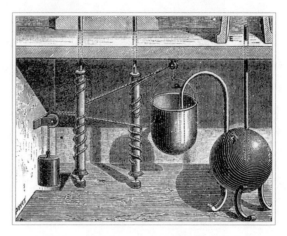

Lighting an altar fire automatically opened the doors.

Here is how they did it: they began the story of magic with references to the trickery of ancient priests. They explained how the gods appeared before their worshippers in ancient temples, with the help of smoke and mirrors. They described how Greek temple doors flew open, accompanied by the sound of thunder, which appeared to be due to supernatural forces but was, in fact, due to mechanical trickery. They revealed how a variety of ancient wonders were produced by optical illusions, hydrostatics, and acoustics. They pointed out that, in ancient times, trickery was used to create apparent miracles.

This kind of magic was designed to be taken seriously, and it probably was. Faced with an unexplained event and told that it was a miracle, ancient folk probably believed the claims of their religious leaders. However, throughout history, countless people have claimed to have supernatural powers, and many have used trickery to fake them. They still do, and many people, too many people, believe that they are real. But this is not the magic of the conjuror. This is a different kind of deception. It is a lie, a scam, a piece of fraud, and we have always been prone to that kind of deception.

So when we talk about the trickery of ancient priests, we are talking about another kind of deception. If we begin the story of magic with the trickery of ancient priests, before moving on to the magic of the conjuror, we create an illusion: first, there were magic tricks that people thought were real; then, there were magic tricks that people knew were trickery. We create the illusion that people used to believe in magic tricks, and then they did not.

That is how the illusion was done, and it is a tad ironic. We accused our ancestors of confusing one kind of magic for another. However, it was us, the historians of magic, who were confusing one kind of magic for another. Of course, it was not an attempt to deceive. The historians simply took it for granted that ancient folk were gullible and then found cases of trickery that ancient folk believed to be real. It is merely an

An early depiction of cups and balls,
a trick that dates back to ancient
Greece, and perhaps earlier.

example of how writing history can be like being in a magic audience: what we see depends on where we look.

Nevertheless, the myth was created, and the story continued to be told. It would become a major theme in the history of magic, which would define magic in a trivial way. Rather than being seen as a source of wonder, magic would be defined, more than anything else, as something that was not real. What was said of our ancient ancestors was also said of our early modern ancestors. It was said that, during the age of witchcraft, jugglers who performed tricks were persecuted as witches. Historians of magic looked for evidence of this, and even managed to find some. We cited cases of conjurors who were persecuted, tortured, and put to death, simply for performing tricks. We regarded this as clear evidence that we had once thought that magic tricks were real, but that we now know they are not. As we shall see, we were wrong about that. This, too, was an illusion. But how did we do it? What really happened? What did people really think about magic tricks during the age of witchcraft?

The story begins, as this chapter did, with the needless death of a bird . . .

CHAPTER 2

FALSE ACCUSATIONS

IN THE EARLY sixteenth century, Thomas Brandon killed a pigeon. He did this at the court of King Henry VIII, and he provoked "wondering and admiration." This is how he did it: he painted a picture of a dove on a wall and pointed to a pigeon on top of a nearby roof. He then asked the audience to watch as he stabbed the picture of the dove with a knife. The pigeon fell from the roof, "starke dead."[1]

The story of Brandon's pigeon trick is told by Reginald Scot in his book *The Discoverie of Witchcraft* (1584). Scot was skeptical about witchcraft, and wrote this book to debunk it. He claimed that witches had no magical powers. He argued that evidence of witchcraft could be explained by delusion and deception. He wanted to show that "a naturall thing [can] be made to seeme supernaturall."[2] One of the ways that he did this was to reveal how magic tricks were done. He exposed the secret of the cups and balls and how to make a coin disappear. He explained how to cut a piece of lace in half and then put it back together. He revealed, with accompanying illustrations, how to thrust a bodkin into your head, or through your tongue, without coming to harm. And he also included an explanation for how Brandon killed the pigeon.

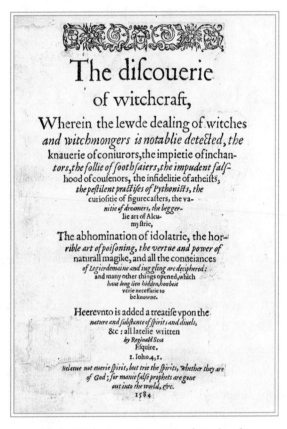

Scot's 1584 book, The Discoverie of Witchcraft.

According to Scot, this is how he did it. The pigeon was secretly given poison, so that it would live no more than a half hour. The bird was released and landed on a roof near to the performance area. The magician then began the performance and started to talk. He continued to talk until the poison kicked in, and the pigeon fell from the roof.[3]

If this were true, however, then Brandon must have been a courageous fellow. After all, the trick depended on the pigeon being in view. What if it had simply flown off or landed out of sight? And how, precisely, did Brandon time the performance to coincide with the bird's demise? Did he stand in front of Henry VIII, a king not particularly known for his patience, and stall for up to a half hour by talking, pointing, and silently praying that the pigeon stayed where it was?

As it happens, Scot was only guessing at how it might have been done. He had not even seen the trick. He was merely reciting a story he had heard, about something that had happened at least four decades earlier.[4] However, for Scot, that did not matter. His main concern was not *how* it was done but rather that it *could* be done. It did not matter which method was used, so long as there was a way to do it. Scot was trying to undermine belief in witchcraft by providing natural explanations for seemingly supernatural events. He was trying to show that a natural thing could be made to seem supernatural.

In the process, however, he suggested that people mistook magic tricks for real magic. He spoke of card tricks that were performed "to the wonder and astonishment of simple beholders, which conceive not that kind of illusion, but expect miracles and strange works." He claimed that, when Brandon performed his pigeon trick, people had thought it was real and that this would still be the case. "If this, or the like feate should be done by an old woman," Scot declared, "everie bodie would crie out for fier and faggot to burne the witch."[5]

This, however, was merely rhetoric. After all, nobody wanted to burn Brandon as a witch. Scot's account of the pigeon trick was based on nothing more than hearsay, but even if we take the story at face value, Brandon was not persecuted. On the contrary, he was licensed by the king to entertain. He was paid the handsome sum of three shillings and fourpence to do so. He became such a successful entertainer that he was made a Freeman of the City of London. Far from being persecuted for performing tricks, Brandon made a rather good living at it.

In fact, when you look at the evidence, you see that early modern people regularly distinguished between magic tricks and witchcraft. Demonologists and witch-hunters, who were adamant that witchcraft was real and evil, also made the distinction. Even the notorious *Malleus Maleficarum* distinguished between witchcraft and the kind of magic that "can be done without devils, since it is artificially done by the agility of men who show things and conceal them, as in the case of the tricks of conjurers."[6] Throughout the sixteenth and seventeenth centuries, the most ferocious enemies of witchcraft distinguished between the work of the devil and the innocent tricks of jugglers. They understood that "divers men, by reason of the agilitie of their bodies, & sleight of their hands, are able to work divers feats, which seem strange to the beholders, and yet not meddle with Witchcraft."[7] "As if a merry Juggler who plays tricks of Legerdemain at a Fair or Market," wrote philosopher Henry More, "were such an abomination."[8] In short, they believed in witchcraft, but they understood that magic tricks were not the work of the devil.

Our ancestors were not as gullible as we have sometimes thought them to be. Of course, they believed in witchcraft, and we (well, most of us) no longer do. But witchcraft beliefs were part of a wider contemporary worldview, in which science and religion, alchemy and chemistry, astrology and astronomy, were not yet separated. In the seventeenth century, the most eminent figures of the "scientific revolution," such as Sir Isaac Newton and Robert Boyle, could study alchemy or believe in second sight. They were Christians who believed that the Bible was true, and several, including Newton, used it to calculate the date of Creation. They took certain things for granted, while they questioned other things.

We now know more about how the world works, and so we see it differently. But if we had lived there and then, we would have believed in God and in the Genesis story of Creation. We would have believed in witchcraft, no doubt, because it would have made sense at the time. God was good, but bad things happened, and evil was the work of the devil. Strange things happened, which demanded explanation, and witchcraft was a popular explanation. It was denounced, at that time, as the work of the devil, but in other ways, it was not so different from later beliefs in spirits and other invisible forces, such as fate or luck.

Like other religious beliefs, of course, witchcraft was exploited for various purposes. It was used to explain natural disasters and to justify social inequality. It was used to seek revenge on a neighbor and to punish unorthodox thinking. There was persecution, and sometimes torture, though it was not as common as we once thought. Magistrates considered the evidence and often found folk innocent. The darker tales are better known, of course, but the worst cases were not typical cases. And when belief in witchcraft declined, we went on to blame other evils for natural disasters and appealed to other unseen forces to justify social inequality. We continued to fight with our neighbors and to punish unorthodox thinking. We continued to persecute and sometimes torture. We did this in the name of one god or another, or one political ideology or another. We continued to justify appalling behavior by appealing to the power of invisible things.

If we look at the world of our ancestors, as they saw it, then we can see that witchcraft made sense at the time. If we had lived there and then, we would have taken similar things for granted. We would have considered evidence according to the standards of the age. This is not gullibility. It is what we have always done, and what we continue to do. It is only in hindsight, when we think we know better, that we wonder how our ancestors could have been so blind. And no doubt our descendants will look back on us and wonder what on earth we were thinking.

Meanwhile, throughout the age of witchcraft, jugglers performed magic tricks without persecution, because their audiences understood that they were watching tricks. Jugglers made a living on the street, at fairs, and sometimes indoors for wealthier company. They entertained the common folk, peasants and town dwellers, merchants and military. Some of them entertained nobility and royalty with similar tricks, for better money, though probably with more polite patter. And those who got the premium gigs were the first magic celebrities.

There was the Frenchman, Gonin, who entertained early-sixteenth-century Parisians, and whose name was kept alive by others who borrowed it, no doubt without permission, hoping to capitalize upon his fame. There was the Italian Scotto, who seems to have performed exclusively for European nobility, from the court of Emperor Rudolf II to that of Queen Elizabeth I. He appeared in the writings of Thomas Nashe and the soon-to-be King James. The most famous of them all, however, was an Englishman, William Vincent, of whom you will have heard. Indeed, he may be the most famous magician in history. His name appears in poems and plays, and he was cited in contemporary satire. He was, on one occasion, compared to Satan, but this was meant in jest. The name by which he was known, however, was not William Vincent. He was known throughout the land, and you will have heard of him by his stage name: Hocus Pocus.

When James became King of England, Vincent became known as "the King's most excellent Hocus Pocus." He was licensed in 1619 to "exercise the art of Legerdemaine." He performed the cups and balls and card tricks, swallowed daggers, and pulled ribbons from his mouth. Along with his company, he presented tumbling, vaulting, and dancing on ropes. He toured the land—or some of it, at least—performing in Leicester, Gloucester, and Coventry. At times of contagious sickness, when strangers were considered particularly risky, he was paid to leave as soon as possible. When he performed, he engaged in strange patter, a mixture of Latin and gibberish:

"Hocus pocus, tontus talontus, vade celeriter jubeo." As he commanded things to disappear quickly ("vade celeriter jubeo"), he opened his hands, one at a time, saying, "Here is nothing and there is nothing."[9] This was the essence of his magic and his script: first there is something, then there is nothing. Hocus Pocus became a household name, a name that became synonymous with magic, while the name of William Vincent disappeared.

These were the most famous jugglers of the early modern period, but there had been others. There are references to jugglers in the early fourteenth century, who performed at the court of Edward II. Indeed, there are earlier references to "jugglers," but these may have been minstrels who did not perform tricks. Those who did, however, continued to perform the cups and balls, as contemporary illustrations reveal. The most famous of these images is *The Conjurer* by Hieronymus Bosch, which shows a fifteenth-century juggler performing the classic trick, while a distracted member of the crowd is having his purse snatched. The itinerant juggler was often regarded with suspicion, though this had as much to do with his being an itinerant as with his being a juggler. In a predominantly rural society, strangers were difficult to miss and harder to trust.

There were also amateurs who dabbled with tricks. There are fifteenth-century manuscripts that reveal novel ways to play with food. One describes how to make an egg move by itself, by previously hollowing out the egg and attaching it to a fine piece of hair. Others describe how to use the same method to make a loaf of bread dance on the table or to cause a dead fish to jump out of the pan. Today, such tricks would struggle to succeed, where modern lighting might reveal the secret hair, but they would have worked better in the darker rooms of late medieval homes. And those who knew about the secret uses of fine hair could still be astonished when an apple moved by itself, with no threads attached. They did not realize that someone had secretly made a hole in the apple and placed a beetle inside.[10]

The Conjuror, *by Hieronymus Bosch, c. 1502,*
shows a cups and balls performance.

By the time that Scot published *Discoverie of Witchcraft*, a few tricks
of the trade had already been revealed in books that were available to
those with the money to buy them and the education to read them. Performing magic tricks might be a diverting hobby for a gentleman, but
legerdemain was a hard profession. Indeed, Scot regretted having to dis-
close the secrets of juggling "to the hindrance of the poore men as live
thereby." He admired John Cautares, a Frenchman in London, who was
"a matchless fellowe for legierdemaine." His sleight of hand, according to
Scot, was the best "of anie man that liveth this daie." Cautares did not
make a living from this, however, and had to "laboureth . . . with the
sweat of his browes."[11] As for those who made it their profession, the
hours were long and the earnings precarious, as they sought tossed

pennies from passersby or took their tricks into the taverns, where the audiences were captive, if not flush.

Nevertheless, performed correctly, feats of legerdemain could astonish some of the finest minds of the age. Girolamo Cardano, the remarkable Italian polymath of the sixteenth century, admitted that he simply could not explain a card trick he was shown. The performer asked someone to select a card and hide it, and then he revealed the name of the card. "Now," wondered Cardano, "perhaps this could have been attributed to manual dexterity, but that does not explain at all what happened next." The card was returned to the pack, more cards were selected, "and we realized that the person who had first drawn the card drew the same one each time." Unable to figure it out, he then brought a clever acquaintance to see the trick, who "confessed he could not understand how it was done." Cardano agreed that he had "never been able to work out a rational explanation," though he nevertheless attributed it to legerdemain, admitting that the juggler "proved cleverer than we were."[12]

In the seventeenth century, Francis Bacon had a similar experience. He was shown a card trick by a juggler, who told him what card he was thinking of. Bacon could not work out how the trick was done, and so he discussed it with a learned man. They considered the possibility of confederacy and of some kind of psychological ruse. They did not discuss the possibility of witchcraft. Nevertheless, the keen eyes of the most systematic of observers, the father of the scientific method, struggled to reveal the mystery.[13]

Meanwhile, early stage-conjuring technology was being used to create theatrical effects. In late medieval Passion plays, the character of Jesus might disappear through a trapdoor or be resurrected with the assistance of a pulley. In Shakespeare's *The Tempest*, Ariel clapped his hands upon a banquet table, and the banquet disappeared, with the help of a reversing tabletop. In numerous popular productions throughout the early modern period, actors were stabbed with trick knives and hanged from gimmicked ropes.[14] These effects were designed to be convincing, but audiences did not rush to help or run from the theater in fear. On the contrary, these effects attracted the public, who enjoyed an entertaining illusion. Indeed, they were sometimes added to the play, even when they were unnecessary to the plot, simply to attract the public.[15]

In the days of Reginald Scot, then, magic tricks could be found on the streets, at common fairs, at royal courts and in Shakespearean theater. At every level, they could be enjoyed as seemingly impossible illusions that were the product of deception. Beyond the world of entertainment, of course, there were always darker forms of deception. This was the case throughout the early modern period, as it has been ever since. There were some who used sleight of hand to cheat at cards or in a game of "fast and loose." There were those who pretended to have magical powers, and some engaged in deliberate fraud. But this is not the magic of the conjuror. This is a different kind of deceit. It is a lie, a scam, a piece of fraud, and we have always been prone to that kind of deception. The story of magic, as we explained, is a story about humans who deceived humans who knew that they were being deceived. That is the story of magic, though it is not quite the story of magicians, because magicians have not always played by the rules.

Consider the notorious Bornelio Feats, a shadowy figure of dubious character. Feats, we are told, loved good liquor and had a red face to prove it. He seems to have been known by different names, as "Hilles" and possibly "Cuts."[16] This may have been a useful strategy, since he had a reputation for great skill at cards, con games, and practical jokes. According to one story, he challenged a man, for the princely bet of £100, to stay in a room for an hour. He then put the man in a room over a stable and set fire to the stable below. Feats was also suspected of indulging in witchcraft and seems to have been good at training performing dogs. In other words, there were many good reasons why he might have wished to remain anonymous.

One of his many victims was a Mr. Powell, who made fun of Feats's red face. After dinner—and a good deal of liquor—Feats asked for a dish of nuts. He then asked a gentleman to think of a card, and if he would like the name of the card in red or black letters. The man chose red, and he was told to take a nut and crack it open. Inside the nut was a small piece of parchment. Written on the parchment was the seven of spades (the card that the man had chosen), and it was written in red letters. Feats then repeated the trick with Mr. Powell. Powell thought of a card, chose a nut, and eagerly cracked it open. This time, however, the nut was filled with "filthy, black, stinkinge stuff," which went into Powell's mouth and over his face and took more than a half hour to remove. Mr. Powell, though covered in filth, was filled with admiration.

But Feats had not yet finished with him. On another occasion, he showed Powell a trick with three supposed virgins. He asked the landlord of an inn if there were any maids in the house, and the landlord said that there were three. Feats asked for a basin of water. To this, he added a special root. He then placed a knife in the water and told it to "get up presently" if the first young woman was a maid. The knife immediately shot upward and stuck in a beam of the roof. He then placed another knife in the basin and demanded similar proof of the second young woman. Once again, the knife flew upward and stuck in the handle of the first knife. But then the knife was asked to confirm the virtue of the third young woman. It did not move at all. When pressed, the landlord finally admitted that the young woman had a secret child. This deeply impressed Powell, who immediately offered to buy the special root for forty shillings. And, or so it was said at the time, he might have tried every maid in Christendom before he got the knife to fly upward again.[17]

Such stories are, at the very least, exaggerations. Similar tricks can be found in Scot's *Discoverie of Witchcraft*, but they would have looked rather less impressive than the stories imply. Nevertheless, the stories suggest something about Feats's reputation. He appears to be the sort of man who used trickery to con and cheat and to pretend to have supernatural powers. Certainly, some suspected that he indulged in witchcraft and that he had magical powers. One man even suggested that Feats performed real magic but disguised what he did, in order to avoid suspicion. He thought that, when Feats performed magic tricks, he sometimes included some genuine magic, so that the audience would not suspect and would think that they were watching tricks. This curious theory made sense, of course, only if you believed that Feats was a witch. But even then, it assumed that audiences, when they watched Feats perform, thought that they were watching tricks.

In other words, even in the case of a dubious character such as Feats, when he said that he was performing tricks, people would believe him. This is what all the evidence shows: when early modern folk watched magic tricks, they did not think it was witchcraft. Nevertheless, historians of magic would later tell a different story. We would claim that, throughout the early modern period, magic tricks were mistaken for witchcraft. We would claim that jugglers were persecuted as witches. We would even conjure up evidence of this and create an illusion of early modern gullibility that many people believed was real.

This is how it was done.

$\circlearrowleft$

REGINALD SCOT WAS trying to show that witches had no magical powers. He was trying to show that a natural thing can be made to seem supernatural. In the process, he claimed that people mistook magic tricks for witchcraft and would want to burn the performer as a witch. But this was rhetoric; he provided no evidence of this. Of course, during the age of witchcraft, if somebody claimed to have magical powers, then they might be persecuted. But all the evidence shows that when magicians were open about their use of deception, audiences believed them.[18]

Nevertheless, following Scot, other books appeared that revealed how magic tricks were done. In the process, they also claimed that magic tricks were mistaken for witchcraft. *The Art of Jugling* (1612), for example, said that "many when they heare of any rare exploit performed which cannot enter into their capacity, and is beyond their reach, straight they attribute it to be done by the Devill."[19] These books were simply copying Scot, however, and taking his claim for granted. Indeed, some copied him literally, because they plagiarized large chunks of his book. They might make references to "silly people" who thought that juggling tricks were the work of the devil, but they provided no evidence of such gullibility.[20]

Nevertheless, the myth persisted. In the eighteenth century, books that revealed how magic tricks were done referred to people who "imagine that many deceptions cannot be performed without the assistance of the gentleman of the cloven hoof," noting that in the past, many had mistaken trickery for the supernatural.[21] This kind of rhetoric was not new, but it was useful. It allowed publishers to justify the work in terms of its educational value, which fit neatly into the popular notion of "rational recreations." The work was not simply a trivial exposure, they claimed, but a lesson in rational thinking. However, they provided no evidence that people had actually mistaken magic tricks for witchcraft.

Nevertheless, the myth persisted. By the nineteenth century, it was taken for granted. The view expressed by Reginald Scot was also expressed by Sir Walter Scott, who claimed that "the common feats of jugglers, or professors of legerdemain" were "wonders at which in our fathers' time men would have cried out either sorcery or miracles."[22] When reviewing the shows of Victorian magicians, the press might remark that, in the past, the conjuror would have been burned at the stake. Meanwhile, Victorian conjurors reinforced the myth by claiming that they were performing a new kind of magic: "modern magic." Modern magic, they said, was for modern audiences, who (now) understood that magic was an illusion. Modern magicians praised science, denounced superstition, and chastised their ancestors for being so gullible as to believe that magic was real. This made them appear to be modern and more respectable, which was very good for the box office. But they provided no evidence that their ancestors had been so gullible.

Nevertheless, the myth persisted, because it was easy for the Victorians to believe. They assumed that they were living in a modern age and that their ancestors had been more primitive. With the growing influence of evolutionary thought, past societies were increasingly assumed to be *naturally* more primitive than modern ones. Victorian psychologists and anthropologists regarded magical beliefs as relics of the distant past and their survival as evidence of insufficient advancement.[23] This was a flattering story for modern audiences: they could watch a magic trick and understand that it was trickery while imagining how their primitive ancestors would have been less rational than them.

It was at this time, and in this context, that the earliest histories of conjuring appeared. When Thomas Frost wrote *The Lives of the Conjurors* in 1876, he simply took it for granted that magic tricks had been mistaken for witchcraft. He described a period prior to the eighteenth century when magic was regarded as genuine and when conjurors were persecuted as witches. He wrote a section on the "persecution of conjurors," though he had no evidence of this at all. Indeed, his only example of a persecuted conjuror was of a man who was actually an occultist.

Nevertheless, the myth persisted, as historians of magic continued to contrast magic past and present. In *Ancient and Modern Magic* (1879), Arprey Vere contrasted "our forefathers," who "flew to the aid of *diablerie* and the supernatural for an elucidation of the mystery," with the present age, "which is distinguished for its matter-of-fact treatment of all that appears mysterious and unusual."[24] According to the introduction to Henry Ridgely Evans's *The Old and the New Magic* (1906), the transformation from the old to the new was an example of evolution, from an old belief that magic was supernatural to a new belief that it was not. "[T]he spread of modern magic and its proper comprehension," it was declared with confidence, "are an important sign of progress."[25]

This story of magic was merely part of a modern origin myth, which told the story of how we became the modern folk that we are. It defined modern people as rational by describing earlier folk as irrational and by telling a tale of progress since. It was a flattering tale, which no modern rational person would wish to doubt. The story of the rise of modern reason was famously told in William Lecky's classic *History of the Rise and Influence of the Spirit of Rationalism in Europe*, published in 1913. And as he told this story, Lecky praised Reginald Scot for his enlightened exposure of "juggling tricks that were ascribed to the devil."[26]

And so the myth continued into the twentieth century, based on the rhetoric of Reginald Scot and subsequent assumptions about the gullibility of others. Throughout the twentieth century, amateur historians of magic took the earlier histories for granted. Nevertheless, there remained the problem that there was no actual evidence. Not a single example had been found of anyone being persecuted for performing magic tricks. However, in the world of magic, anything is possible, and so some evidence was conjured up. And, on the surface, it seemed to be real.

☾

IN THE 1920s, the historian of magic Sidney Clarke finally found evidence of jugglers who had been persecuted for witchcraft. In fifteenth-century Cologne, he explained, "a girl was charged with witchcraft" for having "torn a handkerchief into pieces and immediately afterwards produced it whole and entire." "In 1571," he continued, "a juggler who did card tricks in Paris was imprisoned on a charge of witchcraft." And, around the same time, a man called Triscalinus performed a trick before Charles IX of France. He caused finger rings to fly through the air, and "the company rose against him and compelled him to confess Satanic aid!"[27] Others then found further evidence. The well-known magician and amateur historian Milbourne Christopher found the case of an Italian magician called Reatius, who performed in Mantua and Padua, and was "seized and tortured until he admitted he produced his deceptions with sleight of hand and the help of confederates."[28]

Now, here was a curious mystery, which historians of magic did not even realize was a mystery. On the surface, things appeared to be exactly as they should be. We thought that conjurors had been persecuted, and here, it seemed, was evidence that they had. What we did not realize, however, was that this was not real. Behind the illusion, something else was going on. But in order to see what was really going on, we need to look more closely.

Sidney Clarke provided no sources for his claims, but the sources can be found.[29] The original source of the story about the girl in Cologne is Johannes Nider's *Formicarius*. This is a well-known book on witchcraft, published in the fifteenth century. According to Nider, he had been told the story by an inquisitor, who had heard it from people in Cologne.[30] In other words, it was a third-hand account, but even if we take the story at face value, this was no street entertainer. This was a young woman who claimed that she was Joan of Arc, resurrected by God. She made controversial comments about the church and the monarchy. She carried weapons, drank excessively, and dressed in men's clothing all the time. This was shortly after Joan of Arc had been convicted of heresy for, among other things, wearing men's clothing. As for the tricks, so far as they were mentioned at all, they were described as "frivolities." In other words, there were obviously other reasons for her arrest.

Clarke's next example is a "juggler" who was imprisoned for performing card tricks in Paris in 1571. He has been cited by several historians of magic as one example of how "[c]onjurors, who claimed no demonic powers, suffered along with other innocent victims."[31] According to the modern witch Gerald Gardner, the poor juggler "was tortured until he confessed that he had attended a witches' [sic] Sabbat. He was then burned and as the result of what he said a number of people were burned on the same charge."[32] This tragic case, according to another historian, was a seminal event: "The dark ages for magic had begun!"[33]

Once again, nobody provided any sources, but the sources can be found. The origin of this story is almost certainly in the second edition of Jean Bodin's *Démonomanie* (1587), which mentions a sorcerer by the name of Trois-eschelles.[34] The "trick" involved a deck of cards, but it was hardly a "card trick." In 1571, according to Bodin, the sorcerer accused a priest of being a hypocrite who pretended to carry a prayer book but actually carried a pack of cards. When the priest looked at his prayer book, it seemed to be a pack of cards, and he threw it away. But when it was later picked up, it was seen to be a prayer book after all. Bodin believed the story was real but thought it described a diabolical hallucination that relied on satanic powers. The sorcerer may have been persecuted, but not for performing a magic trick.

Then there was Triscalinus, who was supposedly condemned for making finger rings fly through the air. Clarke had probably gotten this from a nineteenth-century essay (written in English), which had gotten it from Jean Bodin (originally written in French). In the original, Bodin had described a sorcerer who had demonstrated a feat in front of Charles IX, but it was not a trick with finger rings. The sorcerer, we are told, caused several links of a gentleman's gold chain to appear in his hands, but later the chain was found to be in one piece. It also sounds like a diabolical hallucination, such as the case just mentioned. Indeed, the man called Triscalinus (in Latin) had been called (in the original French) Trois-eschelles. It was the same sorcerer who had been responsible for the other diabolical hallucination.

The last on our list of innocent victims is Reatius, who, according to Milbourne Christopher, was a conjuror "who claimed no demonic powers."[35] Christopher gave no source, but he would have gotten it (directly or indirectly) from Johannes Weyer's *De Praestigiis Daemonum* (1563). Weyer refers to a conjuror who was seen at Mantua and Padua, was seized by the inquisition, and later confessed that he used trickery.[36] Weyer, in turn, was clear about his source, which was a book by Pietro Pomponazzi, the Renaissance scholar at the University of Padua, published around 1520. In the original source, Reatius is certainly not described as a conjuror "who claimed no demonic powers." On the contrary, he is described as someone who practiced divination and who cheated when he did. There is nothing to suggest that Reatius performed magic tricks as entertainment, only that he used trickery to pretend that he had clairvoyant powers.[37]

So, when we look more closely, we can see that none of these were actually conjurors who were persecuted for performing magic tricks. They may have used trickery to pretend to have genuine magical powers, but that, of course, is another kind of deception. Yet historians of magic looked at the evidence and saw it in a different way. It was, of course, a case of misinterpretation. We tend to believe what we are told and to see what we expect to see. We notice things that confirm our beliefs and interpret new information in line with our existing theories. As a result, we sometimes believe in things that are not really there. Victorian historians of magic had told us that, during the age of witchcraft, jugglers had been persecuted. We expected to find evidence of this, and when we looked, we found it. We noticed stories that seemed to confirm the theory and interpreted them as evidence of the theory.

Here is a final example. In 1676, one writer claimed that a man who performed some tricks was accused by the audience of being a witch, and had to reveal how the tricks were done to avoid being thrown out a window.[38] Now, on the surface, this looks like evidence of magic tricks being mistaken for witchcraft. Indeed, it has been cited as evidence of magic tricks being mistaken for witchcraft. However, if you look closer, you see that the story appeared in a book containing practical jokes and tricks for the amusement of schoolboys. In the same book, the writer explained how to steal a cloak (and then, if Satan betrays you, how to lie before a magistrate).[39] Clearly, his young, educated readers were not supposed to take this seriously. More generally, would he have seriously taught them how to perform tricks (and would any parents have bought the book) if this were likely to lead to schoolboys (their own children) being accused of witchcraft?[40]

Nevertheless, we took the story seriously, because it confirmed our existing suspicions. We deceived ourselves because we did what a magic audience does. We directed our attention too narrowly and took what we saw at face value. We saw part of the story and thought it reflected the whole story. As a result, we falsely accused our ancestors of gullibility. But our ancestors were not as gullible as we thought, and we are more gullible than we think. Gullibility, after all, is merely a tendency to take things for granted, and no one is immune to that. However, it is a constant theme throughout history that, when we speak of gullibility, we are speaking of other people and of things that we do not believe ourselves. It is, like narrow-mindedness, a term reserved exclusively for those with whom we disagree.

•

HISTORIANS ARE ALWAYS narrow-minded. We focus on particular themes at particular times and particular places. We rely on sources to which we have access, in a language that we can read. We have relied on

English language texts and translations, which so far refer to Europe, primarily England. There were jugglers performing elsewhere, of course, though evidence is harder to find, harder to interpret, and often harder to believe. Travelers' tales are notoriously unreliable, though how unreliable is hard to say. When Marco Polo went to China (assuming that he went to China), he saw (or, rather, he claimed that he saw) Chinese magicians who could raise the winds and calm the seas and make goblets of wine float though the air toward the thirsty lips of the Great Khan.

When Ibn Battuta went to China (assuming that he went to China), he saw (or, rather, he claimed that he saw) a man throw a wooden ball into the air. Connected to the ball was a leather thong, the other end of which remained in the man's hand. As the leather thong hung vertically in the air, a boy climbed up and disappeared. Then the juggler climbed up and disappeared. Then the limbs of the boy fell from the sky, one at a time, and finally the head. The man reappeared, climbed down, placed the various pieces of the boy in position, and kicked the dismembered body, at which point the boy stood up, unharmed.

We do not believe that these were tricks. Controlling the weather has traditionally been beyond the abilities of conjurors. Stories about ropes and cords that rise into the air, then someone or something climbing up the rope, can be found in many cultures. In the late nineteenth century, these tales became associated with the modern legend of the Indian rope trick, though that is another story.[41] If travelers' tales are hard to believe, then these particular tales are particularly difficult. So, in order to separate the wheat from the chaff, we have chosen to stick to feats that we know have been performed because we know how they can be done. In other words, we will be narrow-minded and assume that what we cannot explain probably did not happen.

For example, Ibn Battuta also reported seeing a remarkable levitation in India, in which a man took the shape of a cube and rose into the air above the heads of the audience. A sandal then rose into the air and struck the "cubic figure" on the neck, which then descended to the earth. Ibn Battuta was so astonished that he fainted and had to be given some medicine.[42] Now, when you read something like this, it sounds so incredible that it is hard to imagine how it could have been done. For what it is worth, we do not see how this—the trick that Ibn Battuta described, in the circumstances that he described—could have been done. We therefore assume that it did not happen.

On the other hand, here is an account from a seventeenth-century visitor to India, who had heard about a man who:

> will first go and sit on three sticks put together so as to form a tripod; after which, first one stick, then a second, then a third shall be removed from under him, and the man shall not fall but shall still remain sitting in the air! Yet I have spoken with two friends who had seen this at one and the same time; and one of them, I may add, mistrusting his own eyes, had taken the trouble to feel about with a long stick if there were nothing on which the body rested; yet, as the gentleman told me, he could neither feel nor see any such thing. Still, I could only say that I did not believe it, as a thing too manifestly contrary to reason.[43]

Despite being a secondhand account, and one that the narrator himself does not believe, we actually find this more plausible. It may sound impossible, but there are later accounts of Indian performers sitting suspended in the air. The method they used is now well-known and continues to be used today. The description here is a little misleading, but it is, after all, a secondhand account, and thus quite possibly an exaggeration. But it is easy to imagine that the suspension trick, which we know was performed later, was being performed in the seventeenth century, and that this is what was witnessed here.

An Indian performer sits
in the air in 1832. Perhaps earlier
visitors to India saw a similar feat.

The levitation described by Ibn Battuta, on the other hand, sounds like something quite different. Of course, it may be that Ibn Battuta saw the suspension trick and later completely misremembered or exaggerated the story for effect. If that is the case, then the suspension trick goes back even further. But what he described did not happen, in our view, because it seems too implausible in the circumstances. It is a curious fact in the world of magic that, in certain circumstances, remaining suspended in the air is plausible, but rising into the air is not. And so, based on what we know and what we think is plausible, we will assume that, in this case, we know better than the folk who were there (assuming that they were there).

By the seventeenth century, visitors to India were certainly reporting many wonders. They said that there were men who could read minds or could hatch an egg in minutes, producing any bird on demand. Sir Thomas Roe, the British ambassador to India, reported seeing a clairvoyant ape that could discover the location of a hidden finger ring. Others describe men who could make a tree branch blossom and bear fruit in less than an hour. This feat became known as the "mango trick" and is still performed in India today. On the other hand, the Moghul emperor Jahangir described some extraordinary feats in his memoirs that we do not believe. For example, he described seeing a chain being thrown into the air and a dog climbing up the chain. When the dog got to the top, it disappeared. It was immediately followed by a hog, a panther, a lion, and a tiger, none of which were seen again. Like Ibn Battuta's Chinese thong trick, we regard this as a piece of fiction.[44]

Of course, we can never truly separate fact from fiction, since nothing is entirely factual, nor entirely fictional. Every history is a narrative, which weaves together chosen facts. Every novel is a tale inspired, in some sense, by real events. We can never be certain what really happened. Like Reginald Scot, we treat some reports as the product of delusion and deception. When we have an explanation for how they can be done, we find it easier to believe that they happened. When we do not have such an explanation, we assume that they did not happen. This is the traditional view of the skeptic, and it covers any impossibility. It is in the tradition of David Hume, which is very good company to keep. However, as Hume stressed, it is based on making assumptions and should not be mistaken for certainty. The history of magic, like any history, will always be written from a certain perspective, based on what we believe to be possible. And, while we may pretend that anything is possible, we all know that this is an illusion. If the history of magic reveals anything, it is that we are all narrow-minded.

○

IN 1630, Hocus Pocus was living in the parish of St. Giles, London, where he had two children, a son and a daughter, who both died in infancy. They had appeared, but quickly they were gone, and a few years later, so was Hocus Pocus. He died sometime between 1642 and 1650, when this poem was written:

> Here *Hocas* lies with his tricks and his knocks,
> Whom death hath made sure as his jugler's box:
> Who many hath cozen'd by his leiger-demain,
> Is presto convey'd and here underlain:
> This *Hocas* he's here, and here he is not
> While death played the *Hocas*, and brought him doth pot.[45]

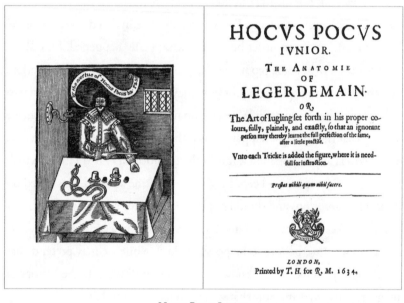

Hocus Pocus Junior,
published in 1634, the first of many editions of this book of secrets.

This was the epitaph of Hocus Pocus, who now was gone, and yet he was not. His name has lived on ever since, and he also left another legacy.

He wrote a book called *Hocus Pocus Junior*, which revealed the tricks of his trade. Reginald Scot had revealed many secrets, but *Hocus Pocus Junior* revealed many more and in considerably more detail. It provided detailed illustrations that showed how to do the cups and balls, as well as other tricks that had never been revealed. It went through more than a dozen editions, and with each new edition, the book revealed more, as new tricks were added and their methods explained. This was the new chapter in the story of magic. If making a living in legerdemain had been difficult, it was about to get even harder. Conjurors would need to survive in a world in which their secrets were increasingly being exposed.

CHAPTER 3

DISENCHANTMENT

IN 1719, AN extraordinary book appeared. It described the remarkable life and adventures of a man who had been shipwrecked on a Caribbean island. He explained how his ship had been sunk in a storm and that he had been the only survivor. He had survived alone, in the face of astonishing adversity from the punishing climate, the threat of cannibals, and the arrival of mutineers. He single-handedly built a fortress and, later, a more secluded retreat. He raised goats, adopted a parrot, shot some cats, and found a servant. In the process, he became religious, killed several people, and learned to regret his previous life of irreligious behavior.

This almost unbelievable account was signed by its author, "Robinson Crusoe." It would soon become clear that he was a fictional character, invented by Daniel Defoe, but this was not immediately obvious. One man felt the need to publish a pamphlet that explained, in rigorous detail, why it was not a true story.[1] *Robinson Crusoe* has often been regarded as the first example of realistic fiction. It tells a story as if it is true, though the audience is supposed to know it is not. The problem with *Robinson Crusoe* was that, like subsequent fictions presented as fact, sometimes people believe it is real.

But magic is not fiction presented as fact. It is a more curious mixture of fact and fiction. The magician does not merely tell you, but actually shows you, the facts. Or at least what appear to be the facts. Here is the ball, and you can see it. Now the ball is gone, and you can see that it is gone. You are supposed to believe what you see: now it is there; now it is not. However, you are not supposed to believe that it genuinely disappeared into thin air. You know that things cannot really disappear into thin air. You know that it is an illusion, because it is presented as fiction. You are supposed to believe what you see, without believing that it is real.

This is a narrow cognitive path, from which it is easy to stray. When a performer pretends that what they do is real, many people believe that it is. Even a little ambiguity can give a false impression. However, for the bulk of history, magicians have been remarkably clear. They have, in fact, told you how it is done: it is an illusion, which depends on trickery. This allows you to resolve the paradox of seeing something happen that cannot happen. The resolution is simple: it does not really happen. If this were normal fiction, then that would be the end of the matter.

However, magic is different. Although you know that magic is fiction (things do not really disappear), it nevertheless appears to be fact (once it was there; now it is gone). In contrast with literary fiction, you have seen this with your own eyes. And this makes you wonder: Where did it go? You understand that it is a trick, but you want to know more details. You want to know the secret. The magician has to deal with the problem of curious folk, understandably, wanting to discover the secret.

Now, you are clearly a curious person, so here is a secret: for anyone who is curious enough, the secrets of magic are available. If you want to know how a trick is done, then you simply have to find out. This is now easier than ever before, but it is certainly nothing new. The secrets of magic were revealed by Reginald Scot and Hocus Pocus. They were revealed in dozens of later editions and in a number of books that appeared throughout the eighteenth century. Since then, they have continued to be revealed, in increasing detail, in books and magazines, on television and the internet.

So, there appears to be another paradox. On the one hand, magic cannot succeed if the audience knows how it is done. On the other hand, the secrets of magic have been revealed for centuries. So magicians have had to survive in a world in which their secrets are available. How did they do it?

IN THE 1720s, if you could read, then you would have heard of *Robinson Crusoe*. And if you had heard of magicians, then you would have heard of Isaac Fawkes. Fawkes was, without a doubt, the most successful conjuror of the early eighteenth century. He had his own booth at Bartholomew Fair, where he was seen by thousands of folk. He also performed for more select company in central London, at the Opera House, where one went to see Handel. He performed for domestic royalty, of course, but he also attracted an international audience. When Indian princes visited London, they went to see Isaac Fawkes. When Algerian dignitaries visited London, they went to see Isaac Fawkes. He was drawn by William Hogarth and became the subject of politics, theology, and, of course, a fair bit of rumor. It was once said that the Catholic Church was trying to recruit him, so that they could make him "Miracle Worker General." It was announced, on another occasion, that he would, for a relatively modest fee, take people to the moon.[2]

If his advertisements are anything to go by, then Fawkes's shows were quite remarkable: "He lays a Pack of Cards on the Table, and while you are

Isaac Fawkes, the popular British fairground
magician who performed by "dexterity of hand."

earnestly looking at them, he causes them to be alive." "He blows the spots of the Cards off or on, and changes them to any pictures." He "turns the Cards into living birds flying about the room." He "conveys living Creatures into any Persons Hand, without their knowing of it, [and] causes several sorts of living Beasts and Birds to appear upon the Table; no Person shall know how or which way they came." And, in what was probably his signature trick: "He takes an empty bag, lays it on the Table and turns it several times inside out, then commands 100 Eggs out of it, and several showers of real Gold and silver; then the Bag beginning to swell several sorts of wild fowl run out of it." These included "Cockatoos, Paraketes, Virginia Nightingales, and others, which no Person in Europe shows but himself, the Birds alone giving an entire Satisfaction to those that are curious."[3]

In addition to this extraordinary repertoire, with cards, coins, and cockatoos, he exhibited a host of curiosities, both mechanical and human. He displayed the contraptions of Christopher Pinchbeck, the maker of remarkable automata. He showed a "curious musical Clock" and an "Artificial View of the World." When he heard of the Indian mango trick, he commissioned a mechanical apple tree that produced a similar illusion. Later, when the Algerian ambassadors went to see him, "he rais'd up an apple-tree which bore ripe apples in less than a minute's time, which several of the company tasted of."[4]

He was often accompanied by his "incomparable Posture-Master, who turns himself into so many different Shapes as is amazing to behold."[5] "He stands upon his own Shoulders, and makes a Seat of his Head, and sits as proper upon his own Head as any person can upon a Chair." "He performs such prodigious Actions, as to surpass Human Faith to believe without Seeing." For a while, Fawkes also exhibited "a Miracle in Nature, being a Woman with a Horn on the back part of her Head," but her career unexpectedly ended when she fell down some stairs, and the horn broke off.[6]

It was, by the standards of any time, a curious kind of entertainment. Cards that transformed into living birds, an empty bag that produced eggs and an international cast of fowl, a boy who could not only stand on his shoulders but also sit on his head, and a poor woman whose physical deformity was only a temporary source of income. But Fawkes had to compete with a host of rival wonders for the attention of the public. There were fire-eaters, stone-eaters, knife swallowers, and water spouters. There were shadow shows, puppet shows, ballad singers, and rope dancers. There were singing cats, dancing turkeys, and sparrows that could spell. There was also the remarkable Matthew Buchinger, the "Little Man of Nuremburg," who had been born with neither hands nor legs, yet performed the cups and balls and a variety of other extraordinary skills.[7] And, in the extraordinary world of eighteenth-century entertainment, things were becoming increasingly competitive. Before long, one would be able to see a blindfolded goose perform card tricks and a pig that could read minds.

In this extraordinary market, Fawkes not merely survived but thrived. He managed to do this by performing the seemingly impossible and telling his audience how it was done. "The famous Mr FAWKS," he explained in his advertising, "performs his most surprizing Tricks by Dexterity of Hand." He did not provide the details, of course, but this was considered adequate. The audience knew that it was trickery, which depended on dexterous manual work. In 1726, it was said that his "Dexterity of Hand" was "quicker than your eyes."[8] Since then, magic tricks have been attributed to the hand being quicker than the eye.

This, of course, is fiction. The hand is not quicker than the eye. Fawkes did things that went unnoticed, but that is not the same thing. There were hidden compartments that could not be seen, no matter how quick the eye might be. There were secret moves that went unseen because they were out of sight. He explained that it was due to the dexterity of his hands, but that was only part of the story. When he promised to make things appear upon the table, he also promised that "no Person shall know how or which way they came." He provided a clue and then challenged the public to solve the rest of the mystery. They would fail, of course, but they had paid to see it, because he had promised them miracles so astonishing "as to surpass Human Faith to believe without Seeing."

Meanwhile, others were making similar promises, but for different reasons. In 1721, an anonymous pamphlet appeared: *The Wonder of All the Wonders that Ever the World Wonder'd At*. It described an unbelievable performance, in which the performer "takes a pot of scalding oil, and throws it by great ladlefuls directly at the ladies, without spoiling their clothes or burning their skins." He will take "any person of quality" up a scaffold, "which person pulls off his shoes, and leaps nine foot directly down on a board prepared on purpose, full of sharp spikes six inches long, without hurting his feet or damaging his stockings." "He gives any gentleman leave to drive forty twelvepenny nails up to the head in a porter's backside, and then places the said porter on a loadstone chair, which draws out every nail, and the porter feels no pain."

The secret author of the pamphlet was Jonathan Swift, whose satirical writings were often a curious mixture of fact and fable. In *Gulliver's Travels*, he had parodied the blurring of truth and fiction in *Robinson Crusoe*. *The Wonder of All the Wonders that Ever the World Wonder'd At* was part of a wider satirical attack on the introduction of paper credit. As we have learned so many times since, money that cannot be seen— and which only exists if people believe in it—can create a dangerous illusion. When confidence is lost, bubbles burst and fortunes disappear.

Isaac Fawkes's advertisements, of course, had a simpler commercial purpose. They were merely exploiting contemporary curiosity, and in the process, Fawkes made a fortune. It was said that, when he retired, he had amassed a sum of ten thousand pounds.[9] Curiosity could be a profitable business, if you could exploit the public's need to see extraordinary things for themselves. And in the 1720s, as Fawkes was performing, this was extremely topical, since other events were taking place that were challenging conventional ideas about what was possible.

OUR BELIEFS ABOUT what is possible are based on what we see and what we are told. We generally believe our eyes and our ears until we encounter something odd. At that point, we wonder if we can believe our eyes or what we are being told. And if we are told something that sounds impossible, because we have never seen such a thing, then we will tend to be skeptical. The English philosopher John Locke gave the example of the king of Siam. The king was speaking to a Dutch ambassador, who described how "the water in his country would sometimes, in cold weather, be so hard that men walked upon it, and that it would bear an elephant." This, of course, was entirely contrary to the king's experience of water in Siam, and so he refused to believe it. "Hitherto I have believed the strange things you have told me, because I look upon you as a sober fair man," the king told the Dutch ambassador, "but now I am sure you lie."[10]

Sometimes, we have to see things to believe them. As Fawkes was exhibiting his curious miracles, the theologian Thomas Woolston published a series of pamphlets in which he denied the miracles of Jesus. This eighteenth-century doubting Thomas did not believe what he had been told. He argued that the Bible should be treated as fiction rather than fact. And, as he challenged religious doctrine, he compared the miracles of Jesus to the tricks of Isaac Fawkes. "It may be true," he wrote, "that *many of the Jews, who had seen the Things that Jesus did, believed in him*, that is, believed that he had wrought here a great Miracle: But who were these? the ignorant and credulous, whom a much less *juggler* than Mr. *Fawkes* could [have] easily impos'd on."[11] Woolston went on to denounce the Resurrection as "the most bare-faced, and most self-evident Imposture that ever was put upon the world."[12] He was charged with blasphemy, imprisoned, and died in confinement a few years later.

Meanwhile, as Fawkes was making a host of strange birds appear, the strangest bird of all appeared. It appeared in Batavia (present-day Jakarta). It was a black swan. There had been earlier claims that one had been seen, but now one had been captured and put on display.[13] In 1726, it was being exhibited to the public, since it had to be seen to be believed. For centuries, it had been assumed that all swans were white, since every swan that had been observed (thus far) had been white. Since nobody had seen a black swan, this was considered an impossibility. But now the seemingly impossible had happened. What else might be possible? What else was to be believed?

A few years later, the Scottish philosopher David Hume discussed these very questions. In one of his famous arguments, on the problem of induction, he said something like this: our knowledge is based on experience, but our experience is always limited. So we assume that things beyond our experience resemble things that we have seen. We assume that the sun will rise tomorrow because, in our experience, it has risen every day. As a result of our daily experience, we expect this to happen in the future. Tomorrow, however, is another day, and so we can never be certain. Like everyone else, of course, Hume expected that the sun would rise the next day. His point was that this is an expectation, one that is based on prior experience. It does not follow from this that our experience in the future will be the same. After all, we once assumed that all swans were white. In that sense, anything is possible.

Nevertheless, according to Hume, miracles should not be believed. His famous argument against miracles went something like this: if we are told that a miracle has happened, then we need to weigh up the evidence. For example, some people might claim that they witnessed a resurrection. However, testimony can be unreliable: we know that people sometimes lie and that people can misremember things. Against this, there is the combined experience of everyone else in history. That is why a resurrection is a miracle: it contradicts our common experience that when people die, they remain dead. When we compare the two options, then, which is more likely: that the testimony is wrong, or that someone rose from the dead? Hume reckoned that it was bound to be the former.

So, according to Hume, anything was possible, but our beliefs should be based on evidence. If something is contrary to common experience and we have not seen it with our own eyes, then we are right to be skeptical. As far as he was concerned, the king of Siam was understandably skeptical, because he was being told something that was contrary to his experience. Nevertheless, he was still wrong, because water can indeed transform into ice. This did not happen in Siam, but Hume knew that it happened, because he was from Scotland. He had seen it with his own eyes. And if the king of Siam had come to Scotland, then he would have seen it, too. For him, it would have been like the discovery of a black swan.

Such are the problems of trying to figure out what is possible. On the one hand, we get a sense of things, of what is possible and what is not. We see what happens, and, in our experience, this is then what always happens. We assume that this must always be the case. But we are wrong, because we cannot possibly *know* what is always the case. We cannot know what is around the corner. We cannot know the future. All we can do is go with what we know and assume that it will continue. But what do we do when we hear of something that contradicts what we think is possible? Should we believe what we hear? Or must we see it with our own eyes?

This was a problem that was being tackled at the time by the eminent members of the Royal Society. Since the seventeenth century, the Royal Society had been in the business of determining facts. In principle, facts had to be observed, but since members could not observe all the facts for themselves, they had to rely upon testimony. Their general view was that facts were facts, however much they clashed with prior experience. Nevertheless, some of the things they were told seemed hard to believe. They were told of monstrous births, of giants and dwarves, and even of a pig that had neither a mouth nor a nose. They were provided with details and shown drawings and sometimes struggled to know how to distinguish between fact and fiction.[14]

As the pioneers of modern science struggled to know what to believe, the public was no less vulnerable. In so-called cabinets of curiosity, the precursors to the modern museum, bizarre objects were put on display; some were real, and some were fake. The line between fact and fiction could be equally fuzzy in live performance. The most notorious example happened in London, in January 1749, when a performer promised to show "a common wine bottle, which any of the spectators may first examine; this bottle is placed in the middle of the stage, and he (without any equivocation) goes into it in the sight of all the spectators, and sings in it; during his stay in the bottle any person may handle it, and see plainly that it does not exceed a common tavern bottle."[15]

Whatever the public might have believed about the "Bottle Conjuror," they were certainly curious enough to go to see him for themselves. They went to the theater in Haymarket; bought tickets, which were far from cheap; and waited with anticipation. After an hour, it became clear that the Bottle Conjuror was a hoax. The audience began to riot. In the crowd was William, Duke of Cumberland, who had recently defeated Bonnie Prince Charlie at the Battle of Culloden. He had earned the nickname of "Billy the Butcher" because of his merciless execution of the Jacobites after the battle. In the commotion that followed, Cumberland lost his diamond-hilted sword. As they destroyed the theater, the crowd were heard to shout, "Billy the Butcher has lost his knife!"[16] We can only imagine what Cumberland might have done to the hoaxer had he caught him and been able to borrow a sword.

Later, historians of magic described the case of the "Bottle Conjuror" as an example of remarkable gullibility. But this is quite unfair. After all, the advert promised nothing more extraordinary than did those of Isaac Fawkes. It is no more impossible to climb into a bottle than it is to turn cards into living birds. And you need not believe that either is possible to be curious enough to go see for yourself. The Bottle Conjuror was merely a case of fiction being presented as fact, then later being revealed as fiction. But, like *Robinson Crusoe*, the fact that it was fiction was not immediately obvious. In hindsight, of course, it is easy to snicker, but hindsight in advance of events is no more possible than climbing into a bottle.

Meanwhile, as the eighteenth century proceeded, it was becoming increasingly difficult to know what might happen. New technologies had already appeared in the process of spinning and weaving cloth, and over the following decades, increasingly efficient machines would gradually transform the entire economy. The rapid population growth, which would fuel this extraordinary transformation, had already begun. The "Industrial Revolution," as it was later called, was not so rapid as the term suggests. Nor was it merely industrial; it affected every sphere of life.

People would come to experience the world in ways that were quite different from their ancestors. They would live in different spaces, both at home and at work, and would distinguish more clearly between work and leisure. As workers were increasingly paid per hour, rather than for what they produced, time became a currency that one could spend, save, or waste. As their experience of time changed, people lived and worked more closely together and came to see themselves differently, in contrast with how they saw others. New distinctions were drawn between men and women, rural and urban folk, between different trades and different classes. In a few generations, we would have a very different sense of our world and of ourselves. But this was not immediately obvious.

Some things, however, were becoming apparent, because they concerned very practical matters of how to get by in a changing world. Some occupations disappeared, and new ones appeared elsewhere. There were more people with money to spend, but there were also more people trying to make a living. For a conjuror, this meant that potential audiences were getting bigger, but the competition was also becoming fiercer. One did not need to be a philosopher to realize that prior experience was no guarantee of future experience. Just because it had always been so did not mean it would continue to be so. Things that would once have been regarded as impossible were now starting to happen. As for those who made a living from performing the impossible, there were two primary problems, the solutions to which were not immediately obvious.

The first problem was that knowledge was changing and, with it, the boundaries of possibility. In the middle of the eighteenth century, scientific advances in physics and chemistry were beginning to change how people looked at the world. Benjamin Franklin's electricity experiments were revealing the nature of invisible forces. The French chemist Antoine

Lavoisier was carrying out research that would lead to a new understanding of the unseen elements of matter. Meanwhile, Europeans were discovering new lands and new people, and new ways to compete with their rivals over the profits that might be made from them. Scientific knowledge and technological advances, fueled by curiosity, economic opportunities, and political ambition, were transforming views of the world and of what it might be possible to do. From the somewhat narrow perspective of the conjuror, it was becoming more difficult to astonish folk.

The second problem was that knowledge was being disseminated more widely than ever before. As printing techniques improved and literacy rates rose, publications grew in number and range. Public lecturers toured the country, educating the public on an astonishingly wide range of topics. In order to sell tickets, they made their talks both educational and entertaining. The spread of "rational recreations," which provided "useful knowledge" in an entertaining way, took both spoken and written form. This knowledge included a growing number of books that revealed how magic tricks were done. These might provide information on physical, chemical, and optical experiments, alongside mathematical puzzles and conjuring tricks. Their purpose was to satisfy curiosity, to explain how things worked and remove the mystery. "We trust," one author declared as he explained the secret of a magic trick, "we have said sufficient to render [it] no wonder."[17]

Faced with so many rival wonders and the dissemination of hidden knowledge, what was the conjuror to do? The most successful performers found a way to transform these problems into advantages. Rather than compete with the wonders of science, they incorporated scientific wonders into their shows. They exploited the demand for rational recreations by providing lectures on philosophical and scientific topics, alongside conventional magic tricks. In the process, they played with the boundary between fact and fiction, and some were accused of quackery. Indeed, some engaged in quackery. However, they made a successful living by providing a host of wonders for an increasingly curious public who were not always in a position to separate fact from fiction.

One of the most successful was Nicolas Ledru, who performed as Comus. In the 1760s, he was performing on the bustling Boulevard du Temple in Paris. In addition to performing magic tricks, he gave demonstrations of electricity and magnetism and offered courses on philosophical and scientific topics. At a time when the scientific profession was not yet established, the line between respectable scientist and vulgar performer was often a fuzzy one. Joseph II of Austria, for example, preferred Comus's demonstrations to those of Lavoisier at the Royal Academy of Sciences. The philosopher Helvétius, on the other hand, regarded Comus's experiments as "more curious than useful," and Denis Diderot described him as a charlatan. Nevertheless, Comus went on to use electricity to treat nervous disorders and managed to gain royal approval. Louis XVI made him a "Professor of Physics to the Royal children of France," at which point he gave up magic tricks and devoted himself to electrical cures. It is said that, on one occasion, he cured a cat of epilepsy.[18]

More conventional conjurors also dabbled in scientific demonstrations. Jonas, known as the "Conjuring Jew," performed tricks at fairs and taverns and achieved an impressive reputation. In the 1760s, he was performing private shows for "the Nobility and Gentry" and public shows for respectable ladies and gentlemen in a room at the West End of London. He performed "dexterity of hand with cards, money and watches, and particularly [though we are not sure what this means] with a bason of water." One of his signature tricks was to decapitate a pigeon: a gentleman was asked "to hang a live pigeon on a string, and Mr Jonas will cut the head off by cutting on the shadow, so that the body shall fall on the ground, and the head shall remain on the string. Mr Jonas will stand at a distance from the live pigeon, as a surprise to the spectators." This sounds like a version of Brandon's pigeon trick and, as in the case of Brandon, nobody wanted to burn him as a witch. Nevertheless, it seems that the old tricks were no longer adequate. Jonas decided to create a mixture of fairground attractions and scientific demonstrations. In 1770, he was accompanied by Mr. Zucker's "Learned Horse" and Mrs. Zucker's "Musical Glasses." He was also now performing, in addition to magic tricks, "Comus' philosophical experiments." This may have worked, since the following year, he performed for George III.[19]

The most notorious of the conjuring quacks, however, was Gustavo Katterfelto. He was a Prussian who came to London and used the title of "Dr." In 1782, he was selling elixirs that, he claimed, cured influenza. He was also performing a daily show, in a "very warm room" in Piccadilly, which may have attracted his customers. Here, he exhibited magic tricks with dice, cards, billiards, letters, money, watches, and medals, along with "surprising Experiments in Natural and Experimental Philosophy." The advert promised "Great WONDERS! WONDERS! WONDERS! WONDERS! and WONDERS!" And wonders are what the audience got when they attended a Katterfelto show. In addition to conjuring tricks, he exhibited an extraordinarily bizarre collection of strange-sounding apparatus, all of which were supposedly educational, though what was learned was not always clear.

Some of the apparatus was used to demonstrate scientific principles in an amusing way. There was a large artificial magnet, "which will lift up a child from the ground," and four different mirrors, which reveal "great powers in optics by the help of fun." Some were exhibited for no clear reason. There was a "new-invented apparatus, whereby he will explain the greatest mechanical powers," and the celestial and terrestrial globes, "their use too tedious to mention." Some were presented as practical inventions, though how practical they were is difficult to say. There was, for example, a model of a house "whereby he explains how a thief may be catched or killed when robbing a house." And some were clearly conjuring tricks, which actually removed the practical function of the apparatus in question. There was also a "new-invented hour-glass," in which "the sand will run or stop 100 times an hour, by desire," and a "new-invented watch-case," "which causes the watch to go quicker or slower, or stop without any person touching or opening the watch."[20]

His prized exhibit, however, was a solar microscope, which he also claimed to have invented, through which the audience could view "many surprising insects in different waters, beer, milk, vinegar and blood, and other curious objects." Unfortunately, the microscope relied on direct sunlight, which made it vulnerable to weather conditions. When he took it to Edinburgh in 1787, he had to apologize to disappointed locals, who were unable to see surprising insects in beer and other curious objects, "for want of clear sunshine days."[21] This may have given him time to write an open letter to King George III, during the monarch's bout of madness, in which the "doctor" suggested a remedy that had helped him recover from a similar condition. The atrocious spelling, however, not to mention the admission of madness, suggests that this may have been a hoax by one of Katterfelto's many detractors.

Katterfelto was a notorious character, but he was not the most famous conjuror of the period. In the late eighteenth century, two other men were better known. One was Giuseppe Pinetti, an Italian who took the now well-established path of combining magic tricks with "philosophical and scientific experiments." This included the "philosophical mushroom," which was produced by combing two different chemicals. Pinetti made his name in Paris, where Benjamin Franklin, then the American ambassador to France, declared himself a fan. Then in London, Pinetti quickly rose to fame. "The wonder, wonders, wonders of Mons Katterfelto are no longer wonderful," the press declared, "of all the jugglers we ever saw, from Bartholomew Fair to Cockspur Street, we never beheld such a wonderful master of the art of deception as Signor Pinetti."[22]

It was in London that Pinetti encountered his main rival, a German performer who had been in Britain for some time already. And this would have been a surprise for Pinetti, since the man had recently been pronounced dead.

〇

IN NOVEMBER 1783, the British press announced that Philip Breslaw was dead.

Breslaw was not British, but he was, at the time, the most famous conjuror in Britain. He had recently completed a long run in London, following a successful provincial tour, and had worked hard to fill the room. The show had provided "various entertainments," from bird imitations to a mechanical clock. Toward the end of his run, he had even promised to teach the audience some tricks. For a half crown, you could learn how to "make an egg jump out of anyone's pocket" and how to "make a ring hang in the air."[23] He had also offered private lessons, for an appropriate fee, of course. At the end of the run, he had left London and presumably gone to Brussels. That was where, according to the *Morning Chronicle and London Advertiser*, "Breslaw, the noted conjuror" had died. Several other newspapers picked up on the story, but no further details were given.

Over the next few weeks, the mystery deepened. In London, a book was published that appeared to exploit his recent demise. It was entitled *Breslaw's Last Legacy*. According to an advertisement for the book, it revealed Breslaw's tricks, along with those of other conjurors, such as Comus and Jonas. However, the title was clearly intended to capitalize on Breslaw's reputation and the fact that he was now gone. Nevertheless, as the book was being published, curious stories began to emerge.

According to some provincial newspapers, there had been a misunderstanding. Breslaw was not dead. He was in Newcastle.

The mystery was solved in January 1784. A letter was published in the *Morning Chronicle and London Advertiser* that announced that Breslaw was "in very good health."[24] It was signed by Breslaw himself. He was now, as it happened, in Edinburgh. He had been performing to Scottish audiences over the Christmas and New Year period and had managed to survive that, too. He was, as he said, in very good health, as he announced his resurrection from an illusory death. As for *Breslaw's Last Legacy*, this had had nothing to do with Breslaw. It had taken his name, without permission, along with some of his tricks.

day by the post :

" S I R,

" I was informed by several Gentlemen, that there has been inserted in several of the London papers, that I died at Brussels ; therefore to make happy my friends, you will oblige me to contradict it immediately in your paper, as I am in very good health, and performing at present in the city of Edinburgh, and in hopes of having the pleasure of seeing you very soon,

And remain, Sir,

Your humble servant,

P. BRESLAW."

Edinburgh, Jan. 2, 1784.

Breslaw reveals, in a letter to the newspaper
Morning Chronicle and London Advertiser,
that he is not dead.

Meanwhile, in Edinburgh, and in very good health, Breslaw entertained the locals with tricks that did not depend on sunny weather. He performed a variety of deceptions with, among other things, "Magical Watches, Caskets, Gold Boxes, Dice, Rings, Pocket Pieces, Lemons, Letters, Numbers . . . and Glass Machinery." In addition to Breslaw's magic, there were "Several select Pieces of Music by a Foreign Lady" and "Whistling the Notes by Sieur Arcalani." There was also "the Imitation of

Various Birds by the Venetian, Rossignol." All of this for the price of two shillings, but then, an Edinburgh audience expected their money's worth.[25]

Breslaw and his company toured Scotland, through to Glasgow, up to Montrose, and back to Edinburgh via Fife, before heading back to England. When he returned to London, however, Breslaw discovered that he had a rival. It was, of course, Pinetti, who had just arrived from Paris. He had already performed for King George and had been described as "astonishing." The London press was describing him as "incomparable" and his feats as "miraculous." "We have seen many masters of legerdemain," the *Morning Chronicle* declared, "but never before witnessed performances so extraordinary and unaccountable."[26]

Like others before him, Pinetti described himself as a "natural philosopher" who performed "experiments." Like Breslaw, he performed sleight of hand with cards, and other tricks with dice and eggs, and exhibited novel machinery. At some point in his show, he even cut off the head of a chicken, though this was considered unpleasant. It "had better be dispensed with in future," advised the *London Morning Herald and Daily Advertiser*, "as the poor fowl's struggling and bleeding did not give rise to the most pleasing sensations."[27] Nevertheless, Pinetti had some knowledge of natural philosophy and was a member of several academic societies. This made him more respectable than the average conjuror, which could attract a better-off audience.

This was a problem for Breslaw. It reflected the essential problem for a conjuror, at that time and since. The public seems to have an endless appetite for artists, musicians, and writers. In the world of magic, however, there is rarely room for more than one star. Perhaps it is in the nature of magic, which provides a series of impossibilities and, with each new impossibility, the impossible becomes increasingly familiar. It suffers from that eighteenth-century notion of diminishing marginal utility. How many times can you watch something disappear before the effect itself disappears? And so, while there has always been room for many performing artists in other spheres, the conjuror has long understood that the demand for magic is limited. To attract an audience in a competitive market, one had to claim to be the original and the best. This often led to public disputes, but then, public disputes can be good publicity.

And so they were, for Pinetti and Breslaw. The rivalry between the two was not simply a matter of competing advertisements. It included anonymous letters to the press, which compared the two performers. In one letter, it was suggested that Pinetti, unlike Breslaw, used a gimmicked table, false boxes, and confederates.[28] Another described how Breslaw had performed one of Pinetti's tricks, and where "the latter failed . . . Breslaw succeeded."[29] Meanwhile, in a bid to compete, Breslaw began to describe his tricks as "philosophical experiments." Pinetti retaliated, or rather "a correspondent" who "professes himself to be perfectly impartial" did. He impartially complained of Breslaw's "pompous, though malignant *self-puff*," denouncing his "worthless production" and accusing him of being a "clumsy copyist." To compare the two was laughable—"ha! ha! ha! and again, and again!"—and he advised this "angry disappointed Quack of Natural Philosophy . . . to keep to his old common tricks."[30]

The feud between Pinetti and Breslaw became a national talking point. It was compared to that of William Pitt, the prime minster, and his main political rival, Charles James Fox. It was compared to the recent dispute between Joseph Priestley and Bishop Samuel Horsley about the doctrine of the Trinity. They were, it was said, examples of the "strange disputes and animosities, which engage the attention of mankind" for which "[t]he present age is remarkable."[31] On a lighter note, it also inspired a comedy play, *The Rival Jugglers*, which was performed at the Theatre Royal Haymarket.

The curious thing was that Pinetti and Breslaw were, in a sense, on the same side. They may have been competing with each other for an audience, but they also had to deal with similar problems. When it was reported that Breslaw was dead, *Breslaw's Last Legacy* had appeared, which explained how Breslaw's tricks were done. Pinetti had had a similar experience in Paris, when he had attracted the hostility of a man called Henri Decremps, who had published a book that claimed to reveal how Pinetti's tricks were done. When Pinetti was in London, an English translation of the book, *The Conjuror Unmasked*, was published. No sooner had Pinetti left London than another book appeared, which was a copy of his own book, though it managed to misspell his name. It was called *Pinneti's Last Legacy*.

Those who exposed the secrets of conjurors always gave their reasons. Decremps, for example, hinted that Pinetti pretended to have supernatural powers. He also made a direct accusation that Pinetti used confederates. He was exposing a charlatan, he claimed, in the interest of truth. But the fact was that there was money to be made in revealing conjuring secrets, and conjurors wanted a share of the profits. They taught the audience some simple tricks and offered private lessons. They published their own books, which explained how some of their tricks were done. They held back their most important secrets, of course, and they kept it all as vague as possible. And they justified their own revelations by countering their critics. When Pinetti revealed his own secrets, for example, it was to refute "[s]ome invidious hints insinuated relative to the means I practiced . . . my experiments, which had appeared complicated to such a degree as to require a confederate."[32]

As information became more accessible, secrets were becoming harder to keep. Unable to resist, and in need of income, conjurors were revealing their own secrets. As long as they did, they could limit the damage, but they could not prevent others from giving away more. They would have to invent new tricks, which relied on new methods that others did not know. Meanwhile, they could counter accusations with denial. They could use the press to make bold claims that few were in a position to question. They could claim to be the originator of a trick or the best performer of it. However, they would also be able to rely on a more general trend: the expansion of information meant that nobody could read everything. There was simply too much information out there, and most of it would have to be ignored. As people became more knowledgeable, they were also learning to be (literally) more ignorant. They would pay attention to certain things and, in the process, would miss the rest. And, of course, they could never be sure that what they read was true.

In May 1803, the British press announced that Breslaw was dead.

$\circlearrowleft$

BRESLAW'S LAST LEGACY was published in 1784, when Breslaw was thought to be dead. However, as he was announcing his resurrection in Edinburgh, another book was being completed just up the road from where he was. This was the second edition of *Encyclopedia Britannica*. The first edition had been popular, but it had not included certain areas of knowledge, such as history and biography. In the second edition, the Edinburgh publishers decided to expand the work. They did not simply make it bigger. They made it truly comprehensive. Indeed, it was later said that this was the first encyclopedia that "covered the whole field of human knowledge."[33]

Of course, it was not the whole of human knowledge. It was merely a selection, most of the content being written by the editor, James Tytler. Tytler was an odd but affordable choice, being both scholarly and in need of money. He was, according to the poet Robert Burns, "an obscure, tippling, but extraordinary body" who "drudges about Edinburgh as a common printer, with leaky shoes, a sky-lighted hat, and knee-buckles as unlike as George-by-the-grace-of-God, and Solomon-the-son-of-David; yet that same drunken mortal is author and compiler of three fourths of . . . [the] *Encyclopedia Britannica*."[34] Tytler read extremely widely but made some errors, which is understandable. After all, as every student knows, reading a book is not the same as understanding it.

Even the entries that were written by experts were unavoidably incomplete. The entry on "History," written by the historian Adam Ferguson, included a historical chart: a timeline of human history. The timeline was on a single sheet of paper. At the top of the chart was a thick black line, which marked the Deluge, calculated to have happened 1,656 years after Creation (it was thought, at the time, that God had created the world in 4004 BCE). The next event to get a mention was the Tower of Babel, followed by the emergence of early civilizations in Egypt, Assyria, and Greece. The Roman Empire then took over, with another thick black line marking the birth of Jesus Christ (4,004 years after Creation). More recent centuries were marked by a succession of kings and queens, emperors and popes. Despite the small writing, the cast was limited. As Ferguson admitted, "to attempt inserting all that deserve being recorded, would crowd and embarrass the whole."

This is the nature of timelines: they provide the illusion of completeness while being remarkably incomplete. This was the illusion of the *Encyclopedia*, too. It appeared to be a comprehensive collection of human knowledge when it was not. It was merely a selection. The *Encyclopedia* sold well and was used as a useful reference by many, but like all reference books, those who got a copy would have read only a fraction of its content. After all, as every student knows, possessing a book is not the same as reading it.

Nevertheless, it was an impressive collection, with far more entries than the first edition. And one of the new topics was "Legerdemain." It explained that legerdemain, or sleight of hand, referred to "certain deceptive performances," and promised to "present our readers with a selection of the best that have been either explained in books, or publicly exhibited." It described tricks with cards and revealed how to use "the pass" (which secretly cuts the cards) and the "long card" (the length of which means that it can be found in a shuffled deck). It included several mathematical tricks and explained how secret messages could be made to appear on paper, by using "sympathetic" (invisible) ink. It was accompanied by some beautiful illustrations, which helped to explain how to palm coins and how some trick apparatus worked.[35]

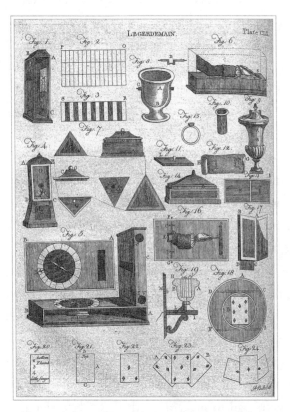

The second edition of Encyclopedia Britannica *revealed some
basic secrets of magic, but not enough for the reader
to truly understand what was going on.*

The secrets of magic were exposed in the *Encyclopedia Britannica*. It was, however, only a selection. Most of those who had a copy would not have read these secrets, because having a book is not the same as reading it. And even those who read the secrets would not necessarily have understood them, since reading is not the same as understanding. For example, if you would like to make several people choose the same playing card, here is the secret, as described in the second edition of *Encyclopedia Britannica*:

> Let a person draw any card whatever, and replace it in the pack: you then make the pass [secretly cutting the cards], and bring the card to the top of the pack, and shuffle them without losing sight of that card. You then offer that card to a second person, that he may draw it, and put it in the middle of the pack. You make the pass and shuffle the cards a second time in the same manner, and offer the card to a third person, and so again to a fourth or fifth.

Having now read the secret, you are free to attempt to perform the trick. This will prove difficult, however, not because the description is inaccurate but because it is inadequate. The *Encyclopedia* was full of knowledge, but it was obviously not all human knowledge.

Human knowledge continued to grow. In the third edition of the *Encyclopedia*, the editors felt the need to pay more experts to write on specialist topics. Amateur polymaths such as Tytler, however well read, were no longer up to the task. It was now impossible to read everything in print, and so the most curious folk would need to rely on experts to sum up what they knew. In summing things up, they missed out on the detail, and nonexperts had to make do with that. They were given the gist, which provided them with a sense that they knew the subject. The availability of some information provided the illusion of knowing all.

This is how magic survived in a world in which secrets were being revealed. Secrets were available to those who were curious enough and ignored by those who were not. Those who were curious were given information, but it was not sufficient. The secrets of magic, even when they were revealed, remained a mystery. The larger problem for conjurors was that, as new discoveries were made and new technologies appeared, the public's understanding of what was possible was changing.

In 1784, for example, nobody in Britain had seen a hot air balloon. But in August of that year, and just a couple of miles from where the second edition of *Encyclopedia Britannica* was printed, the first balloon flight took place. The man who made this happen was the eccentric polymath and editor of the second edition of *Britannica*, James Tytler. As he rose in the air, he saw Edinburgh as nobody had ever seen it before. The original flying Scotsman had an entirely original view.

People were now looking at the world differently. Things that were previously considered impossible were now starting to happen. Swans could be black. People could fly. What other wonders, wonders, wonders might be expected next? For those who made a living from provoking wonder, they would need to raise their game. It was not just a matter of performing new tricks, using methods that the public did not know. It was a matter of how to astonish a public who were starting to take astonishing things for granted.

ꙮꙮꙮꙮ

CHAPTER 4

SECOND SIGHT

T HE IMPOSSIBLE IS never easy. James Tytler's attempts to fly in a hot air balloon were not without problems. On one occasion, the inhabitants of Edinburgh gathered to watch the spectacle. The balloon was unable to support his weight: it rose in the air without him, to a humble height of one hundred yards, then fell sideways to the ground. "It is impossible to describe with what contempt and derision the multitude beheld the balloon ascend without Mr Tytler," the *London Magazine* reported, some spectators suspecting that he had never intended to do so, and "that the whole was a trick."[1] When Tytler made his successful ascent, the balloon traveled only half a mile. It may have been the first in Britain, but the first manned flight had taken place in Paris in the previous year. And shortly after Tytler, Vincenzo Lunardi came to Edinburgh and made a considerably more impressive flight across the Firth of Forth. Tytler's flight may have looked astonishing to people who had never seen a man fly, but astonishment never lasts for long, and one wonder is soon eclipsed by another.

As the *London Magazine* snickered at Tytler, denouncing his attempts as a waste of time, it was full of praise for Pinetti. In a show it described as "a new species of entertainment," Pinetti had performed a mind-reading feat. He asked a gentleman "to write upon a card a *number*, a *letter*, and the name of a *city*; another gentleman, an officer in a royal regiment, went on the stage, a *volunteer*, to assist in this experiment: he had three tickets presented to him, which he was desired to open; the *number*, the *letter*, and the *city* agreed with the card, which still remained in the hands of the gentleman who first had it."[2] The fact that he had used a respectable officer, that he had been a volunteer, and that the card remained in the hands of the gentleman who wrote on it, made it seem inexplicable.

It was certainly not the first mind-reading trick. Such magic tricks could be found in the earliest magic books, which explained how to know things that someone else knew, whether they were thinking of a number or of the location of an object.[3] There were also popular demonstrations in which learned animals and sometimes automata seemed to know what people were thinking. By the eighteenth century, sapient pigs and chess-playing machines were provoking widespread wonder. Indeed, before Pinetti had arrived in London, Breslaw had been performing a mind-reading feat: "the communication of thoughts of any person to another without the assistance of speech or writing." However, this was merely a card trick.[4]

Pinetti began to work on a new mind-reading feat. This would not be easy because he did not speak English and so had to rely on an interpreter. For the most part, this was not a problem since his tricks and exhibitions were visual—things appeared and disappeared, and the scientific demonstrations could be seen. Performing mind-reading in a foreign language, however, is no easy matter. And it did not help that his interpreter was getting some negative press.[5] "In addition to the interpreter's ignorance of English," the *Morning Herald and Daily Advertiser* reported, "he added that of ill manners." On one occasion, he "grossly affronted a lady," whereupon a nearby gentleman, the Honorable Captain William Wyndham, "in the most spirited manner obliged the offender to get upon the stage from out of the Pitt, ask the lady's forgiveness, and apologise to the house for his rudeness."[6]

Giuseppe Pinetti, the popular Italian magician.

Pinetti replaced the interpreter and soon announced that he had, at great expense, engaged a new one who was "most excellent and humourous."[7] Now accompanied by a more competent translator, Pinetti announced a "new experiment," in which his wife, Signora Pinetti, would stand onstage blindfolded, "with an handkerchief over her eyes, and guess at every thing imagined and proposed to her, by any person in the company."[8] In the decades to come, countless conjurors would perform onstage with a blindfolded assistant, who would demonstrate apparent clairvoyance. It would become one of the great feats of mental magic, known as Second Sight.

Pinetti would be praised by historians of magic as a pioneer of this effect. He would also be accused of pretending that it was real, though this appears to be another misunderstanding.[9] However, it is hard to know what audiences thought of it. The feat was advertised prominently for a few nights. After that, it was not mentioned again.[10] If it had been successful, then presumably he would not have dropped it. If it had been controversial, then there would have been a controversy. However, during its short run, reviewers did not so much as mention it. On the other hand, one found the time to mention another of Pinetti's tricks, in which he surreptitiously removed the shirt of a member of the audience: "The Signor has already taken off a *shirt*," the *Morning Herald* noted, "and if the Signora *takes off a shirt*, we do not see what she can well do more towards giving *satisfaction*."[11]

It was, in more than one respect, a disappointing reaction. The most likely explanation for the short run of the blindfold act is that it did not work very well. Pinetti quickly replaced it with a new feature: a "MECHANICAL FIGURE Of the SIZE of a MAN."[12] Perhaps the problem was that the blindfold trick depended on Pinetti communicating information to his wife in such a way that the audience could not tell. When he performed through an interpreter, even an excellent and humorous one, the audience may have suspected that he was secretly communicating to his wife. Pinetti returned to Paris, and Signora Pinetti continued to perform blindfolded, but the feat never quite took off.[13] The blindfold act would later go on to become one of the great feats of mental magic and continues to be performed to this day. However, like Tytler's balloon, its ascent was slow, and its initial excursion was brief.

○

WHEN BLINDFOLD ACTS were performed by others, many would think that they were real. Such feats would tap into a growing interest in the mysterious powers of the mind, one that was already being fueled by the controversy over "animal magnetism." This was the theory of Franz Anton Mesmer, the unorthodox Viennese physician who proposed that living bodies contain an invisible magnetic fluid. Mesmer claimed that he could use animal magnetism to cure the sick. He also put his subjects into a trance and caused them to behave in strange ways. He was very successful, but he attracted hostility. He became a celebrity, was declared to be a miracle worker, and was denounced as a quack.

In 1784, a French Royal Commission was set up to investigate animal magnetism. It was chaired by Benjamin Franklin and included the chemist Antoine Lavoisier. Lavoisier was by then a prominent authority, having managed to isolate a new chemical element and given it a name: oxygen. The commission also included Dr. Joseph-Ignace Guillotin, whose name would be given to the cold apparatus that came to symbolize the brutal aspects of post-revolutionary France. The investigators conducted experiments with subjects who were blindfolded, so that they could not tell if they were being magnetized. As a result, the subjects often reacted as if they had been magnetized, when they had not. The report concluded that animal magnetism was a product of the imagination.

Nevertheless, it continued to be studied, and the mysterious effects of animal magnetism were soon associated with more extraordinary powers. Reports appeared of mesmerized subjects who could "see" without using their eyes. It seems that they were "able to name medals, letters, playing cards and other small objects" that were placed out of sight, even when in the pockets of the investigator.[14] Tests were conducted with blindfolded subjects, who seemed to demonstrate clairvoyant powers. This had to be seen to be believed, and public demonstrations soon appeared. Charismatic lecturers sold tickets to a public eager to hear about this extraordinary ability and to see it for themselves. The lecturers introduced a subject—typically a woman, a child, or a servant—who was put into a trance and who then exhibited a range of extraordinary abilities. Their limbs were made so stiff that it was impossible to move them. They were stuck with pins, yet exhibited no pain. They were blindfolded, yet somehow knew the name of a playing card or what object was being held up.

By the 1830s, these abilities were being demonstrated in London. They were being presented in the context of a scientific lecture and exhibited as real. However, at the same time, conjurors were performing similar feats as entertainment, while employing quasi-scientific language to make it seem more mysterious. They pretended to have exotic powers and tapped into the controversy over mesmerism. By then, of course, Pinetti was dead. It was said that he died in poverty, having lost a fortune on a venture with hot air balloons.[15]

AN EARLY PLAYBILL in the winter of 1831 declared that an eight-year-old boy possessed a faculty that "has defied the research of all the Medical men."[16] This defiant faculty was demonstrated as he stood in a corner of a room in Egyptian Hall in Piccadilly. His back was to the audience, and his eyes were covered with a handkerchief. His father collected items from the audience on a slate and held them up one at a time, asking short questions about what they might be. The boy described the objects in detail, including the dates and types of coins, and also discerned messages that the audience wrote on the slate. He then went next door, while members of the audience were asked to whisper softly. On his return, the boy repeated precisely what they had said.

Some would wonder if this was mesmerism, but the initial response was wonder. In a review of the performance, London's *Morning Advertiser* noted with astonishment that "even when an attempt was made to mislead him, he instantly detected it." It pointed out that "he never made any mistake," that he answered "without a moment's hesitation," and that there "could certainly be no collusion" with members of the audience. As a result, the paper declared, he "excited the very highest degree of wonder."[17]

The eight-year-old boy was Louis M'Kean, and he was billed as the "double-sighted Scotch phenomenon." It was a blatant attempt to exploit the exotic associations with the Scottish Highlands. Presented as a Highland youth and dressed in impressive tartan regalia, he was said to be possessed with something resembling the Highland gift of second sight. Certainly the press made this connection and wondered whether it might be real. The *Morning Chronicle* observed that the performances "differ widely from all the traditions that have reached us concerning the marvellous talent of second sight. He deals with things present, both as to time and space. . . . There can be no doubt that the answers proceed from the boy. By what means he is enabled to give them is a mystery."[18]

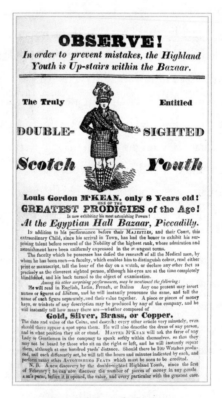

Louis M'Kean, also known as
the "double-sighted Scotch phenomenon."

Mysteries, of course, demand explanation, and explanations were sought. Indeed, when the double-sighted Scotch phenomenon performed for the royal family, his father may have felt the need to be clearer that it was mere entertainment. By then, after all, the royals had savored the ingenuity of Don Carlos, "the Double-Sighted and Beautiful Dog," whose "acquirements consist chiefly of Performances with Cards, wherein he displays the greatest precision. He will also select the handsomest Lady in the Room, according to his judgement (which is seldom questioned) . . . and the Gentleman most partial to the Ladies."[19] Don Carlos also moved on to Egyptian Hall, where any comparison between a double-sighted dog and a double-sighted boy might have led some spectators to conclude that nothing particularly mystical was going on.

The mystery gradually faded, as curious folk tried to figure out what was really going on. If the press is anything to go by, then the public began to take the view that the performance was no more than a display of "amusing and curious feats."[20] By January 1832, the previously mystified *Morning Chronicle* noted, rather more condescendingly, that M'Kean had proved a "most attractive amusement during the past week, particularly to the rising generation about to take their departure for school."[21] By May, when the *New Monthly Magazine* described the "extraordinary exhibition, that puzzles the public not a little," it recommended their "readers to see him and try to discover his secret, or rather his father's secret, for he, of course, communicates with the boy, in some way or other, although we have failed to ascertain how."[22]

As the double-sighted Scotch phenomenon was subjected to a second look, M'Kean Senior began to attract attention. In 1833, he got drunk, charged into his landlord's room, and threatened to "smash his *heed* into the consistency of a well-made haggis." When appearing before the magistrate, he admitted to having been "not *althegither* sober," but he assured him that the landlord's head had been "as safe from him as a glass of cold water would be, were a glass of warm toddy standing by its side."[23] Nevertheless, the following month, whilst "in a glorious state of intoxication," he assaulted a member of his audience "by breaking a violin across his nose."

Apparently, prior to a performance at Saville Palace in Leicester Square, the victim had failed to show his ticket, so M'Kean Senior "came reeling up to him, took him by the collar, and nearly shook the breath out of his body; at the same time spluttering forth some Scotch." The victim, unhappy with this treatment, produced his ticket and demanded his money back. This threat to his income so enraged the stereotypical Scotsman that "he immediately smashed the violin which he had in his hand across the young man's face." The violin, we are told, "appeared to have been a valuable one. It was smashed into many pieces."

Back in court, M'Kean Senior claimed self-defense but was nevertheless found guilty. On hearing this, "he put his hat on in a rage, and said that he had been in the company of the King four times, and could have a character [reference] from a Duke." Such connections, however, did not excuse his breach of protocol, and "[t]he gaoler desired him to pull off his hat." When M'Kean refused, "it was pulled off for him, in doing which his wig came off with it, which put him in a greater rage than ever. He was conveyed to the lock-up."[24] Such was the fate of M'Kean Senior, the excited double scotch phenomenon.

◎

THE PERFORMANCES OF Louis M'Kean were naturally compared to the phenomena of mesmerism. Indeed, as M'Kean Senior was being locked up, J. C. Colquhoun, a chronicler of magical phenomena, was reporting on the most recent investigations into animal magnetism. He had read of experiments into "eyeless vision" and had little difficulty in "assenting to the reality of the phenomena." And when he heard about Louis M'Kean, he strongly recommended that he be investigated, as it sounded like a similar phenomenon.[25] He was aware, of course, that it might be a trick, but that was a matter to be determined. This is what happens when people wonder if the magic is real: they want to look into the matter.

This was certainly the case in the early nineteenth century. By the 1840s, demonstrations of "eyeless vision" were becoming common. They were presented by mesmerists, who claimed that these were examples of "lucid somnambulism." The most famous of the somnambulists was Alexis Didier, who became a household name in France before achieving international fame. Didier gave some quite extraordinary demonstrations of "lucid somnambulism." While blindfolded, he played cards and read the titles of books. He read from the hidden pages of books and from cards inside an envelope. He divined the context of closed boxes and described distant places that he had not visited.

He was, of course, investigated. His investigators, of course, came to different conclusions. The arguments over Didier were the arguments that we have had ever since. Some argued that trickery was possible, while others argued that it was not. They claimed that it was a genuine phenomenon, because they could not see how it could be a trick. Or they claimed that it was trickery, though they did not know how it was done. They admitted that some of it might be trickery, but some of the phenomena were genuine. Or they assumed that, because some of it was trickery, the rest of it was trickery, too. Since everyone thinks that they are "skeptical, but open-minded," they accused one another either of gullibility on the one hand or of narrow-mindedness on the other. The argument has been going on for a very long time, and it continues to this day.[26]

As long as magicians have performed such tricks, the argument has never been far away. The problem for magicians is that, if you pretend to be real, then you can get into trouble. In the early modern period, this might have been very serious trouble. In the 1840s, you were unlikely to be denounced as a witch, but if you pretended to be real, then you would be denounced as a fraud. Few Victorians believed in magic, except for the miracles in the Bible. They were far too modern for that sort of thing. So if someone claimed to have magical powers, then they could expect a hostile reaction.

But that was not the only problem. Pretending to have genuine powers is a different kind of deception. You might involve accomplices, who help you to fleece the unsuspecting, but accomplices can turn on you and reveal you as a fraud. This has happened on many occasions, some of which we will come to later. Alternatively, you may keep it to yourself and lie to everyone around you. Sincere believers will think that you are genuine, and they become your supporters. They defend you from your enemies and help you when times are difficult. They do this because they believe in you, as you lie to them every day. This is not an easy thing to do.

But some have managed to do it.

○

THERE WERE MANY who claimed clairvoyant powers in the age of mesmerism. These were rarely the mesmerists themselves but rather the subjects who were put into a trance. The mesmerists, no doubt, believed that it was real, but the subjects knew if they were cheating. We cannot be sure that Didier was cheating, unless we are certain that such things cannot happen. Some of his feats may be easily explained, while some remain mysterious. If he was cheating, then he was deceiving not only his critics but also his supporters. This was also true for his brother, Adolphe, who did very similar things. However, in the interests of open-mindedness, we will consider a lesser-known but more straightforward example of cheating: the curious case of George Goble.[27]

Goble had been on the lecture circuit with two of the best-known exhibiters of mesmerism, W. J. Vernon and H. Brookes. They exhibited the phenomena of mesmerism in various towns and cities in southern England. Their exhibitions consisted of part lecture and part perfor-mance. They began by talking about the new science, denouncing their critics as ignorant and narrow-minded. They declared that facts were facts, however extraordinary they might seem. They then proceeded to demonstrate the facts. They placed their subjects into a trance and demonstrated the phenomena of catalepsy, insensibility to pain, and lu-cid somnambulism. The latter demonstration was usually a simple one: the subject was blindfolded but was able to read, or "see," an object held up in front of him. The lectures attracted a curious public, who had seen the advertisements that promised, in enormous font, "EXTRAORDI-NARY PHENOMENA." Price of admission was sixpence.

These demonstrations also attracted hostility. Hecklers were com-mon, and sometimes fights. In Greenwich, one of the subjects was as-saulted, which led to an "exchange of blows, and for a few minutes the confusion was indescribable." The police were called, calm was restored, and the assailant was taken into custody. Some of the more vociferous of critics even began to give lectures on the subject of "Anti-mesmerism." One of these was J. C. Rumball, a Fellow of the Royal College of Sur-geons, who denounced Vernon and Brookes as frauds. When Vernon gave a lecture on mesmerism, Rumball would book the same venue to give a lecture on the "Fallacies of Mesmerism." He would demonstrate "eyeless vision" and then reveal how the subject could peek below the blindfold.

Public demonstrations could be profitable, for mesmerists and for their critics. But the matter of whether it was real was something to be determined by science. Mesmerists were keen to embrace the challenge, and their subjects went along with this. After all, the endorsement of a scientist was a way to enhance your reputation. And if the blindfold turned out to be effective, then you could always say that your powers were weak and apologize for "want of sufficient lucidity." But scientists had heard about how subjects could circumvent a blindfold and were not easily impressed. When Adolphe Didier exhibited the ability to play cards while blindfolded, it was said that he played "wonderfully well for a man who did not see—rather badly for a man who did." Such evidence was considered worthless: "the facility of 'playing tricks' afforded by cards is the staple of the vulgar conjuror."

So scientists introduced more tightly controlled conditions into their experiments. Subjects were tested with target messages, which were written on folded paper or sealed within an envelope. Some were even challenged to read messages written on a piece of paper that was inside a wooden box. This was when George Goble, a veteran of the lecture circuit, decided to rise to the challenge. He claimed that he could see objects in a wooden box more easily than he could see through paper. He quickly gained a reputation. "Unlike any other patient we have seen," London magazine *The Critic* observed dramatically, "he has never failed in a single instance."

Goble was now working as a clerk for a barrister. Perhaps he missed the attention. So he managed to convince his employer that he possessed clairvoyant powers. The barrister wrote to John Forbes, editor of the *British and Foreign Medical Review*, inviting him to put Goble to the test. Forbes had already tested Alexis and Adolphe Didier and had been impressed by neither. Nevertheless, he decided to display his open-mindedness one more time. The initial experiments seem to have gone very well. Forbes wrote to a colleague, "in some excitement after the first of them, that at last he seemed to have got hold of a genuine case of clairvoyance."

However, his hopes, like Tytler's balloon, were not raised for very long. He soon became suspicious that Goble was secretly opening the box out of sight. When he used boxes that could not be opened, Goble simply gave up. At one point, in a display of "bold confidence," Goble "selected one of the best secured" boxes, then "proceeded to a desk standing in the room, placed the box within it, locked it, and gave [Forbes] the key!" He then wrote down six marks (to indicate six letters), then the letters "cas" twice. Had the message been "cascas," it would have been a miracle. Unfortunately for George, the message written on the paper was "1787."

In the end, Goble, caught in an embarrassing attempt to cheat, "confessed his roguery and implored forgiveness." As a result, he became, for a short time, something of a household name. As for the barrister, despite all this, he continued to believe that Goble was genuine. He claimed that Goble had been in a mesmeric state throughout the entire proceedings, including his cheating and confession. He had later awakened "in an agony of tears, quite unconscious of what had passed." The barrister conceded that Goble had cheated but insisted that he had genuine powers. Goble had assured him that, though he had cheated many times, he had done so "only occasionally, when his powers failed him."[28]

Such is the remarkable power of belief. We want to believe in magical things, and sometimes the wish is enough. But perhaps more than that, we need to believe in people. Many more trusting souls would be deceived by folk who pretended to have genuine powers and to be genuine people. They were deceived not simply because they did not know how it was done. They trusted that the person was not deceiving them. It is hard to believe that people we have come to trust can be so dishonest. Perhaps it is easier to believe in magic.

We do not know what happened to Goble, but we do know what happened to the barrister. His name, it transpires, was Edward Cox, and he had a successful career in publishing. He was proprietor of many periodicals and launched a few, including *Law Times* and *Exchange and Mart*. He tried and failed on four occasions to become a Conservative MP. But he continued to believe in magic. He became one of the most prominent advocates of what became known as "psychic" phenomena. He was, as it happens, the man who first proposed the term "psychic." He founded the Psychology Society of Great Britain, the first psychological society of any kind. He wrote about the nature of the mind, about the mental faculties of animals and humans, about memory, sleep, and dreams. But the Goble episode would continue to haunt him. It would still be cited, twenty-five years later, as evidence that he was "one of the most gullible of the gullible."[29]

MEANWHILE, AS HOSTILE arguments over the magical phenomena of mesmerism continued, magicians had to figure out what to do. On the one hand, they had to sell tickets. After all, their living depended on it. And tapping into topical interest was certainly one way to do it. On the other hand, they did not wish to make serious claims, since this might attract animosity. They did not want a hostile skeptic trying to figure out how their tricks were done, revealing them publicly, and denouncing them as frauds. So they presented themselves as entertainers and tried to sound mysterious but not too serious. The most successful of these, and perhaps the most mysterious, was "The Mysterious Lady."

The Mysterious Lady was mysterious for two reasons. The first, and apparently the more important one, was that she exhibited "eyeless vision." She performed very similar effects to M'Kean, describing "minutely objects which are placed in such a situation as to render it wholly out of her power to see any portion of them," and displaying the ability to "repeat sentences which have been uttered in her absence." But she was also surrounded by another mystery that captivated early Victorian audiences. Nobody knew who she was. Printed images of her showed only the back of her head, and, when she performed, she never revealed her face. This was a clever marketing ploy,

*The Mysterious Lady conceals her identity
during a performance in Paris.*

since the less the public knew of her, the more they could imagine the possibility that she had unknowable abilities.

At the same time, however, she advertised herself as a mere entertainer. Her performances were billed in the contemporary language of rational recreations, being "interesting, surprising and instructive." The show included "some sleight of hand tricks, performed with dexterity" and was written up in the "Entertainments" section of newspapers.[30] She also appeared, at times, alongside, "for the amusement of juvenile visiters [*sic*], the interesting performance of the Canine Philosopher, Don Carlo."[31] *Punch* described her act as an "amusement," and when Queen Victoria saw her in Brighton, she was, contrary to stereotype, "greatly amused."[32]

The Mysterious Lady even found a way to exploit the topical interest in mesmerism, while keeping a safe distance from it. She presented herself in direct competition to those who claimed to do it for real. In March

1845, as W. J. Vernon and Adolphe Didier were publicizing their demonstrations of "Mesmerism and Clairvoyance," the Mysterious Lady was advertising (on the same front page of the same newspaper) her performances, which threw "completely into the shade the wonders of Mesmerism and Clairvoyance."[33] Nevertheless, despite this, some spectators attributed her abilities to mesmerism.[34]

Such are the problems of pretending to have extraordinary mental abilities. It is not the same as conventional magic, which deals primarily with physical stuff. Physical objects can be seen and touched. We know they are solid and that they are real. We can see (with our own eyes) that something is there, and then that it is gone, and we know that this is impossible. But thoughts are invisible. We need to rely on metaphors of vision—we can see what others mean, but we have our own views, according to how we look at things—precisely because we cannot see thoughts. The brain can be seen, prodded, and sliced. Now, of course, it can be scanned. We can see changes in blood flow in the brain and assume that this correlates with thinking. But we cannot see a mental thing. This remains something of a mystery.

So, when magic tricks are about the mind, they have a more mysterious air about them. Audiences assume that physical objects cannot appear from thin air or disappear into it. But they are not sure what the mind can do. After all, there is a genuine sense in which we can know what others are thinking. We can tell when people are happy or sad, when they like us and when they do not. We can often predict what others will say or do in certain circumstances. Demonstrations of mind-reading, then, tend to seem more plausible. Audiences do not wonder if the cups and balls is genuine magic, but they often wonder if a demonstration of mind-reading might be real.[35]

When other conjurors performed tricks of the mind, then, they did so as part of a wider repertoire that consisted of more conventional magic tricks. Surrounded by physical objects that appeared and disappeared and floated in the air, these demonstrations were firmly framed as no more real than the rest of the show. Later, other performers would emerge who specialized in reading minds and who would provoke another controversy, but we shall get to that.

As for the other mystery surrounding the Mysterious Lady, that was later revealed. Her name was Georgiana Eagle, daughter of Barnardo Eagle, a professional conjuror. Her father gained a reputation of his own, as it happens, as someone who copied the tricks of others. But this was not particularly unusual. Indeed, his main source of inspiration, John Henry Anderson, did the same. He gained a reputation not only for plagiarism but also for puffery, of the most extraordinary kind. He was, according to his own playbills, the "Emperor of All the Wizards." But when it came to John Henry Anderson, you could not believe everything that you read.

⟲

THERE WAS LITTLE mystery surrounding John Henry Anderson. Everyone knew who he was. And, when he performed a demonstration of clairvoyance, nobody thought it was real. His version of Second Sight was the sort of thing that only a conjuror would do. He asked a gentleman to write a message on a piece of paper and place it into a case. Other members of the audience were requested to place small objects into the case. He revealed which objects were in the case and what was on the paper. Then the objects vanished from the case and appeared in a different case. And the piece of paper with the message on it reappeared inside an egg.[36]

Anderson was an entertainer. That much was unquestionable. He made the most extraordinary claims, which were certainly questionable. He exploited every trick of the trade thus far and invented some new ones. He cited testimonials from the great and the good, some of whom he had never met. In addition to an astonishingly varied repertoire and a host of novelty acts, he exhibited a range of curiosities that Fawkes would have paid good money to see. He gave himself the title of "Professor," presented his show as a "philosophical exhibition of natural magic," and described his apparatus with language that would have made Katterfelto blush. He claimed that he had extraordinary powers and aggressively debunked the powers of others. He was more competitive than Breslaw or Pinetti and was as Scottish as the M'Keans.

Anderson had hailed from humble roots.[37] He had been a young boy when his father, a tenant farmer near Aberdeen, had died. After working as a blacksmith, he had joined a troupe of traveling players, and his career had begun. He was not, it seems, very good at acting, but he discovered another way to pretend. He put together a magic act and performed in the towns and cities of Scotland as the "Caledonian Conjuror." He attracted large audiences, particularly in the rapidly growing industrial city of Glasgow. In 1840, he headed south and arrived in London with a new persona: the "Great Wizard of the North."

Anderson claimed that he was given this title by Walter Scott, who was known himself as the "Wizard of the North." But there is no evidence, and it is highly unlikely, that they ever met. In fact, Anderson indulged in a variety of playful deceptions. He performed with "Gorgeous and Costly Apparatus of Silver" that was actually made of tin. He sold what he called a "magical dye" to "Any Gentleman with a head of Grey Hair that he wishes changed to a glossy black." He also claimed to be endowed with second sight. But this, at least, was not meant to be believed.

After all, he also presented himself as an advocate of science and an enemy of superstition. He published booklets in which he was clear that "everything he exhibits can be accounted for on rational principles," and he denounced those who "attribute their feats to some extraordinary and mysterious influence. There are few persons at the present day credulous enough to believe such trash, even among the rustic and most ignorant."[38] He nevertheless complained that, once in the Highlands, he had been arrested for suspicion of having committed murder by witchcraft.

But his audiences were unlikely to think that they were in the presence of a genuine wizard. His show included, among other things, an incomprehensible guinea pig trick, and he was a pioneer of a new trick in which a rabbit was pulled from a hat.[39] His feature attraction was his gun trick, in which a gun was loaded and fired at him. He claimed, of course, to have invented this and described it as an "impenetrable mystery," but he also assured the public that it was entirely safe. An Anderson show was many things and might have included bell ringers and a group of Virginia minstrels, but it was not the kind of thing that suggested dark forces were at work.

John Henry Anderson, the Great Wizard of the North,
pulls a rabbit from a hat.

It was, however, remarkably successful, and his success had as much to do with puffery as talent. Anderson developed new publicity techniques, using huge posters declaring, "Anderson is coming!", and butter pats were supplied to local hotels bearing the news: "Anderson is here." He advertised conundrum contests, offering a silver trophy as a prize, which encouraged participants to come to his shows. He even traveled with his own printing press, so that he could print booklets containing the best conundrums and then sell them to the people who had supplied them. And when he advertised the illusions themselves, he gave them truly irresistible titles: "The Birds of Fire!", "The Grand Metamorphesian Wonder," and the "Phoenixestocalobian."

The impossible, of course, is never easy. Others tried to cash in on his success by taking the title that he had taken. They advertised themselves as the "Wizard of the North," or the "Wizard of the South," or the "Wizard of the East." One of these was Barnardo Eagle, father of the Mysterious Lady, who copied his style and his tricks and threatened to reveal how they were done. But Anderson was made of sterner stuff, and none of his rivals could match him in puffery. Indeed, he made sufficient money that he was able to realize his dream. He invested his fortune in the construction of Glasgow's City Theatre. The young pretender, who could not act, would now be able to put on plays for which he would need no audition. In July 1845, his theater opened. Just four months later, it was destroyed in a fire.

Nevertheless, Anderson rose from the ashes, like a Phoenixestocalobian. The following year, he tapped into the political buzz surrounding the repeal of the Corn Laws. The Corn Laws had placed tariffs on imported grain, which allowed landowners to make larger profits from agriculture but made food more expensive. When they were repealed in July 1846, it was seen as a huge defeat for protectionism and a great victory for free trade. The heroes of free trade, in the eyes of many, were Sir Robert Peel, the prime minister at the time, and the anti–Corn Law activist Richard Cobden.

That month, Anderson advertised a "Free Trade Demonstration" on playbills that included, in enormous font, the names of Sir Robert Peel and Richard Cobden. If the public had read the small print, then they would have seen that he was merely claiming that he had performed for them in the past. But Anderson understood misdirection, and that font size was one way to focus attention. He also promised to make a "Grand Free Trade Pudding" appear and, in the spirit of free trade, offered a reduction in prices. It was a remarkable success.[40]

*An Anderson bill exploits topical interest
in trade reform.*

He then took advantage of the rapidly improving forms of transport, crossing the North Sea and touring the European cities by train. He performed for the crowned heads of Sweden, Denmark, and Prussia and became the first British conjuror to appear before the tsar. Indeed, according to Anderson, Tsar Nicholas was an amateur magician who discussed the wonders of conjuring with him, and then taught him a trick that he had learned "while travelling among the Kirgees."[41] When Anderson returned to London, it was as Napoleon returned from Elba. In fact, he actually put out a poster based on Steuben's painting *Napoleon's Return from Elba*, which showed Lord Nelson genuflecting to the "Napoleon of Necromancy."[42]

It was a rather odd symbol and, in hindsight, an ironic one. As it happens, he was about to do battle with a Frenchman, and he was going to lose. His French rival would establish himself as the most important conjuror of the modern period and be hailed as the "King of Conjurors." Anderson would make a tactical retreat and find new territory to conquer before he returned home again. And so the story of magic might continue, if it were nothing more than a series of battles between great wizards. However, this is only a fraction of the story. Behind the biggest names, further down the bill and in smaller font, there were many others. They were in, and from, various parts of the world, and they did the most extraordinary things. And, depending on the context, many folk believed that the magic was real.

≋

CHAPTER 5

SEPARATE SPHERES

A S THE MIDDLE of the nineteenth century approached, London was the largest city in the world. In other words, it was the biggest stage. It attracted conjurors from far and wide and provided a useful springboard from which to launch a career elsewhere. If you could make it here, then you could make it anywhere, though if you could not make it here, then you could always make it somewhere else. For those who tried to make it in London, however, it was not a single place. There were different spaces that attracted different audiences, and finding an audience was the bottom line. So conjurors found the audiences that they could, wherever they might be.

The Great Wizard of the North had risen to fame by playing every available space. He had worked the small towns with a traveling troupe and performed outdoors for the common folk. He had found rooms in the larger towns and attracted the better-off. He had built his reputation in London, through hard work and brass-necked impudence, and had managed to raise sufficient money to build his very own theater. And, when that burned to the ground and his fortune was lost, he had started over again. He had traveled across continental Europe and had entertained its crowned heads. He may have come from humble roots, with neither wealth nor education, but his humble past was now in the past, along with his humility.

Anderson had climbed this slippery slope by making the most of new opportunities. As modern, industrial Britain developed during the early nineteenth century, leisure pursuits were becoming more respectable. Traditional fairs could be rowdy outdoor venues for drinking, fighting, and wenching. This kind of disorderly and immoral behavior was concerning for the new middle class, who worried about the morality, sobriety, and proximity of the mob. Outdoor spaces were increasingly enclosed, and urban streets were policed more strictly. Meanwhile, rational recreations were encouraged to foster self-improvement.

The saloons and early music halls remained rough and ready venues, where working men drank in their leisure time and perhaps met a woman who was still at work. In the context of such competing goods and services, the conjuror struggled for attention. But lecture halls were contained spaces, which people paid to enter so that they could see and hear what was going on. Meanwhile, theaters were becoming more respectable, with seats and carpets being installed, and the "lesser sort" being relegated to the galleries. It was becoming easier to find a sober, attentive, and paying audience rather than hope for a few tossed coins from a transient, intoxicated crowd. And the more respectable the venue was, the higher the ticket prices could be.

The Great Wizard of the North climbed to the top, but few conjurors rose so far. Some made a living performing on the street, in the rowdy taprooms, or the politer parlors. They performed sleight of hand with cards and coins and other easily portable props. On a good day, they might make a few shillings, perhaps a bit extra from selling a booklet that explained how the tricks were done. But not every day was a good day. They left behind little by way of legacy, but a couple of them were interviewed by the social commentator Henry Mayhew and provided some insight. One described how, on a single day, he could walk twenty miles, busk at every parlor that he found, and make as little as a shilling and sixpence. Another explained the importance of good patter and how he made a large die penetrate the crown of a borrowed hat. He called himself a "wizard," too, which he felt was "the polite term for a conjurer."[1]

An early Victorian street conjuror, described by Mayhew,
who sought tossed coins from passersby.

Some had the education and means to find work in lecture halls, presenting scientific demonstrations as respectable entertainment. In order to attract an audience, however, they had to be genuinely entertaining. They exhibited "physical and chemical magic," along with more conventional tricks. One of the more successful was Mr. Henry, who transformed the color of liquids as if turning water into wine. He also exhibited a phantasmagoria, a modern form of magic lantern. He made a borrowed wedding ring disappear, then reappear on the neck of a canary. He borrowed a watch and made it disappear, then reappear inside a bottle. But his feature attraction was laughing gas, which was inhaled by members of the audience, who then exhibited the hilarious, high-pitched consequences of nitrous oxide.[2]

Some decided to specialize by exhibiting single illusions in fixed spaces. The most famous of these was the "Invisible Girl." This was an odd-looking piece of apparatus. What the public saw was a small metal ball, suspended from wires, with four horns extending from it, pointing north, south, east, and west. A spectator asked a question into one of the horns, placed his ear to the opening of the horn, then heard a whispering voice provide the answer to his question. It was the voice of a girl, which seemed to come from the ball, but there was no girl to be seen. It relied on ancient acoustic principles, which had been given a clever marketing twist. Strictly speaking, it was a talking ball, but it was transformed, through modern presentation, into an invisible girl. And who would not wish to see an invisible girl?

Some invested on a grander scale, with extravagant apparatus onstage. They dressed in fine costumes, provided music, and presented illusions that had narrative plots. When Ludwig Döbler walked onstage, he was dressed in a costume that resembled that of "a German student at the time of Faust."[3] On the stage were two hundred candles, each of which had been soaked in turpentine and contained a fine stream of hydrogen gas, ready to be ignited by an electrical spark. This allowed Döbler to open with a spectacular illusion: he fired a pistol, and instantly, two hundred candles lit up the stage.

Döbler, who performed in a theater with an impressive array
of magic apparatus, was regarded as a "skillful artist"
who elicited "wonder."

Meanwhile, Phillipe, a French performer, offered something more exotic by exploiting a growing fascination with the Orient, while relying on the fact that few of his audience knew anything about the East. He advertised "Indian and Chinese experiments" and performed in what was supposed to be a large Chinese-style robe to present "a night in the palace of Pekin." It may have looked exotic, if not authentic, but there were other advantages to wearing a large robe. A bewildered spectator watched how he produced, from under a shawl, "a glass bowl filled with water, in which goldfish swam about." Then another bowl of fish, and another, and another, and finally "several animals such as rabbits, ducks, chickens, etc."[4]

Magic appealed to the rich and the poor, from the dukes and duchesses who saw it at the West End theaters to the unemployed laborer, who stood at just the right distance from the humble street wizard, close enough to see, but not so close that he felt obliged to pay. They may have watched similarly impossible feats, but they watched them in a different way. After all, what the audience thinks of magic depends not only on how it is done but also on where it is done. On the street and in the rowdy taprooms, it was viewed as cheap entertainment. In the context of a lecture hall, however, it could be seen as a rational recreation. Meanwhile, in a legitimate theater, the conjuror might be described as a "skillful artist" whose performances elicited "wonder."[5] Depending on the context, magic could be seen as a cheap trick, a curious puzzle, or a genuine source of wonder.

However, its popular image continued to suffer from comparisons to "real" magic. Not that anyone thought that conjuring was real. On the contrary, what continued to make it culturally relevant was the fact that it was not real. In the age of witchcraft, it had been a way to distinguish between what was real and what was not. For Reginald Scot, it had been a way to argue that witchcraft was a delusion. By the early nineteenth century, of course, the age of witchcraft was now seen as an age of irrational thinking. However, modern kinds of magic had appeared, most noticeably in the phenomena of mesmerism. And so, once again, conjuring tricks were used to debunk beliefs in real magic. When John Forbes reported his experiments into lucid somnambulism, he referred to the conjurors of the day as a way of explaining why even educated, modern folk could be convinced by mesmerism. "If Herr Döbler and Monsieur Phillipe can puzzle and perplex a whole theatre," he wrote, "surely George Goble may bamboozle the erudite."[6] Conjurors continued to be held up as proof that magic was nothing more than trickery.

This would become a larger theme. It would reinforce the view that conjuring, rather than being a source of wonder, was merely a trick. But it would not prevent people from believing in other kinds of magic. Forbes was underestimating the importance of context. In the context of a theater, the audience knew that what they were seeing was an illusion. In the context of a lecture on the science of mesmerism, however, the audience did not know this. On the contrary, the purpose of the lecture was to convince the audience that it was real. Vernon argued that "eyeless vision" was real, even though it seemed impossible. Then he exhibited George Goble, who seemed to demonstrate that it was possible. If the audience believed what they were being told, then they would believe what they saw.

The problem of context was becoming more obvious, as the most profound beliefs of Christians were coming under increasing scrutiny. When Thomas Woolston had denounced the miracles of the Bible in the seventeenth century, he had been imprisoned. When David Hume, in the eighteenth century, had published his argument on the problem of miracles, though he was widely criticized, he had not been imprisoned. As the nineteenth century proceeded, the problem of miracles was becoming increasingly problematic. Recent geological findings were challenging the view that God had created the world in 4004 BCE. Meanwhile, theologians in Germany were questioning the historical accuracy of the Bible. The miracles at the core of the Christian faith were becoming harder to believe.

Less skeptical Christians found a way to believe in the miracles of the Bible while at the same time renouncing other kinds of magic. They did so by appealing to context. The reality of the particular miracles in the Bible was based on the truth of Scripture. Once the truth of the Bible was taken for granted, anything could be believed. So fossils could be understood to be relics of the Deluge and Jesus's miracles could be seen as genuine because the Bible told them so. Meanwhile, similar feats in different contexts could be dismissed as trickery. Thus, when Mr. Henry transformed water into wine, the audience knew that this was "natural magic." After all, as David Brewster explained in *Letters on Natural Magic* (1832), "[s]uch transformations present no difficulty to the chemist. There are several fluids . . . which should produce a change of colour at any required instant." However, when it happened in the Bible, Brewster regarded it as one of "those events in sacred history which Christians cannot but regard as the result of divine agency."[7]

Modern folk still had the capacity to believe in magic, when it took place in certain contexts. When they saw a conjuror on the streets of London; in the saloons, parlors, or lecture halls; or on the West End stage, they understood the rules of the game. This was a piece of theater and was not to be taken literally. The conjuror, with his props and patter, was a familiar figure in London and the provinces, across the European continent, and, of course, farther afield. The audiences did not know how it was done, but they knew that it was not real. However, in an unfamiliar context, the rules were not so clear. When Europeans looked at the mysterious East and in the shifting frontiers of the West, it was harder to be certain about what was possible.

◯

INDIA, IN THE eyes of the West, would come to be seen as the home of magic. This had less to do with Indian magic, however, than with how Western eyes looked at India. Increasingly, they saw it as a mysterious place. Europeans had long been there, of course. They had fought with one another in the interests of trade and profit, and had aligned themselves with local rulers who had enlisted their people to fight for them. By the early nineteenth century, the British had become the dominant European power, though their power remained limited, as did their knowledge of the land and its people. Some attempted to understand the languages, religions, and cultures of the subcontinent and wrote about these as well as they could for a domestic audience who knew so much less. Others attempted to make "improvements," by trying to convert the heathen into the British way of thinking. But they often failed to understand their hosts and frequently failed to convince them. In the process, they created a view of India as a land of magic and mystery.[8]

When the magic of India came to London, however, it was not particularly mysterious. It came in the form of the Indian jugglers Ramo Samee and Kia Khan Khruse. They had arrived in 1815, as part of an Indian troupe: "The Four Surprising Indian Jugglers just arrived in this country from Seringapatam." They had created a sensation with their balancing feats as well as juggling brass balls and swallowing swords. The demonstrations were impressive to anyone, but they also provided the opportunity for the middle classes to engage in polite dinner conversation about the Other. They regarded themselves as intellectually superior, of course, but conceded that Indians might be better at other things. The jugglers were discussed in table talk as evidence of a natural Indian superiority in physical dexterity. They did, wrote the essayist William Hazlitt, "what none of us could do to save our lives, nor if we were to take our whole lives to do it."[9] It fitted neatly into a more general trend of attributing certain stereotypes to non-Europeans. "The dexterity of the Hindoos," it was often said, was "so much superior to that of Europeans," and that "such proficiency is so common in India, that probably it excites no interest there."[10]

There were also Chinese jugglers in London, promising "singular conjuring tricks never before seen in Europe."[11] They attracted "fashionable and crowded audiences," but they did not gain the same level of appreciation.[12] When a troupe performed at Drury Lane, one critic sarcastically remarked that this was "a worthy use for the greatest of English theatres!"[13] Chinese jugglers may not have seemed so novel, because British audiences struggled to distinguish between different kinds of "Oriental conjuring." Apart from the costumes, one historian reckoned, there was "practically no difference between Indian and Chinese jugglers."[14] Meanwhile, the various mysteries of the East were further obscured by cultural confusion. Phillipe performed "Indian and Chinese experiments," while another performer described himself as an "Anglo-Chinese juggler a la Ramo Samee."[15]

Indian and Chinese jugglers continued to perform around the country, but it was Indians who gained wider recognition. Ramo Samee inspired a mechanical toy and was referred to in the House of Commons. He was on the bill in Hull alongside a production of *Nicholas Nickleby*, and Charles Dickens certainly knew of him: he later wrote of an English conjuror "practicing Ramo Samee with three potatoes."[16] Kia Khan Khruse became famous for catching a bullet in his hand, particularly when the public heard that he had been shot dead in Dublin. However, like Breslaw, he was in very good health and continued to deny the fact that he was dead as he "walk[ed] on his hands with his foot in his mouth" and transformed "three shillings into a horse's foot."[17]

Ramo Samee and Kia Khan Khruse also provided an odd form of inspiration for Dickens. Dickens was an avid magic fan. He watched the performances of street conjurors and went to see magic in the theater. He was a fan of Döbler and almost certainly went to see the Great Wizard of the North. Dickens saw the Invisible Girl. He wrote about magic in several articles and gave a street conjuror a cameo appearance in *The Old Curiosity Shop*. Indeed, he was an enthusiastic amateur who delighted his friends by "playing the conjuror." In one private show, he cooked a plum pudding in a hat, produced a pocket handkerchief from a wine bottle, and transformed a box of bran into a guinea pig. And, in a private show for friends, he blacked up his face and hands, dressed himself in exotic robes, and presented himself as "The Unparalleled Necromancer Rhia Rhama Rhoos."[18]

It was not until the 1860s, as Japan was beginning a new era of economic and cultural contact with the West, that Japanese jugglers arrived in London. They excelled in spinning tops and in a Japanese specialty: the butterfly trick. Pieces of paper were torn into the shape of a butterfly and thrown in the air. The juggler waved a pair of fans, and the paper butterflies seemed to flutter around, as if they were alive. Occasionally, they would settle on a bouquet of flowers or dart in and out of a vase. The jugglers performed with unhurried grace, but some thought it too slow for European tastes and that, while they "do a few conjuring tricks . . . in these there is no great novelty."[19] By then, troupes of Indian jugglers had already become a familiar sight in Britain and were also suffering from a lack of novelty. When Dickens's friend Wilkie Collins featured a group of Indians as characters in *The Moonstone*, he had them disguised as jugglers so that they would blend in with other "strolling Indians who infest the streets."[20]

Nevertheless, India became known as the home of magic. This was not because of Indian jugglers in Britain, who gradually became too familiar. It was because of reports of magic that took place in India itself, a distant place that seemed so much more mysterious. The feats of jugglers in India, it seems, were more difficult to explain. Perhaps there was a reluctance to accept that one had been deceived by a perceived inferior mind, and it was easier to imagine that something more mysterious was going on. Some performers, for example, exhibited a feat in which they sat cross-legged in the air, with only a hand resting on a staff.[21] This provoked astonishment in visitors to India, who wondered if it might be due to "some wonderful discovery in magnetism" or perhaps was a demonstration of yogic powers.[22] As one writer conjectured, it may be due to "the art of fully suppressing the breath, and of cleansing the tubular organs of the body, joined to a peculiar mode of drawing, retaining, and ejecting the breath."[23]

Other feats of Indian magic also seemed to be taken seriously. Many Indian jugglers, for example, performed the Basket Trick, in which a girl was placed into a basket and the performer plunged a sword through the wicker. One British visitor to India described how the sword was "plunged with all the blind ferocity of an excited demon," how his "first impulse was to rush upon the monster and fell him to the earth," but he had been "pale and paralyzed with terror."[24] Then the girl vanished from the basket and appeared nearby, in very good health, and he realized that it was a trick. Nevertheless, it remained an Oriental mystery, the secret to which "no European that witnesses it can discover."[25]

An Indian conjuror performs the Mango Trick in 1888. Behind the performer is the famous Basket Trick, in which an assistant enters the basket and then a sword is plunged through the wicker.

There were also accounts of jugglers in Egypt and China that seemed rather less mysterious. The English Orientalist Edward William Lane described how an Egyptian juggler drove a spike into a boy's throat, as well as other feats that "I must abstain from describing: some of them are abominably disgusting." However, most of the Egyptian juggler's repertoire was less shocking. He produced large quantities of silk from his mouth, put cotton in his mouth, and blew out fire. He put a finger ring into a small box, which then changed into a different ring and, from a larger box, produced a rabbit, two chickens, and a stack of pancakes. He cut a muslin shawl in two and then put it back together. According to Lane, "[m]ost of his sleight-of-hand performances are nearly similar to those of exhibiters of the same class in our own and other countries."[26]

In China, visitors saw jugglers demonstrating knife-juggling, sword-swallowing, and fire-eating. One performer put sewing needles into his mouth, then a piece of thread, and when it was removed from his mouth, the needles were strung upon the thread. Another produced a melon and a bowl of vegetables from under a blanket. In one "particularly wonderful" trick, the juggler appeared to dismember his son, placed the parts beneath a blanket, and when the blanket was removed, the boy had "seemingly vanished." Later, of course, the boy appeared from beneath the blanket in very good health.[27] One visitor to Peking was astonished when he saw a street performer produce dozens of pieces of bamboo from his mouth, nose, and eyes.[28] In a Cantonese drawing room, a juggler exhibited an empty basin, then placed it behind his back. A few seconds later, he "displayed to the astonished spectators the basin filled to the brim with pure clear water, and two gold fishes swimming therein."[29]

So many wonderful feats of magic from distant and exotic lands, yet it was Indian jugglers who came to represent the mysteries of the Orient. India gained a special place within the British imagination as a land that was increasingly familiar and yet increasingly mysterious. The more they learned, the more they realized what they did not know. The seemingly strange customs and beliefs, which felt so alien to the Victorian mind, provoked a general sense of wonder. This enhanced the reputation of Indian jugglers, and many believed that their magic was real.[30]

Indeed, European conjurors would reveal the secrets of their Indian colleagues to convince the public that it was not real. But they would also dress up in Oriental costumes and claim that they had discovered the esoteric secrets of the East. They would try to exploit some of the mystery surrounding an imagined India by dressing up in what they imagined to be an Indian look. It may even have worked, to some extent, but the true mystery of India remained in India and in what was imagined could happen over there. It was, once again, a matter of context.

Meanwhile, a new kind of magic appeared in the West, which was more familiar and more easily transported. It provoked another argument about whether magic was real. It became, like witchcraft and mesmerism, another battle between believers and skeptics, and conjurors were once again forced to stress the obvious point, which should go without saying: magic is not real. However, this was not immediately obvious.

UNTIL THE EARLY nineteenth century, American magic was a foreign affair. European conjurors might struggle in London, but if they were prepared to make the journey, they could find new audiences in New York, Boston, or Philadelphia. Indeed, they often exploited their foreignness, in order to appear exotic or to appear familiar to fellow immigrants from the home country. Meanwhile, they could also exaggerate the extent of their fame in a distant place. A variety of "famous," "noted," and "celebrated" conjurors arrived from across the Atlantic, where they had entertained, they assured their new audiences, the great and the good.

They toured the East Coast, from Maine to Georgia, and visited the West Indies. As the population began to move westward, they headed for the frontier. For the most part, they performed "dexterity of hand" in private homes or public taverns or whatever room might be available. Some performed in temporary venues while others, such as the ingenious Signor Falconi, presented "Natural and Philosophical Experiments" in legitimate theaters. They were resourceful, adaptable, and multitalented, providing a variety of entertainments, from fire-eating to puppetry.

Since the end of the eighteenth century, illusions with guns had been popular. In 1790, New Yorkers could witness "the shooting of a man, in appearance to the Eye." Meanwhile, in Jamaica, the Young Hollander promised that "Any Lady or Gentleman may think upon a card, [and] he will throw the pack up toward the roof, and shoot the card flying." Signor Falconi would allow anyone to write a question on a piece of paper and load it into a pistol. He then fired the pistol out of the building and, instantly, a dove would appear with the answer to the question in its bill. He also presented "AN AUTOMATON, Representing an INDIAN, armed with a BOW and ARROW," which would shoot an arrow into a selected number on a board a dozen feet way.[31]

Native Americans performed their own magic, of course, though this was in a different context. Shamans from Alaska to Tierra del Fuego simulated magical powers. If the writings of later ethnologists and anthropologists are anything to go by, then they had an impressive repertoire. They made snakes appear. They made pebbles disappear. They brought dead rabbits back to life. They could, while tied up securely inside a tent, cause the tent to shake violently. They made small dolls, leaves, and feathers appear to move by themselves. These were tricks, in the sense that they relied on secret moves and gimmicked props. However, they were not mere entertainment but part of the world of ritual. In the world of entertainment, the audience watches. In the world of ritual, they participate. In ritual, however, one can go through the motions without thinking that it is real. And there seems to have been many who understood that deception was involved.

But whatever they thought about how it was done, the magic of the shaman was more than that. Shamans also acted as healers and as a link between the material and spiritual spheres. As a healer, they might remove a diseased agent from a sick body. As a spiritual guide, they might have communications with the spirits. So far as the sick recovered, which sometimes they did, we might explain this as placebo. When the spirits provided advice, we might dismiss this as ventriloquism. But the shamans knew what they were doing, and it was more than an act. It served purpose, and it represented something larger. It mattered in a way that European magic did not, because it was seen as more than a trick.

This was about to become a significant matter for other Americans and also for Europeans. A new kind of magic, which also relied, in part, on secret moves and gimmicked props, was about to emerge in New England. However, for the moment, east of the Mississippi, magic continued to be pure entertainment, dominated by visitors and immigrants. Those who had enjoyed success in London, such as Ramo Samee and the Mysterious Lady, also enjoyed success in America. Those who had struggled to make it there managed to make it here. John Rannie, a Scotsman who had had limited success in Britain, had much greater success in America. According to one American critic, his legerdemain "is not less to be admired than the skillful performances of Brisloe [Breslaw]."[32]

The first American conjuror to have domestic success was Richard Potter.[33] This was a particularly impressive achievement, not least because he was the son of a black house servant in Massachusetts. He had gone to sea as a cabin boy and had learned his trade abroad. He returned home, however, and worked with John Rannie for a while before going on to become a successful entertainer in his own right. He had an extensive repertoire, which included conjuring, ventriloquism, and comic songs. He promised a range of light amusements, an "evening's brush to sweep away care." But he could demonstrate more serious material. He might, for example, "PASS A RED HOT BAR OF IRON OVER HIS TONGUE, Draw it through his Hand repeatedly, and afterwards bend it into various shapes with his naked Feet, as a Smith would an anvil. He will immerse his hands and feet in Molten Lead, and pass his naked feet and arms over a large body of Fire."[34] He also did bird imitations.

When Potter performed his bird imitations, he claimed that "none or few will be able to distinguish his imitation from reality."[35] A similar problem emerged concerning his reputation as a conjuror, as rumors gradually emerged about his ability to crawl through a solid log or to make a rooster appear that was able to pull a wagon that horses could not budge.[36] But his genuine talent was more than adequate to win over more skeptical folk. He performed a run in Mobile, Alabama, where, on account of the color of his skin, he was refused a hotel room, but where he nevertheless attracted large audiences who paid to see his show.[37] His success allowed him to buy a farm in Massachusetts, where he joined the masons, and he helped to found Prince Hall Masonry.

As the frontier reached the Mississippi River, conjurors followed in search of audiences. In 1806, John Rannie was performing in Natchez and New Orleans. By 1814, conjuring was being performed in St. Louis, the largest of the frontier towns. The pioneering performer was the extraordinary Colonel Eugene Leitensdorfer. Leitensdorfer, if we are to believe his colorful life story, had joined the Habsburg imperial army, but deserted when he killed a fellow soldier in a duel. He had then enlisted in the French army but had been suspected of being a spy, been imprisoned, and then escaped. Later, he went to Egypt, bought a coffeehouse, raised a family, deserted them, joined a monastery in Sicily, left the monastery, and became a dervish. At some point between being a monk and being Muslim, he had learned some card tricks. After assisting the United States army in the First Barbary War, he had come to America and settled west of the Mississippi, where his new wife had been intimidated by hostile Native Americans.[38]

And so, following a series of unbelievable adventures, Leitensdorfer had ended up in St. Louis. He now made a living presenting a "Spectacle of Recreative Sports of Mathematicks and Phisicks." He performed conjuring tricks, such as "The Magic Picture" and "Dancing Eggs," and exhibited an automaton of an "Egyptian prophet," who would predict which cards would be selected by members of the audience. He also ate burning coals and performed a gun trick in which a chosen card was burned, shot at him, and appeared on his chest, while his hands were tied behind his back.[39] One can only imagine what stories he told his audience and what they believed.

Conjurors continued to face danger and then tell stories about it. That most reliable of chroniclers, P. T. Barnum, recalled the dangers that he had faced when working as a conjuror's assistant. On one occasion, he was hiding beneath the conjuror's table, holding a squirrel. He and the squirrel were waiting for the conjuror to borrow a watch and chain, which he would secretly pass to them through a hidden trapdoor in the top of the table. When Barnum received the watch, he wound the chain around the squirrel's neck and waited to pass it back up through the trapdoor to the conjuror. However, despite his many talents, Barnum lacked any experience in winding a chain around a squirrel's neck. As a result, "the squirrel bit me severely; I shrieked with pain, straightened my neck at first, then my back, then my legs, overthrew the table, smashed every breakable article upon it, and rushed behind the curtain!" Meanwhile, the squirrel, taking advantage of this unexpected misdirection, "galloped off with the watch around his neck."[40]

As Barnum faced the perils of squirrels, others contended with loaded guns. Catching a Bullet had always been a risky trick, but so far, nobody had been killed. Kia Khan Khruse had survived in Dublin, Anderson seemed to be indestructible, and Leitensdorfer, if we are to believe his tales, had survived considerably worse. Nevertheless, the trick was dangerous, and the sense of danger was what made it a draw. Performers had to weigh up the pros and cons and then take their chances. One of those forced to decide between profit and survival was Signor Antonio Blitz, who arrived in the United States in 1834 and soon made his reputation. Before long, he had made acquaintances with John Quincy Adams, Millard Fillmore, and Martin van Buren, who, at the time, was known as the "Little Magician."

As Blitz quickly made a name for himself, he also made it for others. After a few months, he had spawned many imitators, and "Blitzes were represented in all parts of the country," who used his name and copied his handbills, in which they claimed to be the "original." It was, he said, an "incalculable annoyance." Like other conjurors of the time, including other Signor Blitzes, he played in whatever space he could find, be it a theater, masonic hall, museum, lecture room, garden, or courthouse. Like others, he offered experiments in "Natural Magic," alongside more lighthearted amusements. He demonstrated plate spinning and exhibited trained canaries. His bullet-catching trick, however, became too dangerous when a member of the audience in Savannah, Georgia, "drew his loaded revolver and earnestly requested to shoot at me." "So determined was he in his desire to shoot," Blitz recalled, "that it required much effort to prevent his firing." And so, despite the feat being "the most adroit in my performance . . . it became attended with so much danger, that I found it necessary, for self-protection, to abandon it."[41]

By now, of course, it should be obvious that the history of magic, like so many others, can become a story of famous men. It is true that the vast majority of performers were men, as were the most famous. However, there has been a persistent stereotype of the woman in magic as the assistant. Like many stereotypes, it is not untrue: women have frequently worked as assistants. The problem, of course, is that this became seen as the proper role for women in magic. Like the whiteness of a swan, what was commonly seen was taken to be what was natural. The persistence of this particular stereotype, despite so many black swans, has been remarkable, and the reasons for it are not entirely clear.

There have been various explanations offered, some more useful than others. There have been rather weak historical explanations, which hark back to the age of witchcraft and claim that there was a continuing fear that women practicing magic would seem dangerous.[42] There have been unthinking sexist explanations, of course, about women not being good at that sort of thing and feminist analyses of the ways in which it reflected a wider patriarchy.[43] It has certainly been bound up with gender stereotypes—and stereotypes can be self-perpetuating—but stereotypes also change over time, and in magic, the change has been remarkably slow. The reasons for the ongoing gender imbalance are surely to do with magic itself. After all, to become a magician, you need to have access to secrets. Until recently, these were discovered in magic books, which were largely written for boys, and in magic clubs, which were largely gentlemen's clubs. The stereotype of the lovely assistant who is crushed, impaled, and sawn in half can hardly have been an incentive for women to think of magic as a profession. But, as we will see, that came later.

Meanwhile, in the first half of the nineteenth century, women were performing as conjurors on both sides of the Atlantic. There was, of course, the Mysterious Lady, but there were many others before her. Mrs. Brenon appeared with her husband in New York at the end of the eighteenth century, performing sleight of hand in her own right. Cecilia Blanchard performed the cups and balls and also played the musical glasses. In 1839, Madam de Lago, "the Magic Queen," was performing magic in New Orleans with cards, money, rings, oranges, lemons, birds, rabbits, coffee, rice, and an automaton fortune-teller. In Philadelphia, Madame Kowasky, "the celebrated Polish enchantress," demonstrated fire-eating, in which she "produced from her mouth the most brilliant fireworks of various colors, and which colours were changed at the will of the audience."[44] And, as the nineteenth century proceeded, many more women would have success.

Nevertheless, it was the case that women in magic would frequently appear as assistants and then disappear from view. It was, in a sense, a microcosm of the growing ideology of "separate spheres," which increasingly placed men in the public arena and women in the private realm. The home, it was thought, was a woman's natural habitat, where she could focus on feminine matters such as reproduction and domesticity. Women were, it was thought, dependent on men and expected, like a conjuror's assistant, to play a supporting role. However, the logic of separate spheres dictated that in certain contexts, women had more influence. While the view of women as passive creatures limited their material power, it also conceded to them a degree of moral and spiritual authority. Their passive nature, it was thought, made them naturally more spiritual.[45]

Women, according to William Wilberforce, were "the faithful repositories of the religious principle." They should, in his view, be "the medium of our intercourse with the heavenly world."[46] For some women at least, this provided an opportunity. They could exploit what was widely seen as their naturally spiritual disposition. Women had long been witches and seers. They could now be the modern mediums of intercourse between the earthly and spiritual spheres.

It began in 1848. It began in a house in Hydesville, New York, a small town near Rochester. According to the standard story, Kate and Maggie Fox, two young sisters, heard some mysterious knocking noises. They began to interact with the sounds, as if they came from a spirit. They snapped their fingers, and the spirit responded. They asked questions, and the spirit answered. The communications continued, word quickly spread, and many became convinced that the girls were talking to the dead and that the dead were talking to them. The "Rochester Knockings," as they were called in hindsight, led to the emergence of a movement that would be known as modern Spiritualism.

*Kate and Maggie Fox, whose strange phenomena are
typically seen as the origins of modern Spiritualism.*

This is the origin story of Spiritualism. The roots of Spiritualism, of course, were deeper. We have been communicating with spirits for millennia. Knocking noises had been heard before, and spirits had been suspected of making them. The Rochester Knockings, however, took place in a rather different context. In the wake of the Second Great Awakening and the rise of Adventism, Shakerism, and Mormonism, supernatural encounters were commonly reported. The feats of mesmerists were now well-known in America and had influenced the transcendentalist views of Ralph Waldo Emerson. When the mesmerist Phineas Parkhurst Quimby turned from mesmerism to "mental healing," it would inspire the birth of Christian Science. Meanwhile, Andrew Jackson Davis, the "Poughkeepsie Seer," had already set the stage for the birth of Spiritualism with his own spiritual writings.

Nevertheless, histories of Spiritualism would invariably begin with the

Fox sisters. The origin story, as origin stories do, defined Spiritualism in a particular way: as something that was, at the end of the day, based on demonstrable evidence. It was the phenomena of the mysterious raps and the spirit messages that they seemed to communicate that demonstrated the truth of Spiritualism. So when the Fox sisters began to give demonstrations of the phenomena to the paying public, they attracted enormous attention. And, of course, it was the phenomena that became the target of debunkers. They soon came up with natural explanations for what was going on. They claimed that the noises were merely the result of cracking the joints of their knees and feet. They said, as Reginald Scot had said, that it was merely a case of how natural things can be made to seem supernatural. And conjuring would once again be used to show that magic was not real.

MEANWHILE, in 1848, there was another revolution in France, and the Emperor was replaced, for a few years at least, with a President of the Republic. As revolutions spread across Europe, London was the safest stage for a conjuror. So one French conjuror left Paris for London and began a little revolution of his own. In his "Soirées Fantastiques," he performed a version of Second Sight that was clearly superior to that of Anderson. He suspended his son in the air, in a way that would have seemed impossible even to jugglers in India who suspended themselves in the air. He also performed original illusions, which he had actually invented himself. "We have seen many conjurors in our time," the London *Morning Chronicle* declared, "but we certainly never saw one who came up to this one."[47]

Anderson responded to his newest rival by copying his tricks. But this did not solve the problem. The Frenchman was hailed as "the original inventor, while the other dealers in marvels have been decked in his plumage."[48] "His contemporaries may copy his tricks," wrote a reviewer in the London *Standard*, "but they should also emulate the subtle and tranquil ease of his manipulation"; in short, he "defies all competition."[49]

So Anderson decided on another tour and announced his "farewell performances." He had been advertising "farewell performances" for many years, and would do so for many more years to come. It was another method for attracting an audience who had not yet come to see him. The Frenchman decided to go to see him. He wrote a note to the theater manager, asking for tickets to see the show, though he made it clear that he was not fooled by Anderson's advertising gimmick. "Can you be so good to get me an order for Lyceum theatre—for to-night," he wrote, then added sarcastically, "You know that the Great Wizard of the North, King of all Kings, gives now his last three performances. I have seen that in his bills."[50]

As the Frenchman continued to conquer London, Anderson toured a now more settled Europe. He then decided to find fresh territory, a new and different world in which he could be seen as a pioneer. He arrived in New York in 1851 and began an American tour. In his first show, Anderson performed the illusions of the Frenchman in what, despite being a Scotsman, he also called: "Soirées Fantastiques." Following his "farewell performances" in New York, he took the "Soirées" to Philadelphia, where he was praised for "entirely new" illusions, and to New Orleans, where they were described as "altogether original and novel."[51] He played Boston, Charleston, and Savannah, and then traveled back to New York for another series of "farewell performances." His audiences would gradually learn that, when Anderson said "farewell," it was not "good-bye." It was "au revoir."

This time, however, Anderson had found an original and particularly topical attraction. He announced that he would exhibit the phenomena of Spiritualism and explain how it was done, so that "the matter was set at rest." According to the *New York Daily Tribune*, in words that Anderson might have written himself: "The excitement to hear Prof. ANDERSON'S EXPOSE of the GREAT SPIRIT RAPPING HUMBUG!! filled Metropolitan Hall to overflowing, with the most fashionable and learned audiences ever assembled within its walls. Many were unable to gain admission. Never were the Spirit Rappers so nonplused [*sic*]. His explanation of the raps, the manner in which, and the machinery whereby they are produced, convinced all of the shallowness of the pernicious and fatal delusion."[52]

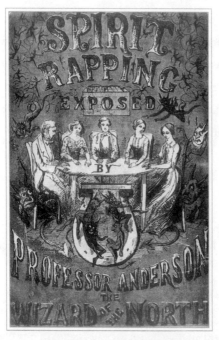

Anderson debunks Spiritualism in
a booklet of exposures.

The matter, however, was not "set at rest." Those who believed in Spiritualism continued to believe in it. They pointed out that fake spirit raps did not disprove the reality of actual spirit raps, just as counterfeit money did not disprove the existence of real money. On the contrary, it took only one real phenomenon to show that such things could be real. After all, it took only one black swan to prove that swans could be black. They pointed out that just because something seemed extraordinary did not mean that it could not happen. After all, if you have never seen ice, then you may doubt that water can transform into ice, but then, of course, you would be wrong. Meanwhile, debunkers accused them of gullibility, a term reserved exclusively for those with whom we disagree, while they continued to believe in the miracles of the Bible, which had taken place in a different context.

Spiritualism grew despite debunking, but Anderson did not particularly mind. His primary purpose was not to debunk but rather to publicize his shows. He was doing as he had always done: finding new ways to attract an audience, wherever that might be. The growth of Spiritualism was an ongoing opportunity to present his show as topical. He could now appear to be a moral crusader, in the business of publicly defending both science and religion from this "absurd and remarkable delusion." His duty, he explained, was to "fearlessly communicate his knowledge for the benefit of his fellow-men."[53] The conjuror, as an expert on deception, could now be seen as a defender of Truth. This made conjuring culturally relevant, but it did so at a price. It was based on stressing, more than ever, that magic was not real.

By the time Anderson returned to London, the Frenchman had already retired to France. His career had been short, remarkably short. Nevertheless, he would shape the history of magic in a way that no conjuror before him had done. He would do this by telling a story that was extraordinary, a story that was not real, but that people would believe was real. As a result, despite his short career, his name would be remembered. His name was Jean-Eugène Robert-Houdin. And, though he was retired from the stage, Robert-Houdin was about to give his own farewell performance.

It would be the performance of his life.

 llllll

CHAPTER 6

THE CONFESSIONS

B Y 1858, the French wizard Jean-Eugène Robert-Houdin had carefully considered the end of his performing career. He was still middle-aged at just fifty-two years old. In fact, his work as a magician, as he calculated it, had lasted just over six years, first on his own stage in Paris, and then in tours of European capital cities. In that era, as today, that represented a remarkably and mysteriously short period of time—barely a blink of an eye for someone whose success depended upon building a rapport with the public and perfecting the niceties of showmanship, let alone the intricacies of sleight of hand. Six years. Stardom. Renown. And he retired with a small fortune to a pretty estate just outside of his hometown of Blois.

But as befitting a careful wizard, Robert-Houdin saved his very best trick, his most astonishing creation, for the very end. It's the mystery that has made him famous today, the coup de theatre that forever enshrined his name upon the history of the art. And fortunately for us, we have a firsthand account of the performance—a detailed explanation of just how, and why, he accomplished this grand finale.

"Eight o'clock has just struck; my wife and children are by my side," he wrote. "I have spent one of those pleasant days which tranquility, work, and study can alone secure." But he had an inspiration.

> Shall I confess to you, reader? And why not? . . . During my professional career, eight o'clock was the moment when I must appear before the public. . . . Then, as now, my heart beat, for I was proud and happy of such success. Do you now understand, reader, all the reminiscences this hour evokes in me, and the solemn feeling that continually occurs to me when the clock strikes?
>
> At times I even mentally transport myself to my stage, in order to prolong [these feelings]. . . . I see my audience again, and, under the charm of this sweet illusion, I delight in telling them the most interesting episodes of my professional life. . . .
>
> But why could I not convert this fiction into a reality? Could I not, each evening when the clock strikes eight, continue my performances under another form? My public shall be the reader, and my stage a book. . . . I imagine they are waiting for me—they are listening eagerly.[1]

His last magic show, the fat pile of reminiscences that he neatly penned at his desk in Blois, was a brilliant success—a warm, dazzling glow that provided a beacon of inspiration. That book, more than anything else, has served to cast Robert-Houdin's shadow over the art of magic for the past century and a half. In the meantime, his devoted readers have managed to divert the spotlight from a dozen important early Victorian magicians. Yet it's a puzzle to understand what this French conjuror accomplished, what he did not accomplish, and what the world of magicians have hoped—and then imagined—was accomplished during that brief, notable career.

*The famous French magician
Robert-Houdin in retirement.*

There is a simple explanation, and it's convenient to start there. Robert-Houdin was something that a magician had never been before. He was a writer. Today we might debate his skill with a wand, but we can easily evaluate his skill with a pen. He provided literate and fascinating memoirs of his career. Those memoirs were intelligent, interesting, and novelistic—in a sometimes picaresque and sometimes gossipy Victorian way, a model of the age. It presented the magician as an insightful critic and demonstrated how the skills of a magician entitled him to important and unique judgments. It made pronouncements about magic as an art.

All of that was new.

Before these memoirs, a magician was often characterized by his peripatetic shows, offering amusements that might be broad and common, if not always relevant or tasteful. Magicians lived a catch-as-catch-can existence; their shows were among many novelties and entertainments that competed for the attention of the public.

Was it art? For a long time, it would have been presumptuous to even ask that question. But Robert-Houdin, he was quick to tell us, was trained as a skilled watchmaker. He invented his own tricks, built them like exquisite works of art, and then carried them onstage to perform them with a seemingly effortless sangfroid. He held himself apart from many of the performing magicians of the day, criticizing their crudities as inartistic and demeaning to the public. He performed in Paris at a sophisticated and exquisite little theater of his own design. His associates were literati and artists; he made numerous appearances before European royalty.

He was an artist.

At least, that is the story that he described in his book—and for many, many years, magicians were first inspired by his story and then disappointed when they personally fell short of his artistic ideal.

Finally, and most important of all, Robert-Houdin's career concluded when he was summoned out of retirement to represent the French government in colonial Algiers. The commanding colonel felt that the Marabout, an assertive native group that claimed magical powers and could apply pressure to the local chieftains, might be suitably intimidated by a display from a real French magician. Robert-Houdin accepted the assignment and demonstrated his magic, including an astonishing effect that utilized electromagnetism to mystify and impress the natives. He earned the praise of French officials and a scroll of admiration from the Algerian tribal leaders. This Algerian adventure would serve as the grand finale of his book.

That story is usually recalled as the modern wizard who used a bit of showmanship and a dose of clever science to conquer a world of daunting superstition. In his memoirs, we can read his description of the precise moment in that Algerian theater when modern conjuring successfully shattered the ancient belief in the supernatural. It's such an important moment that it's subsequently been fictionalized and mythologized beyond recognition. Depending upon the enthusiasm of subsequent storytellers, Robert-Houdin "destroyed an influence . . . very dangerous to the French Government,"[2] or persuaded "the Algerians [to give] up their continual fighting,"[3] or "did the most for the pacification of Algeria,"[4] or was personally summoned "by Louis Napoleon," so he could present a "display of French supernatural power," and "the rebellion was put down," miraculously "avoiding a war in Algeria."[5]

It has taken us a long time to figure out that he did none of those things. Meanwhile, Robert-Houdin became the modern magicians' creation myth. Avoiding a war? No wonder every other magician seemed to fall short. Overestimated or undervalued, fact or fiction, this incredible mystery—the magical creation of "Robert-Houdin" that was conjured forth by Robert-Houdin—is the best way to explain how the Victorians wrestled with magic.

◯

In 1858, the magician had retired to Blois, France, his hometown, where he published *Confidences d'un Prestidigitateur*, which can be translated to *Secrets, or Confessions, of a Magician*. When the book was first translated into English in 1859 by Lascelles Wraxall and then edited by Robert Shelton Mackenzie, it was retitled *The Memoirs of Robert-Houdin*, and that's how it's known in the English-speaking world. The book used to be a popular nineteenth-century biography, but since it's seldom read today, and since the author began by analogizing that he was not just writing a book but performing another magic show, we'll start with the story he told.[6]

Jean-Eugène Robert was born in Blois in 1805. (As we'll see, he later took the hyphenated name Robert-Houdin by adding his wife's name to his own.) His father was a watchmaker and mechanician. Jean Robert similarly became obsessed with his tools at the workbench, "making filings," as his father said. He was sent to school at Orleans, where he first encountered an itinerant magician on the street, a Professor Carlosbach, who blew on a trumpet to gather a crowd, performed the cups and balls, and then sold booklets of magic secrets. Jean eagerly bought one, but when he went in search of the professor for more instruction, he found that he had left his lodgings without paying the bill.[7]

Jean was happily sent to learn from his cousin, another watchmaker in Blois. It was there that he was miraculously called to magic a second time. He was sent to a bookseller's shop to purchase a set of volumes on clockmaking. The bookseller, distracted by another conversation, reached up to the shelf and hurriedly wrapped the requested books. When he returned to his room with the package, Jean was surprised to find two volumes of *Dictionnaire Encyclopedique des Amusmens des Sciences, Mathematiques et Phisiques*.[8] It was a book that described and diagrammed various sleight-of-hand tricks. Fascinated to discover this fateful mistake, the boy stayed up all night studying its contents. Day after day, he secretly practiced the various maneuvers with coins and balls, his hands deep in the pockets of his coat.

Once he'd finished his apprenticeship, he was sent to Tours as a journeyman to a clockmaker named Noriet. Treated like one of the Noriet family, he entertained at parties with his newfound skills at conjuring. One day in July 1828, after the Noriets had visited a nearby fair, Jean Robert returned home with them and hungrily ate from a pot of ragout. He was stricken with food poisoning, and as he slowly recovered, he had a delirious obsession to return to Blois. Early one morning he stumbled from bed, dressed, and boarded a coach for his hometown. The journey was, he recorded, "a horrible martyrdom to me. I was devoured by a running fever, and my head seemed to burst asunder by every jolt of the vehicle." In desperation he leapt from the moving carriage, collapsing on the road.

He awoke, days later, "in a capital bed, and the room was exquisitely clean . . . the sight of a strange man, standing at my bedside . . . this moving room [bearing] a close resemblance to the cabin of a steamboat."

He had been miraculously rescued on the road by a traveling magician, Torrini, and his young brother-in-law, Antonio.

○

TORRINI WAS A DARK, distinguished performer in his late fifties who was living a nomadic existence. He and Antonio crossed Europe from town to town in a special wooden wagon of Torrini's own design. The wagon contained his bedroom and workshop, but the rectangular structure could be pulled opened like a telescope to form a tiny auditorium and stage for his show. Taking an instant liking to Jean, the traveling magician nursed the boy back to health and impulsively explained his own story.

Torrini was born Edmond, the Count de Grisy, a French nobleman. His father, from Languedoc, was killed fighting for Louis XVI during the siege of the Tuileries. Edmond was trained as a physician in Florence. While treating a friend, a dying gambler, he discovered a special piece of apparatus hidden beneath his friend's sleeve, strapped to his arm. It was a metal box that could imperceptibly switch one pack of cards for another.

The physician took this ingenious metal box and used it to accomplish a conjuring trick. A magician named Comus specialized in playing a blindfolded game of piquet at the time. Using just sleight of hand to manipulate the cards, Comus invariably won the game. Torrini took offense at Comus's posters, which arrogantly boasted that Comus alone was able to accomplish this astonishing feat. Torrini challenged Comus, using the gambler's special box up his own sleeve to switch the deck. He amazed Comus and won the contest.

As Jean Robert recovered from his illness and took lessons in conjuring from Torrini, he volunteered to repair a broken automaton so that Torrini could use it once again in his shows. This Acrobat in the Box was an elaborate mechanical acrobat, about a foot tall, that would somersault out of a small chest and perform handstands or sit on the edge of the box, smoke a pipe, and then nod or shake his head to answer questions posed by the audience.

IT'S PROBABLY IMPORTANT to pause the story here, to consider the idea of magic automata. These were fashionable in magic for about a century, and they became important elements in Robert-Houdin's career. Torrini's Acrobat in the Box was, the author recounted, his first encounter with magic automata.

Automata are technically automated machines, at that time operated by spring motors, that could imitate natural motions. They were the predecessors to robots. They were expensive toys, the sorts of things that wealthy people would have on their mantles or in their drawing rooms, covered with a glass dome. Usually, they would repeat a short sequence of movements: birds that flapped their wings and chirped, a clown that strummed a mandolin, a little magician that moved the cups in a performance of the cups and balls. Some, showpieces for their creators, were given especially intricate motions, like the watchmaker Jaquet-Droz's drawing figure, a small boy who could draw several different images on a piece of paper. By Jean Robert's time, these automata were offered for public demonstrations.

During the eighteenth century, automata had become subjects for magic shows. A magician's automaton was made to imitate automata that the public had seen: small figures that moved with the expected snaps and pops of a clockwork device. But magic automata did impossible things. Either they moved in bold, muscular ways, unlike a delicate clockwork device, or they apparently interacted with the performer and the audience, as if reading the minds of the spectators or responding directly to their requests. For example, an early magic automaton, a bell ringer, would strike the bell to answer questions from the audience.

These magic automata are often called "false automata," because they did not use clockwork motors. Instead, an actual person operated them from some remote location, almost as one would operate a puppet. That person might be offstage to one side, pulling on an array of strings, leading to small pistons that had been arranged inside the magician's table. The pistons connected to levers inside the figure. This was how a magician's automaton apparently listened to the audience's questions, and then nodded or shook its head in response. This remote-control operation meant that although the magician's automaton was far simpler in its operation, it used deception to perform its routines.[9]

◯

Returning to Robert-Houdin's story, Torrini recognized the young man's interest in magic and taught him some of his best tricks. In Aubusson, when the wagon was involved in a crash and Torrini suffered a broken leg, the young pupil filled in for his mentor, performing the show and raising money for the necessary repairs. This was, the author noted, his first public performance.

Jean sat by his bedside as the old magician recovered; Torrini then confessed the most tragic details of his career. After his adventure with Comus, Torrini worked as a physician in Naples. There he frequented the shows of Giuseppe Pinetti, the famous Italian magician. Studying many of Pinetti's tricks, he quickly became a rival. Pinetti responded unexpectedly by befriending the new conjuror, even tempting him to take part in a special benefit show before King Ferdinand IV of Naples. Of course, Pinetti's extravagant offer was a trap, and Torrini ended up humiliated in front of the king with failed tricks. When a playing card was selected by the king, he found "a coarse insult to his majesty" written across its face.

Torrini related this story of treachery in operatic terms: "Pinetti, like the coward he was, had fled after the atrocious insult he had offered me. To have challenged him would be doing him too much honor, so I vowed to fight him with my own weapons, and humiliate the shameful traitor in my turn." He devoted himself to six months of study, so he could become more skillful than the famous Pinetti. He spent lavishly, building a show that it would be more beautiful, with apparatus even more decorative. Then, he carefully tracked Pinetti's tour, beating him to every city and winning the public's favor. Pinetti was ruined in Italy and desperately fled to Russia, where, "reduced to a state of abject misery," he died.

Torrini's triumph inspired his new career, and he appeared before Pope Pius VII in Rome. He married a young opera singer, Antonia Torrini. (This was the occasion of the Count de Grisy taking the name Torrini.) Her twin brother, Antonio Torrini, also joined the show. They traveled to Constantinople, performing a prestigious and innovative show, which is the very first suggestion in the literature of a Sawing a Person in Half effect.[10]

This special performance was before Emperor Selim III and the mysterious women of his harem, who watched from behind a gilt lattice screen.

In an effort to remain before the public, Torrini felt the pressure to create more and more innovative magic, noting, "I made a complete reform in my program. The card tricks no longer possessing the charm of novelty, as the meanest jugglers could do them, were nearly all suppressed, and I substituted other experiments." He created a dramatic scene he called the Son of William Tell, using his young son, Giovanni. A pistol was loaded with a marked bullet. A spectator took aim at his son, who held an apple between his teeth. The gun discharged, and the marked bullet was found inside the apple when the fruit was cut open.

The gun trick brought Torrini even more success, but one night he carelessly confused the lead bullets with the specially prepared wax bullets, which were designed to crumble as the gun was loaded. Giovanni was accidentally shot dead. Torrini was jailed, his wife, Antonia, died of a broken heart, and he fell into a deep depression. During Torrini's imprisonment, Antonio, his brother-in-law, offered steadfast support. When Torrini was released from jail, the two men took to the road in their special wagon, vowing to rebuild their fortune. That is when he encountered young Jean Robert at the side of the road. Torrini confessed that he noticed in the young man a resemblance to his own dead son, Giovanni.

Despite their dramatic friendship and these intensive lessons in magic, Jean Robert's adventure with Torrini did not initially influence him to become a professional magician. He felt that he was still too young to become a successful conjurer. He returned to his family after six months of travels with Torrini and Antonio and took a job with a Blois watchmaker.

⟲

THIS IS PROBABLY a good spot to stop Robert-Houdin's story and explain how you've been completely misled—how his readers had been lulled into an incredible fiction. The Torrini adventure occupied nearly one-fifth of the text in Robert-Houdin's *Memoirs,* and it explained his education and appreciation of magic. But there never was a Torrini.

Maybe you weren't fooled. There's all that suspicious stuff about taking a gambler's gimmick out of his sleeve and instantly becoming a great magician; Pinetti's melodramatic treachery (an insult written on a playing card!); and even that impossibly large wagon, supposedly lumbering down the country roads of France.

But a lot of people were fooled, and for a while—about a century—a lot of magicians were fooled. Besides all that blood and thunder, Torrini's account was strung together with names and anecdotes of historical magicians (for example, Comus and Pinetti), of actual rulers and some real events. It sounded like history. On Robert-Houdin's authority, Torrini was often listed as one of the great magicians of the past, his biographical details treated as fact, and included in histories of magic.

Why would a great magician bother with such an exaggerated story about his youth? For Robert-Houdin, this fiction actually accomplished a great deal. Being saved by a traveling showman, and then obliged to travel with him and return the favor, he could excuse his own fascination with the lower classes of show business, despite being raised in a successful family and being educated for an honored trade. Torrini linked the young man to the previous generation of magicians and made him an inevitable heir to the profession. The author could also criticize magic and magicians by using Torrini, a voice of authority, as a surrogate. Finally, and most important, Torrini provided a pedigree and nobility for magic—adding drama and relevance to conjuring. After shedding a tear over Torrini's histrionic contretemps, could there be any doubt that magic was an art?

Suspiciously, the Torrini adventure is filled with several strange points of view about magic that are particular to Robert-Houdin's *Memoirs*, more novelistic than realistic. One of those is the obsession that magic demands constant novelty: a trick becomes stale after a very short period of time, and the public will then abandon a performer. Another unexpected motif is the free-and-easy manner that if a trick is understood, it can quickly be performed, with mastery, before an audience. It was as if magic—in and of itself—could overwhelm an interested subject and imbue instant expertise. Any professional magician would laugh at these ideas, but once they were introduced as part of Torrini's lessons, they formed the roots of the mythologizing about Robert-Houdin.

The Torrini myth was finally exposed in 1943, as the biography of the magician was being researched in France. There was no history of the de

Grisy family—not a single family tree, birth record, or newspaper article. There was neither royal decree nor advertisement.[11] This revelation took many years to accept, partly because the Torrini fiction had been so attractive to magicians and partly because it had, embarrassingly, been already tightly woven into histories of magic.

After his *Memoirs* were published, as Robert-Houdin composed one of his magic books, he included Torrini's name in a list of past magicians. It must have seemed easy to continue the fiction. A recently discovered unpublished manuscript, from much earlier in Robert-Houdin's career, consisted of his brief history of the art. In this list of past magicians, Torrini was not mentioned—presumably because he had not yet been invented for the *Memoirs*.[12]

The question remains: What was the real story? How did Robert-Houdin really learn magic? A chapter in the first edition of the *Memoirs* provided a clue. Late in the book, there was a chapter that seemed to be a complete non sequitur. It was titled "Physionomy of the Mountbank-Conjurer" and was included, presumably, to draw a distinction with the author's growing success in Paris. The chapter began as if an unnamed traveling magician were relating his travails, but then this pretense fell away as the author described the traveling magician in first-person observations. He colorfully and lovingly detailed his ragtag existence, arriving in a town, begging the officials for a license, wearing a special costume of old clothes so as not to look too successful, then running back to change into good clothing before engaging the theater, in order to appear safely prosperous. His success relied upon cheap publicity stunts and then hoary old jokes to amuse the crowd. After the show, celebrating a coin purse that bulged with profits, the conjurer's family treated themselves to dinner; they laughed and argued, recalling the highlights of the day over a bottle of champagne.

It's apparent that Robert-Houdin had lived this life and flourished in this simple, enjoyable setting. More than likely, he had apprenticed with just such a showman—now unnamed, because history would have demonstrated that his mentor was as ordinary as Torrini was exceptional. At another place in the book, Robert-Houdin briefly mentioned that he had worked as a confederate for a magician; perhaps this was another clue to his early experience. When his book was translated to English, however, this chapter was omitted. Robert-Houdin had successfully concealed enough of his early experience to make the "Physionomy of the Mountbank-Conjurer" seem completely superfluous.[13]

○

RETURNING TO THE *Memoirs*, after leaving Torrini, the author was finally working in his chosen trade of watchmaking, but he discovered he was bored with the mechanical labor. He amused himself by forming an acting company with a group of friends and specialized in comedy roles. While he was working as an actor he met Josèphe Cecile Elegantine Houdin, the daughter of a successful Blois watchmaker, Jacques Houdin, who had moved his business to Paris. They married, and Jean Robert added his wife's prestigious name to his own, becoming Robert-Houdin.

He joined his father-in-law's business in Paris and told him about his plan to open a sophisticated little parlor in the capital, selling his mechanical toys and offering demonstrations in sleight of hand. His father-in-law, he wrote, supported the idea. His work as an actor and his early plans for the magic shop in Paris were mentioned briefly in the *Memoirs* but have been ignored by later authors. Clearly, he was a skilled performer and magician, with aspirations to succeed in this field, from the earliest years of his marriage.

In Paris he was visited by Antonio, Torrini's brother-in-law, who announced the death of the old showman. Antonio encouraged Robert-Houdin's plans to create his own magic show.

Robert-Houdin visited the magic dealer Rujol, and there met many of his fellow magicians. He studied his competition and commented on their shortcomings. Comte, a sweet old conjurer and ventriloquist who had famously performed before the king, had a magic theater in Paris. He was gallant and poetic to the ladies but insulting to the gentlemen. His strengths seemed to be as a marketer, a master of coupons and gifts to sell tickets at his box office.

Phillipe's show combined automata with Chinese tricks, but Robert-Houdin was sarcastic about the magician's unusual costume, a long, jewel-encrusted robe, and his flashy finale, the production of a bowl of water "performed, if not gracefully, at least in a way to excite the lively admiration of spectators."

*The French conjuror Phillipe, with his fanciful
Oriental show.*

Finally, the Italian magician Bosco was grudgingly complimented for his sleight-of-hand skills but criticized for his overly dramatic performance of the cups and balls onstage, a trick only suitable in a town square for tossed coins. Bosco's many crudities were noted: his odd costume with short sleeves, his coarse accent, and his gruesome tricks, such as his decapitation of a pigeon. "Zhall it be, ladies, wiz blood or wizout?" Robert-Houdin quoted him.

Once again, a fictional character allowed the author to politely disguise his criticisms. Antonio Torrini accompanied Robert-Houdin to Bosco's show and was nauseated by his bloody deceptions. When the show was only partly finished, Antonio stood and announced to his friend, "Let us go, for I am turning sick."

Comte, Phillipe, and Bosco were all still alive when the *Memoirs* were published in 1858.

FOR ABOUT SIX YEARS Robert-Houdin concentrated on his own business, producing automata and novelty clocks of his own design. One of his specialties was a pretty clock with a clear glass dial and no visible clockwork, gears, or springs: seemingly no connections to the hands themselves. Still, the hands on the dial mysteriously turned and kept perfect time.

Historians now understand that, during this time, he also manufactured apparatus for other successful magicians and started building apparatus for his own shows. He performed magic shows at private homes and for parties. These shows would have primarily drawn upon his skills at sleight of hand.[14]

The *Memoirs* don't mention this early work in magic, but the author did write about his father-in-law's failure in business, which forced him to focus on commercial enterprises. An additional hardship was the death of his first wife in 1843; Robert-Houdin remarried the following year. He accepted a commission for five thousand francs to build a complicated automaton, a writing and drawing figure. In order to devote his efforts to this invention, he rented an apartment in Belleville, a working-class neighborhood just outside of Paris, where he could avoid the distractions of his family.

Robert-Houdin's creation is described in his *Memoirs*. It was a figure of a man, about a foot tall, seated at a fancy Louis Quinze desk. The cams and motors of the mechanism were, presumably, in the large chest hidden beneath the figure. When requested, the figure would draw a picture or write out a phrase. From Robert-Houdin's description, it seems that the automaton could have written out at least a dozen different responses and appeared to answer questions extemporaneously.

It is worth pausing to carefully consider his account of this invention. In fact, three examples of writing or drawing automata—purely clockwork—preceded Robert-Houdin's. The Pierre Jaquet-Droz Draftsman and Writer (two separate figures) were built in Switzerland between 1768 and 1774. Maillardet's Juvenile Draftsman (one figure that wrote poetry or drew pictures), was built in England sometime around 1800. These figures are still in existence. They have been exhibited for many years and are considered some of the finest and most intricate automata ever constructed. It's impossible to believe that Robert-Houdin could have constructed a figure equal to, or surpassing, these astonishing examples—even with eighteen months of intensive work, as he described. Quite simply, such an achievement would have earned him a lifetime of fame.

So it is possible he made a careful copy of Maillardet's figure, which disappeared from public view around this time. Or perhaps we should ask if this was actually a magic automaton, operated by a concealed assistant?

Robert-Houdin's description sounds like a magic trick, with the automaton responding to the audience's requests. In contrast, the Droz Draftsman could draw only four different images; the Maillardet Juvenile Draftsman wrote three different poems and drew four different images. And there are other clues that Robert-Houdin's automaton was a deception, including the inventor's use of a rattling motor to make the device sound more complicated and a casual remark about the machine's triviality, when it was exhibited for judges at the Paris Exhibition of 1844. There, it was shown to King Louis Philippe and his son, the Comte de Paris.

In the *Memoirs*, Robert-Houdin described that he won a silver medal for the automaton at the Exhibition. This would have been an especially bold achievement if the device were actually a deception. But perhaps he was in good company. The *Memoirs* recorded Robert-Houdin's fascination with Wolfgang von Kempelen's famous Chess Player, a false automaton with a man concealed inside that was built to amuse Empress Maria Theresa in 1770, which toured around the world and convinced audiences that a machine could actually think. Although the history of the Chess Player was well-documented, Robert-Houdin included his own fictional history of the Chess Player, a fantastic, melodramatic tale similar to his Torrini invention.

After the 1844 Exhibition, Robert-Houdin's automaton was purchased by P. T. Barnum and displayed in London, then taken to Barnum's Museum in New York. It was lost when the museum was destroyed by a fire in 1865. Barnum's interest doesn't necessarily inspire confidence. A magic automaton, operated by a hidden assistant, would have been right at home amid Barnum's well-known grab bag of exhibits.[15]

LATE IN 1844, Robert-Houdin decided to open his own magic theater; he wrote how he took a lease on a theater space, a gallery in the second floor of the Palais Royal, and began converting it to an auditorium to hold about 180 people. He opened his exclusive little magic shows, christened the "Soirées Fantastique," in July 1845, when he was thirty-nine years old. By minimizing his experience with magic and focusing on his work as a clockmaker, his expertise in magic seems surprising and unexpectedly successful. But a careful reading of the book suggested that he had been gaining experience with magic throughout his life.

A famous section of the *Memoirs* was the magician's list of "proposed reforms" for his art.

Remembering Torrini's principles, I intended to have an elegant and simple stage, unencumbered by all the paraphernalia of the ordinary conjurer, which looks more like a toyshop than a serious performance.... Apparatus of transparent or opaque glass, according to circumstances, would suffice for all my operations. . . . Real sleight-of-hand must not be the tinman's work but the artist's, and people do not visit the latter to see instruments perform.... I quite did away with [accomplices].... Jets of gas ... were to be substituted on my stage for the thousands of candles ... only intended to dazzle the spectators.... [I abolished] those long tablecloths reaching to the ground, beneath which an assistant is always suspected. . . . I substituted consoles of gilt wood after the style of Louis XV.... Of course, I abstained from any eccentric costume [but chose] the attire civilized society has agreed to accept for evening dress, for I was always of [the] opinion that bizarre accouterments, far from giving the wearer any consideration, on the contrary cast disfavor upon him.... [I would] make no puns or play upon words.... Finally, I wished to offer new experiments divested of all charlatanism, and possessing no other resources than those offered by skillful manipulation.[16]

The author boldly proposed this as "a complete regeneration in the art of conjuring," and then included his fictional friend Antonio for a judgment; the magician would be like the famous French actor Talma, who appeared "suddenly at the Théâtre-Francais clothed in the simple antique toga, at a time when tragedies were performed in silk coats, powered perukes, and red heels." Robert-Houdin claimed that he "did not recognize the justice of the comparison . . . [as I] held no brevet rank in the army of conjurers [and] trembled to see my innovations badly received."

FOR GENERATIONS after the *Memoirs*, these reforms were quoted by magicians and waved like a battle flag; they are what earned the author the soubriquet "The Father of Modern Magic" from his fellow conjurors. And it wasn't just magicians. In 1860, *The Saturday Review* praised the *Memoirs*, pointing out how, "Robert-Houdin may be considered to have done for the art of conjuring what Beau Brummel did for the dress of his day, in making simplicity and elegance his study, instead of the pompous, complicated style in fashion with his rivals. . . . So rigidly, in fact, does he advocate purity of conjuring that the solemnity of Bosco, the puffery of our own Wizard of the North, and even little complimentary speeches to the ladies, are all involved in one common condemnation as unworthy of the true artist."[17] In 1877, an article in *Harper's New Monthly Magazine* proclaimed Robert-Houdin "The King of Conjurers."[18]

Beau Brummel was an apt analogy, for in 1860, this dandy was famous for having simplified men's dress, though that reputation doesn't quite translate to the modern age—Brummel was also famous for taking hours on his toilette, spending lavishly on the perfect linens and tailored clothing, and preening over every detail of his appearance, in a perfectly unreal way. Today we probably think of Brummel not as innovative but as a needlessly fussy adjustment of the old, tired fashions.

Robert-Houdin and his son, depicted in his Paris theater.

When Robert-Houdin premiered at his Paris Theatre on July 3, 1845, the show quickly earned praise and established his prominence in Paris. Those first reviews give interesting insights into his appeal.[19]

Le Moniteur Universel: "All of artistic and fashionable Pairs will want to go and admire [Robert-Houdin's] charming automata, which walk, act, listen, and hear as if they were animated, intelligent beings. This little theatre is good fortune for lovers of tasteful pleasures and for fathers of families."

Le Charivari: "M. Robert-Houdin, a mechanician of the first order, a clockmaker of precision . . . and who makes all the mechanical pieces which the most celebrated French and foreign prestidigitators use for their best tricks . . . has wished to become a master in his own turn. [He] does not only execute his tricks himself. Oh, no! That would be too easy! He makes the automata conjure. . . . It is the science of Vaucanson, [and] Maelzel . . . combined with the art of Bosco, Comus and Philippe; it is mechanism and conjuring conjointly united."

L'Illustration: "Walking in the footsteps of Vaucanson and Maelzel, [Robert-Houdin] is less a physician than a clever mechanician, who, tired of constructing for all past and present magicians [now offers] many more improvements for his own use . . . to prove his talents as a mechanician. However, without pretending to be a prestidigitator, M. Robert-Houdin . . . seduced the spectators by his most complicated mechanical pieces."

We know that he was skillful at sleight of hand—his later books demonstrated that—and he used these abilities subtly in his show. But the reviews made it clear that his appeal was as an inventor who was now taking to the stage to exhibit his own creations. There was very little emphasis on prestidigitation (the popular French word, then in vogue, for sleight of hand).

The reviews demonstrate that Robert-Houdin's show was deemed more sophisticated—apparently more honest—than if he had appeared as a common magician. His good taste, good will, and self-awareness made this a prized theatrical novelty for Paris sophisticates. Like Beau Brummel, it was not about a new fashion so much as using old, reliable fashions to give a sense of quality.

In fact, if we step back and look at his "reforms," we see that they were not particularly novel. Evening clothes had been worn by magicians before Robert-Houdin's time, and in the *Memoirs,* the author actually wrote about Philippe entering in black evening wear for the first section of his show.[20] The long tablecloths had already been eliminated from magicians' tables in Pinetti's time, before Robert-Houdin's birth.[21] The Louis XV rococo furniture chosen by Robert-Houdin, carved filigree and heavily gilded, was the fashion one hundred years earlier, when Parisians wore knee breeches, satin coats, and lace cravats. In Robert-Houdin's time, it was enjoying a revival as a safe, old-fashioned, and ostentatious display of French taste.

And finally, his plea for minimalism—"I intended to have an elegant and simple stage, unencumbered by all the paraphernalia of the ordinary conjurer, which looks more like a toyshop than a serious performance"—is virtually impossible to reconcile with the previous century and a half of magic. Engravings demonstrate that few magicians had a stage as decorative as Robert-Houdin's; or one as crowded with gold furniture and toy-like automata; or with more reliance on mechanical devices.

We can see from his reviews that the automata were beautiful and amazing, but they were the last gasp of a century-old tradition in magic, a specialty of magicians like Christopher Pinchbeck and Isaac Fawkes. Nonetheless, those gilt furnishings gave polite society permission to see a magic show. According to the *Journal des Femmes*, Robert-Houdin's show was "full of respectability and good taste," and "an elite society meets every evening in this lovely candy box too small for the number of people who would like to fill it."[22]

○

ROBERT-HOUDIN BECAME FAMOUS for a number of wonderful deceptions, and we can get a sense of his show through the accounts of these mysteries.

One of his favorite effects, dating from the premiere of his Soirées Fantastique, was the Miraculous Orange Tree. The routine represented the epitome of his art, "mechanism and conjuring conjointly united," as *Le Charivari* cleverly expressed it. Robert-Houdin showed a small, round, green-leafed tree in a square planter. He borrowed a handkerchief from a lady, rubbing it in his hands and causing it to disappear. After a brief display of sleight of hand, he applied a mysterious vapor to the automaton tree. As the audience watched, it sprouted white blossoms, and then, as the leaves parted, he revealed the growth of a handful of oranges. Most of these were picked and distributed to the audience. The final orange, at the top of the tree, split open, revealing the missing handkerchief inside. Two automaton butterflies lifted the corners of the spectator's handkerchief, displaying it as the magician took his bow.

The Enchanted Orange Tree, a Robert-Houdin automaton.

Another popular magic automaton, from the first performance of the Soirée Fantastiques, was the Pastry Cook of the Palais Royal. This was a tiny, dollhouse-size pastry shop, artistically made. The audience could see automaton bakers inside, rolling out the dough and tending to the ovens. A tiny chef, about nine inches tall, appeared at the front door and took the orders from the audience, nodding or shaking his head in response to their questions, disappearing through the front door, and then quickly emerging again with the requested sweets, cakes, and liqueurs on a tiny tray.[23]

After his first season in Paris, he introduced the Inexhaustible Bottle, a dark glass wine bottle that could pour various samples of spirits, as called out by the audience. The trick was a popular favorite, first for the complimentary refreshments and second for the amazing way that the bottle could apparently accommodate every request.

Another incredible feat was the Ethereal Suspension. The magician introduced his young son, then about seven years old. He apparently showed a bottle of the new drug, ether, holding it beneath his son's nose to induce a hypnotic trance. The magician enhanced this illusion by having an assistant backstage pour ether on a hot plate, allowing the audience to smell the sweet, distinctive fumes. Once under the spell, the

The Ethereal Suspension, the boy suspended atop a single cane.

boy seemed to be as light as a feather, balanced upright on two vertical poles that touched his elbows. Robert-Houdin then removed one pole and lifted the boy gently from his ankles. His son floated horizontally, as if sleeping on his side, with only one elbow supported by an upright cane.

One of his most successful effects, introduced several years later, was Second Sight. This was the mind-reading feat in which Robert-Houdin had personal objects offered to him in the audience, while his blindfolded son instantly identified the objects. His son, Emile, had a quick mind and a remarkable ability to learn the secret codes used in the act. The magician coded information to his son in the casual conversation he carried out with the audience: looking for objects, thanking the spectators, or asking his son if he could identify what he was holding in his hand. Although Robert-Houdin's show involved many pieces of complicated apparatus, the *Memoirs* made it clear that Second Sight was distinctly different. This performance didn't require any of Robert-Houdin's elaborate furniture or complicated mechanisms. After one of their shows at the Palais Royal, the father and son could dash across town and begin a performance at variety theaters in Paris or in private homes, not only expanding the magician's repertoire but also expanding his audience.

In later years, as audiences gradually became aware of a code, the magician improved on the trick by not speaking when he was in the audience. Instead, he used electric wires and batteries to secretly signal his son. An offstage assistant watched the magician carefully, identified the objects, and signaled the boy, using a sort of quiet, concealed telegraph.

❦

SEVERAL TIMES IN his career, Robert-Houdin packed up his Soirée Fantastique and took it on the road, performing in other European cities. In 1848, when he first encountered John Henry Anderson, he had left Paris because the theaters were closed during the February Revolution. He accepted an engagement in London and earned particular praise from his critics, who considered him every inch a conjuror: "Much as we have thought of M. M. Döbler, Philippe, Herrmann, et cetera, we must confess that M. Robert-Houdin is superior to them all. He has for a long time enjoyed a high Parisian reputation, and is the originator of most of the clever tricks with which we have been made acquainted by other 'wizards,' none of whom, however, perform them with the same admirable dexterity."[24]

He was also asked to perform before royalty—in France he devised a clever trick for Louis Philippe, in which borrowed handkerchiefs were discovered buried in a box on the grounds of St. Cloud. In England he appeared several times before Queen Victoria and produced a special garland of flowers that spelled her name. Some of his most entertaining anecdotes originated with these command performances—from the Russian ambassador in London who followed him into his theater to learn how the tricks were done, to Robert-Houdin's desperation to eat a meal in a room without candles. After his successful performance at Buckingham Palace, Victoria's servants had forgotten to light the room. The magician, too tired and too hungry after his efforts, made his best efforts to devour his dinner in the dark.

The *Memoirs* include many charmingly self-effacing stories, which perfectly leaven the boastful claims. The author manages to put an entire audience of friends to sleep at his first dress rehearsal. He endures the foolish exaggerations of agents, who attempt to charm him into touring. In Hertford, at the end of an English tour, the magician overstayed his welcome, and his third and final performance attracted an audience of exactly three people. In a long, funny anecdote, he related how he performed the entire show and then treated all three spectators to dinner with him, having prepared a table with a delicious feast that was pushed onto the stage at the conclusion of the show. His lesson, he wrote, was "in offering a farewell to the public, you should not wait till there are none left to receive it."

After a short and spectacular six-year career, Robert-Houdin retired to Blois in 1852, naming his son-in-law as his successor in Paris. In Blois, he was able to devote his time to optical and electrical experiments. It was during his retirement that he was summoned to travel to Algeria on behalf of the French government.

○

AT A CLIMACTIC POINT in the *Memoirs*, just before the Algerian adventure, Robert-Houdin concluded his performing career by recalling an anecdote from 1844. This was the stinging remark at the Exposition: the jury considered Robert-Houdin's writing and drawing automaton, novelty clocks, and mechanical toys. When Robert-Houdin told the gentlemen of the jury the long hours that were spent in creating his amusing automaton, he was disappointed to be told, "It is a great pity, Monsieur Robert-Houdin, that you did not apply the talent you have evinced in fancy objects to serious labors."

Robert-Houdin described his pique, and as readers, we prepare for a magnificent defense of the art of amusement: the insights of a great conjuror. Here is his response, as he proudly recalled it:

> Sir, I know no works more serious than those which give a man an honest livelihood. . . . At the period when I devoted myself to chronometers, I hardly earned enough to live upon; at present, I have four workmen to help me in making my automata; and as the least skillful among them earns six francs a day, you can easily form an idea what I earn myself. Now, sir, I ask you, if I ought to return to my old trade?[25]

Another jury member, the famous Baron Seguier, replied, "Go on, Monsieur Robert-Houdin—go on; I am convinced that your ingenious works, after leading you to success, will conduct you straight to useful discoveries."

In other words, congratulations on making money. Someday, you'll probably be able to do something important. To which Robert-Houdin gave this final response: "I thank you for your encouraging prediction, and will do my best to prove its correctness."

It's not an anecdote that we want to read from our artists; it's not a defense of art. The jury members' remarks had an impact. Although he claimed to have won a medal for his automata, in retirement, Robert-Houdin devoted himself to serious experiments with timepieces. He returned to display his electric pendulum clocks in 1855.

○

WHAT DID ROBERT-HOUDIN achieve? One of his legacies is his most famous quote, "A conjurer is an actor playing the part of a magician," which has often been cited to demonstrate magic's essential place in the theater. But like many of the magician's achievements, the actual inspiration was muddled and later overstated. This observation was actually buried in a short chapter defining the terms "escamotage" and "prestidigitation," in his magic book, *Secrets of Conjuring and Magic*, and debating a short-lived fashion for magicians, moving their hands quickly to give their movements special attention.

A conjurer is not a juggler; he is an actor playing the part of a magician; an artist whose fingers have more need to move with deftness than with speed. I may even add that where sleight of hand is involved, the quieter the movement of the performer, the more readily will the spectators be deceived. The conjurer claims to possess supernatural powers; why then should he need to exaggerate the quickness of his movements?[26]

His verdict was sensible, but it's a disappointment that this famous definition of a magician was actually arguing "deftness" over "speed." Even Professor Hoffmann, Robert-Houdin's defender and the translator of his books, thought the chapter "will have but little interest."

What did he create? There's no question that he has inspired magicians, but much of this was done with a puzzling series of exaggerations about his career. Quite honestly, he may not have realized that he did not make reforms. He made choices and selected fashions, which then made him popular with Paris audiences.

He also was the first to suggest a curious construction, which we will conveniently modernize from Robert-Houdin's starched Victorian prose, because it's still useful today, whenever magicians want to call attention to themselves: "I know you don't like magic. It isn't cool. It's disreputable. It's tacky. In fact, straight-up, I don't even like it. But I am an artist. And I have completely revolutionized magic!"

Frustratingly, in an effort to ignore his years spent learning magic and to discount his associations with other magicians, he minimized the training of a good performer—suggesting an almost magical way that someone can step onstage without needing experience. And by continually emphasizing the need for novelty, he gave the impression that his own career exemplified genuine innovation and novelty in magic.

○

WHEN WE EXAMINE the famous Algerian adventure—the climax to the French magician's book and his lasting lesson for modern magicians— we can see how fact and fiction were finally confused in the *Memoirs*.

However, when the book was first actually analyzed, it was not the obvious fictions—like the Torrini story—that inspired doubt but his cavalier treatment of other magicians, his claims to have invented his own effects, and his reforms for the art of magic. Those were the inconsistencies that could be easily examined by a curious magician in the twentieth century.

Enter Houdini, just exactly where we don't expect him and completely out of chronological order. Maybe that's the perfect way for a famous conjuror to appear on the scene—as if by magic.

CHAPTER 7

THE UNMASKING

T HE REASON YOU'VE been stumbling over that name, Robert-Houdin—the reason you are trying to pronounce it as a French name, but it somehow doesn't sound right to you—is because it reminds you of another famous magician.

Erich Weiss was born in 1874 in Budapest, Hungary, three years after Robert-Houdin's death. His family immigrated to America. His father was a rabbi, and they first settled with a small Jewish community in Appleton, Wisconsin, and then moved to New York City when Erich was thirteen years old.[1]

The boy became intrigued by magic and, when he was still a teenager, found a copy of Robert Shelton Mackenzie's English edition of *The Memoirs of Robert-Houdin*. Erich fell under its spell, greedily reading the book and committing long sections of it to memory. Using Robert-Houdin as a model, he decided that magic would be his life's goal. In the words of the former Erich Weiss:

From the moment that I began to study the art, he became my guide and hero. I accepted his writings as my textbook and my gospel. What Blackstone is to the struggling lawyer, Hardee's *Tactics* to the would-be officer, or Bismarck's life and writings to the coming statesman, Robert-Houdin's books were to me. To my unsophisticated mind, his *Memoirs* gave to the profession a dignity worth attaining at the cost of earnest, life-long effort. When it became necessary for me to take a stage name, and a fellow-player, possessing a veneer of culture, told me that if I would add the letter "I" to Houdin's name, it would mean, in the French language, "like Houdin," I adopted the suggestion with enthusiasm. I asked nothing more of life than to become in my profession "like Robert-Houdin." [2]

Houdini, with his book in which he "unmasked" his idol, Robert-Houdin.

"Add the letter 'I' " doesn't make sense, but proving that the *Memoirs* served as Erich's gospel, the actual formula can been prized out of Robert-Houdin's text. The French magician wrote of an early-nineteenth-century "custom of most conjurers of the day, who thought an Italian name more attractive."[3] Torrini was the name of Robert-Houdin's mentor. By combining Torrini with Houdin, young Erich Weiss intended to symbolically link himself to this great tradition of wizards. He became Harry Houdini.

◌

IT WAS NOT just Erich Weiss. Once he had been proclaimed "The Father of Modern Magic," Robert-Houdin became the champion and the model for Victorian magicians. He provided a new origin story. Once his book was studied, students of the art had a blueprint and an inspiration for the role of a magician in modern society.

His pleasant career, his interesting inventions, and his tasteful reforms would not have meant much without the final chapters in his book, the story of his adventure in Algeria. This was the tale that proclaimed the importance of magic and the potential of a wise magician—the apparent capstone to a career that demonstrated the soundness of the foundation. Six years of shows in Paris and other European cities made Robert-Houdin a popular French magician. Two performances in Algeria secured his legend. Like any legend, every retelling has provided new emphasis and carefully omitted the inconsistencies, defining, in gradual steps, its apparent importance. So the story of Algeria has been affectionately retold over the past century.[4]

Sometime in 1856, when he was in retirement, Robert-Houdin was summoned to Algeria "at the special request of the French Government."[5] It was suggested that a performance in colonial Algeria might cleverly "counteract the influence of the marabout miracle-mongers over the ignorant Arabs. It seems that the marabout priests were continually fanning the flames of discontent and rebellion against French domination,"[6] as they believed that "their magic coupled with continuous fighting would shortly drive the French from the country."[7] "The French government, therefore, requested [Robert-]Houdin to visit Algeria and perform before the natives in order to show them that a French wizard, using only sleight-of-hand and the resources of science, was greater than the greatest of marabouts who pretended to occult powers."[8] His show could prove that "the French had not only more powerful armies, but magicians who were infinitely better than native ones."[9] In this way, the diplomatic mission would be "a great service for the homeland."[10]

The magician and his wife sailed from Marseilles, arriving in North Africa in September of that year. "The day he arrived in North Africa, a revolt erupted, [and] the scheduled fetes for the Arab chieftains had to be postponed."[11] Robert-Houdin used the time to carefully prepare his program. On the appointed evening, the chieftains arrived at the theater, curious to witness French magic. Robert-Houdin produced cannonballs from an empty hat, "visual evidence of France's limitless armaments." When he produced flowers from the same hat, the deception "suggested his magic controlled nature." A handful of silver coins passed from his hands into a crystal box, hanging over the stage; this "implied that the strongest fort could be penetrated by French ingenuity."[12]

For the climax of his show, for his final lessons to the chieftains, he planned three of his greatest feats. "If the audience suspected he had supernatural powers, they were right, Robert-Houdin asserted. He could deprive even the most powerful man of his strength. Anyone who doubted this should come forward."[13]

A muscular Arab accepted the challenge and swaggered to the stage. Robert-Houdin displayed a small wooden box, like a jewelry chest or a cashbox with a handle on the top. He placed it on the stage and said, "Lift the box." The interpreter made these instructions clear. The Arab nodded, stooped, and picked up the box effortlessly. He placed it back on the stage and "then stood with folded arms, as if asking, 'What next?'"[14]

The magician announced that he would make the man "weaker than a woman,"[15] and commanded him to lift the box again. The muscular volunteer stooped to pick it up, but the chest would not budge, even when he wrapped both hands around the handle. He tugged and strained, and "it seemed that if he could not lift the chest, he might manage to rip it apart. However, Robert-Houdin was prepared for that, too. He waved his hand, and the strong man's efforts were turned to frantic contortions. As he writhed about, still clutching the box handle, Robert-Houdin gave another gesture. The Arab, suddenly letting go of the handle, reeled back, jumped to the aisle and raced out of the theatre, covering his head with his robe and screaming."[16]

The trick relied upon the latest technology. The magician had concealed a powerful electromagnet beneath the stage, and the little wooden chest had an iron plate concealed inside. "Wires from the magnet ran to a switch backstage. When the current was on, it was impossible even for a Hercules to move the box. The Arab's cry of agony? He had received an electric shock, generated by an induction coil, through the metal handle."[17]

The magician then began a series of masterful illusions. "Having demonstrated his own incredible powers, Robert-Houdin now proceeded to match those of the marabouts."[18] He challenged someone from the audience to come onstage, mark a bullet with a distinctive scratch, load it into a gun, and take aim at the magician's heart.

An Arab eagerly volunteered: "With a gleaming smile, the Arab exclaimed happily, 'I will kill you.'"[19] The magician held an apple, impaled on a knife, as his magic talisman. He stood several paces from the Arab, posed with the apple, and told the man to fire. The gun exploded. As the smoke cleared, Robert-Houdin was still standing, smiling broadly. He showed how the marked bulled had lodged in the apple, so that "dividing the apple [he extracted] from it the marked bullet."[20]

His Algerian audience was shocked to see the magician defy death. The magician invited another spectator on the stage and instructed him to crouch on a tabletop, concealed under a large wicker cone. "[O]n the cone being removed, [the volunteer was] found to have vanished."[21] The magician's seeming ability to make men disappear was met with a gasp from the audience. "That broke up the show. The spectators raced from the theatre, each fearful that he would be the next victim of Robert-Houdin's magic."[22] "There was pandemonium in the theatre as terrified spectators raced to the exits."[23]

In the following days, Robert-Houdin was presented with a precious scroll from the chieftains, "extolling his baffling demonstrations."[24] He later toured the interior of the country, demonstrating additional feats of magic, and overall "his trip as special Ambassador Magician was completely successful; when the native magicians were shown to have inferior miracles, the Algerians gave up their continual fighting."[25]

"How well the famous French wizard succeeded in his mission is a matter of history."[26] He left Algiers with the admiration of his audiences. "Their amazement deepened into awe, and one and all acknowledged that the Frank was a more powerful magician than any of their own people."[27] The residents of Algieria "lost all faith in the miracles of the marabouts."[28]

That composite history, taken from some of the most influential books on magic, will give a good impression of the result of this creation myth. That's the story that made Erich Weiss's heart race and cast Robert-Houdin as a hero.

◯

THERE IS NO contemporaneous account of Robert-Houdin's mission, simply a few newspaper articles that confirm it. So the best evidence has always been the *Memoirs*, although details have probably been exaggerated, and the story has been told from the perspective of colonialism, racism, and a prejudice toward native beliefs.

He told a good story, but by examining the details, we can see that the truth was far more interesting. The inconsistencies and adjustments, which have been clearly written in the *Memoirs*, suggest Robert-Houdin's muddled purpose and the real responses to his magic.

According to the *Memoirs*, Robert-Houdin received a letter sometime in 1854 from Colonel de Neveu, the head of the political office in French colonial Algiers: "The distinguished functionary begged me to proceed to our colony, and give my performances before the principal chieftains of the Arab tribes."[29]

Colonel De Neveu, the man who brought Robert-Houdin to Algeria.

Robert-Houdin was then enjoying his retirement near Blois, so he explained that he was unable to accept the invitation. A year later, in 1855, Colonel de Neveu wrote again, asking the magician to come to Algeria. Again, Robert-Houdin was unable to accept; he had submitted his electric clock designs to the Universal Exhibition and was awaiting the decision on medal winners. In June 1856, de Neveu wrote a third time, reminding him of the invitation and stating that the mission was of a "quasi-political" nature. From the *Memoirs*:

> It is known that a majority of revolts which have to be suppressed in Algeria are excited by intriguers, who say they are inspired by the Prophet, and are regarded by the Arabs as envoys of God on earth to deliver them from the oppression of the Roumi (Christians). These false prophets and holy marabouts, who are no more sorcerers than I am, and indeed even less so, still contrive to influence the fanaticism of their co-religionists by tricks as primitive as are the spectators before whom they are performed. The government was, therefore, anxious to destroy their pernicious influence, and reckoned on me to do so. They hoped, with reason, by the aid of my experiments, to prove to the Arabs that the tricks of their marabouts were mere child's play and owing to their simplicity could not be done by an envoy from heaven, which led us very naturally to show them that we are their superiors in everything, and, as for sorcerers, there are none like the French. [30]

What was the point of the mission? According to the *Memoirs*, the invitation was dismissed for two years. There was no uprising that would need to be put down by magic. There was no imminent war. The invitation was clearly going out in one-year increments, and Robert-Houdin then described how he had been brought at a specific time, "[traveling on] the Mediterranean in the worst month of the year," so that he arrived to entertain at the annual fete, or autumn festival, in the city of Algiers. In other words, he was being brought as an entertainer for a specific event, without any clear need to prevent an uprising.

It's also not explained whether he was supposed to present himself as a genuine French sorcerer—a man with greater magic than the marabouts—or as an expert in scientific deception, who could have demonstrated scientific marvels and exposed the marabouts' fraud about sorcery. If Robert-Houdin pretended to perform real magic, for the first time in his career, it would have been difficult to argue to the Algerians that magical powers did not exist. This confusion is written into Robert-Houdin's first description of the mission: "they hoped . . . to prove . . . that the tricks of the marabouts were mere child's play, and owing to their simplicity could not be done by an envoy from Heaven." In other words, he wanted to demonstrate that there was nothing magical about the marabouts' feats. But Robert-Houdin concluded that very same sentence with a contrary view: "we are their superiors in everything, and, as for sorcerers, there are none like the French."[31] There he suggested that the point of his sorcery was to be convincingly superior.

HE TRAVELED TO Algeria with his wife and an assistant, carrying boxes of special apparatus that he'd used in his Paris shows. They arrived in Algiers on September 17, 1856. *The Globe and Traveller*, a London newspaper, reported, "M. Robert-Houdin, the well-known sleight of hand performer, [is] proceeding to Algiers, at the request of the Governor-General, to give some representations before a number of the Arab chiefs, who are shortly to assemble in that city."[32] The magician was immediately informed that the plans had been changed. A portion of Kabylia had re-volted some time earlier, and troops had been sent to that region to sup-press the insurrection. The annual autumn festival would be postponed for a month, and Colonel de Neveu asked if Robert-Houdin would be willing to wait in the city until his shows were rescheduled. Robert-Houdin agreed, joking, "I consider myself in military employ." This delay actually turned the trip into a commercial enterprise. As they waited for the festival, the magician was offered the use of a prominent theater where he could perform three nights a week, sharing the stage with an opera company.

Robert-Houdin accepted the offer, as it would allow him to practice his show in front of the Arab population, and also "to pocket a very wel-come sum of money" from the box office. Colonel de Neveu suggested that the magician's performances would be useful "by employing the minds of the Algerines [and] prevent them speculating on the eventuali-ties of the [Kabylian] campaign."

The legendary duel of magic has been often described (and sometimes even illustrated) as taking place in the middle of an outdoor stage or in a clearing surrounded by native tents. But Robert-Houdin's shows were per-formed at the Bab-Azoun Theatre, a modern European-designed audito-rium that the author described as "a very neat house, in the style of the Variétés at Paris, and decorated with considerable taste." The building still stands today, as the Théâtre National Algérien Mahieddine Bachtarzi.

Despite Colonel de Neveu's desire to "employ the minds of the Alger-ines," the magician wrote that his show failed to attract the desired crowd: "I may say the Arabs who came were very few; for these men, with their indolent and sensual temper, consider the happiness of laying on a mat and smoking far above a spectacle." When the festival resumed and Robert-Houdin's official performances were rescheduled, "the governor, guided by the profound knowledge he had of their character, never invited them to a fete: he sent them a military summons."

Six Algerian chieftans, photographed just a few years after Robert-Houdin's appearance before them. Bou-Allem, who hosted the magician at his home, is in the front row, third from left.

His shows for the Arab chieftains were scheduled for October 28 and 29. The magician went to the front of the theater and watched the parade of anxious guests who had been ordered to attend. He described the spectacle:

These caids, agas, bash-agas, and other titled Arabs, held the places of honor, for they occupied the orchestra stalls and the dress circle. . . . Then came the turn of the chiefs. These sons of nature could not understand that they were boxed up thus, side by side, to enjoy a spectacle, and our comfortable seats, far from seeming so to them, bothered them strangely. I saw them fidgeting about for some time, and trying to tuck their legs under them, after the fashion of European tailors.... This strange medley of spectators was indeed a most curious sight. Some sixty Arab chiefs, clothed in their red mantles (the symbol of their submission to France), on which one or more decorations glistened, gravely awaited my performance with majestic dignity.[33]

In a box to one side, the French governor-general, Marshal Jacques Louis Randon, sat with his family. Other civilian authorities filled the boxes.

As soon as I walked on the stage, I felt quite at my ease, and enjoyed, in anticipation, the sight I was going to amuse myself with. I felt, I confess, rather inclined to laugh at myself and my audience, for I stepped forth, wand in hand, with all the gravity of a real sorcerer. Still, I did not give way, for I was here not merely to amuse a curious and kind public, I must

The European-style theater where Robert-Houdin performed his supposed duel of magic.

produce a startling effect upon coarse minds and prejudices, for I was enacting the part of a French marabout.

At this point, just moments before the show began, Robert-Houdin understood that he was to present himself as a real wizard. But as his account continued, he quickly changed his mind. Beginning the show in grave silence, which he thought would be staid and threatening, only made the performance uneasy. So, he began to address the audience directly, through the translators, soliciting laughter that made him more comfortable in front of his guests.

He recorded that the production of iron cannonballs from an empty hat received "delighted admiration," as did the production of flowers. Gold coins disappeared in his hands and reappeared in a crystal box hanging over the stage. Robert-Houdin ascribed no special symbolism to these tricks; they were popular successes that he had performed at his Paris theater. Instead of the Inexhaustible Bottle—which was impractical as his Arab audience refused to drink liquor—Robert-Houdin showed an empty, large metal punch bowl, and then found it to be filled with sweetmeats. As the last of the sweetmeats were distributed, he found that the bowl was filled with hot coffee, a favorite in Algeria.

To accomplish his mission, to "startle and even terrify them by the display of supernatural power," he concluded with several specific effects. The first of these was a reprise of his Light and Heavy Chest, which he'd used during his early Paris performances.

It's interesting to note that the trick had been part of his Paris repertoire, and was later described in Robert-Houdin's book *Secrets of Stage Conjuring*.[34] In Paris, he had showed a small wooden box, about the size of a wooden jewelry box, and placed it on the stage. He pointed out that the box was his own particular invention and could become heavy—apparently too heavy to pick it up. He passed his hand over the box, and then a man from the audience was invited to try to lift the chest. But it now couldn't be raised from the stage. He passed his hand over the box again, then reached down and lifted it with his little finger through the handle. It was all accomplished with an electromagnet, installed beneath the floorboards of the stage.

In Algeria, the magician performed the trick with an important difference. He introduced it with this presentation:

"From what you have witnessed, you will attribute a supernatural power to me, and you are right. I will give you a new proof of my marvelous authority, by showing that I can deprive the most powerful man of his strength and restore it at my will. Anyone who thinks himself strong enough to try the experiment may draw near me." (I spoke slowly, in order to give the interpreter time to translate my words.) An Arab of middle height, but well built and muscular, like many of the Arabs are, came to my side with sufficient assurance.

The magician quizzed his volunteer. "Are you very strong?" The Arab assured him that he was. "Are you sure you will always remain so?" "Quite sure." "You are mistaken, for in an instant I will rob you of your strength, and you shall become as a little child."

In Paris, he had gestured over the box. In Algiers, he gestured over the man. "Behold! You are weaker than a woman. Now, try to lift the box."

In the *Memoirs*, he described the man's futile efforts, "exhausted, panting, and red with anger," as a result of the magical duel: superstition versus science.

Deriving fresh strength from the encouragements his friends offered him by word and deed, he bent down once again over the box. His nervous hands twined round the handle, and his legs, placed on either side like two bronze columns, served as a support for the final effort.

But wonder of wonders! This Hercules, a moment since so strong and proud, now bows his head; his arms, riveted to the box, undergo a violent muscular contraction; his legs give way, and he falls on his knees with a yell of agony!

An electric shock, produced by an inductive apparatus, had been passed, on a signal from me, from the further end of the stage into the handle of the box. Hence the contortions of the poor Arab!

It would have been cruelty to prolong this scene. I gave a second signal, and the electric current was immediately intercepted. My athlete, disengaged from his terrible bondage, raised his hands over his head.

"Allah! Allah!" he exclaimed, full of terror then wrapping himself up quickly in the folds of his burnoose, as if to hide his disgrace, he rushed through the ranks of the spectators and gained the front entrance.

With the exception of my stage boxes and the privileged spectators [that is, the French audience], who appeared to take great pleasure in this experiment, my audience had become grave and silent, and I heard the words, "Shaitan! Djnoum!" passing in a murmur round the circle of the credulous men who, while gazing on me, seemed astonished that I possessed none of the physical qualities attributed to the angel of darkness.

The secret of the Light and Heavy Chest:
an electromagnet beneath the floorboards.

☾

THE POPULAR TWENTIETH-CENTURY science fiction author Arthur C. Clarke famously said, "Any sufficiently advanced technology is indistinguishable from magic." And that's the unflattering way that the Light and Heavy Chest has been recounted through the years: the clever white man brings a new piece of technology to the brown people, who are awed and cowed. They quickly see their foolishness, supplanting their own superstitions with new superstitions.

The actual story is much more interesting. It's a story about the presentation of magic. The Light and Heavy Chest, the electromagnetic trick, had been used in Paris years earlier with a very polite presentation, suggesting that the chest could be heavy. And, of course, in Paris he didn't finish by electrocuting his society audience; he finished with a very different climax. The box was hung from a rope and a large pulley, and when it was lifted up, it became heavy again, pulling a man on the other end of the rope off the ground. The magician used a trick pulley, that allowed additional force to pull against the rope. Had he performed it just this way at the Bab-Azoun Theatre, as an interesting magic box, Robert-Houdin would have perfectly fulfilled his duties as a scientific wizard and demonstrated the fraud of the marabouts. Instead, he chose to present himself as a wizard who had powers unlike other human beings.

☾

THE NEXT TRICK performed in Algiers, the magician recounted, was a version of the gun trick, the tragic deception that had supposedly ruined

Torrini's career. Colonel de Neveu had informed Robert-Houdin that one of the marabouts' tricks was to prevent a pistol from firing by secretly plugging the vent, or touch hole. He thought it would be important for the magician to discredit this miracle "by opposing to it a sleight-of-hand trick far superior to it."

The magician informed the audience that he had a talisman that rendered him invulnerable and invited a marksman to fire at him. Instantly, one member of the audience, identified as a marabout, climbed over the seats, pushed aside the instruments in the orchestra, and clambered to the stage. "I will kill you," he told the magician in excellent French, and then repeated this phrase several times.

The pistol was examined and loaded with powder and a marked bullet. Robert-Houdin held a knife with an apple impaled on its tip. "Do you feel no remorse, no scruple about killing me thus, although I authorize you to do so?" "No," replied the marabout, "for I wish to kill you!" The man aimed at Robert-Houdin's heart and fired. The bullet "lodged in the center of the apple." The magician apparently accomplished the trick by switching the marked bullet for another, cast in wax. The wax bullet crumbled when the gun was packed. The magician inserted the palmed bullet into the apple as he impaled it on the knife.

> The spectators, palsied by surprise and terror, looked round in silence. . . .
> The marabout, though stupefied by his defeat, had not lost his wits. . . .
> He seized the apple, thrust it into his waist-belt, and could not be induced
> to return it, persuaded as he was that he possessed in it an incomparable
> talisman.

The gun trick formed a dramatic theme in the book; this was the source of Torrini's tragic downfall, but Torrini's student was now able to use it to represent modern magic. Unfortunately, the inclusion of the marabout gunman appearing mysteriously in the crowd sounds suspiciously dramatic. We need to pay attention to the setting. It was unlikely that this sort of threatening duel ("I wish to kill you!") would have been allowed during a European-style show, in a pretty new theater, in front of Governor-General Randon and his family.

For the final trick, the magician asked for another volunteer:

A young Moor, about twenty years of age, tall, well built and richly dressed, consented to come on the stage. Bolder and more civilized, doubtlessly, than his comrades of the plains, he walked firmly up to me.

The magician showed an ordinary table with a tablecloth. The tablecloth was raised to show that it was an ordinary table, and then the tablecloth was lowered again. The boy crouched on the table, and a large cone, a woven-wicker construction covered with cloth, was lifted over him, so he was covered.

Robert-Houdin and his assistant onstage then dragged the cone and its contents onto another plank, which they held between them, and slowly walked with their "heavy burden" to the front of the stage. There, they gave the plank a toss. The cone tumbled onto the stage, and the audience saw that the boy was gone:

Immediately, there began a spectacle which I shall never forget. . . . Impelled by an irresistible feeling of terror, they rose in all parts of the house and yielded to the influence of a general panic. The audience scrambled for the doors, and one courageous Caid stood and protested: "Stay! Stay! We cannot thus lose one of our co-religionists. Surely we must know what has become of him, or what has been done to him! Stay!"

But just outside the theater, they found the missing boy, who had been miraculously transported to the front of the building. As the audience peppered him with questions, the enchanted Moor became so flustered that he ran away from the crowd.

The magician reported, "The next evening, the second performance took place and produced nearly the same effect as the previous one."

The description of this trick sounded perfectly accurate, but the nature of the trick tells us a great deal. The disappearance of the boy was an old one, performed by a number of magicians.[35] Robert-Houdin had used it in Paris at his own theater to make his son disappear. The tablecloth was raised to show that the table was an ordinary one, but when the tablecloth was lowered, a second panel fell in place. This second tabletop was arranged with accordion-pleated fabric on the sides, so that a secret hiding place for the boy was formed between the two surfaces. The boy passed through a trapdoor in the table. When the curtains closed on the table, he escaped from the hiding place and ran to the front of the theater.

The trick violated two of Robert-Houdin's personal rules—it used an old-style table with a tablecloth (hiding the boy), and the boy who volunteered for the trick was, we can be sure, a confederate. He would have been carefully rehearsed so that he could escape from the cone and appear in the front of the theater—and his flight from the theater and apparent confusion was part of the act.

✺

IF ROBERT-HOUDIN HAD been inspired to impersonate a real wizard, we can see the army officials adjusting this opinion in a sort of "course correction." He wrote in the *Memoirs*:

> The blow was struck: henceforth the interpreters and all those who had
> dealings with the Arabs received orders to make them understand that

my pretended miracles were only the result of skill, inspired and guided by an art called prestidigitation, in no way connected with sorcery.

This correction was clearly written in a newspaper article several days after the show. The public would now be "aware of the truth," and apparent wizards would be exposed:

> [None of the festival events could] produce as vivid an impression on the Arabs as Robert-Houdin's performance. The Marshall's goal was not simply to provide new entertainment for them. In showing the Arabs a Christian superior to the fake sharifs who have tricked them so often, the Marshall believed he would likewise expose and subvert such trickery, which the public, aware of the truth, could resist in the future.[36]

In the *Memoirs*, Robert-Houdin wrote that "the Arabs yielded to these arguments, for henceforth I was on the most friendly terms with them. Each time a chief saw me, he never failed to come up and press my hand." But as a storyteller, he could not resist portraying himself as a genuine wizard who inspired fear. Just a page later in his text, he described a ceremony at the governor's palace, in which he was hosted by a group of the most important chieftains. He recalled the meeting fondly:

> I went round the group, offering my hand to each in turn. But my task was remarkably abridged, for the ranks thinned at my approach, as many of the company had not the courage to take the hand of a man they had seriously regarded as a sorcerer or the demon in person.

Sixteen chieftains presented him with a beautiful scroll of tribute, written in Arabic and translated into French, and then they solemnly affixed their seals to the document. Colonel de Neveu affixed his own seal in the seventeenth spot. Robert-Houdin proudly quoted part of the scroll:

> "He has known how to stir our hearts and astonish our minds, by displaying to us the surprising facts of his marvelous science. Our eyes were never before fascinated by such prodigies. What he accomplishes cannot be described. We owe him our gratitude for all the things by which he has delighted our eyes and our minds."

This romantic account has, in recent years, been slightly spoiled by a careful reading of the scroll, which still exists. Robert-Houdin did not quote the other, more ambiguous parts of the document: "Generous and knowledgeable men went to admire the marvels of his science." A careful translation of the original Arabic demonstrates that he "entertained" or "diverted the thoughts" of his audience. "The overall connotation," a recent author concluded, "is that Robert-Houdin's act was seen as a prodigiously amusing curiosity of knowledgeable performance—not terrifying sorcery as the magician's narration implies."[37]

◯

AFTER THE SHOWS IN ALGIERS, Robert-Houdin was "curious to witness a conjuring performance of the Marabouts, or other native jugglers," and also to visit with several of his new friends, the Arab chiefs. Colonel de Neveu arranged a party of staff officers and their wives to accompany their French visitors.

They were taken to an inner court, where they were an audience to the strange rituals of the Aissawa, a group of religious mystics. The group began with slow and solemn chants, then songs, cries, and shouts of "Allah."

The Aissawa's demonstrations were feats of physical endurance. They chewed and ate glass or cactus thorns, ran daggers through their cheeks, or walked on red-hot iron. The magician's explanations of these feats, offered in an appendix to his book, were dismissive and unconvincing. Here Robert-Houdin was out of his element, speculating about possible tricks while insisting on the gullibility of the primitive audiences.

The party traveled inland, visiting several of his Algerian hosts. This chapter read like a travelogue, as he recounted the modest local dwellings, the local food and customs. At the home of one of the chieftans who had watched Robert-Houdin's performance, Bou-Allem, he encountered another angry marabout, who felt threatened by his demonstrations of sleight of hand and challenged the magician to repeat the gun trick that had been performed in Algiers. Robert-Houdin insisted that he required a full six hours of prayers for such a feat. That night, instead of praying, he prepared several special bullets and slept soundly.

In the morning, he accepted the challenge in an outdoor courtyard, with an audience of curious locals as well as the traveling party. Robert-Houdin again successfully caught the marked bullet, this time in his teeth. As the marabout fumed, the magician picked up a second pistol, firing it at a whitewashed wall and producing a splash of blood. When the Arab dipped his finger in the blood to test it, "It was evident that for the moment he doubted everything, even the Prophet."[38]

Returning to France, the magician stopped to fulfill an engagement in Marseilles. When he returned to Blois, he happily put aside his magic and returned to his experiments with electricity and clockwork.

○

In fact, this Algerian adventure gained no traction as a diplomatic story, nor a political story. It caused barely a ripple of recognition from other sources and is almost ignored in French military accounts. There is one report to the head of the Bureau of Arab Affairs, just days after the performances, noting that the "marvelous tricks made a profound impact on the local imagination."[39] And a French author later recalled the opinion of a General Devaux, who had met the magician in Algeria: "The two men who did the most for the pacification of Algeria were Jules Gerard, the famous lion killer, and especially the incomparable Robert-Houdin."[40] The inclusion of Gerard made the remark suspect. He literally hunted lions in areas surrounding Algiers, so Devaux was using the word "pacification" with a wink.

Thanks to another newspaper interview, we can start to see the seams in Robert-Houdin's story. On October 9, 1857, a year after the performances in Algeria, *Le Moniteur Universel* published an interview with Robert-Houdin, at Blois.[41] The magician discussed his show before the chieftains. Within days, the article was edited and translated by the *London Times*'s Paris correspondent and reprinted in various newspapers around the world.

It's a very interesting newspaper article. Although *Le Moniteur Universel* provided the first public explanation of what happened at the Bab-Azoun Theatre, and was the only other contemporaneous account from Robert-Houdin, this interview has never been quoted, nor compared to the famous account in the *Memoirs*.

From the first mention of the mission, the magician clearly cast himself as the colonial master. *Le Moniteur Universel* credited him with a surprising position of power over the natives. Here's the description from that newspaper:

> Before his arrival, the Arabs were told that a man of extraordinary power was coming, a man who would make miracles. When everything was prepared on the stage, the marabouts were not the first to go and see him; instead, they made an effort to discredit what they were seeing, because they understood he was someone who could strip them of their influence.

Robert-Houdin depended upon his surprising choices to confuse them and defy their reason.[42]

At the time of this interview, the magician would have been at work on his autobiography, and the elements of the story were still malleable. For example, in *Le Moniteur Universel*, the gun trick was given precedence. A typical trick of the marabouts to gain domination was taking a pistol and causing it to fail when the trigger was pulled. Robert-Houdin watched a demonstration. This was the 1857 newspaper account:

At the first glance, Robert-Houdin understood the mystery. He proved that the gun did not explode because the marabout had cleverly blocked the touch hole. Furious that his halo had been knocked off, the holy man was enraged.

Robert-Houdin remained calm, and saw at that moment a way to establish his superiority. "Do you want revenge?" he asked. "Then take a pistol. Whichever one you'd like. Load the gun yourself. Here are the bullets. And to make sure you don't exchange it, put a mark with your knife, so that you know it's yours." The Arab followed the directions, one by one. The magician said, "Are you sure now? Are you sure your gun is well loaded and will fire? Tell me. Don't you feel a little bit of regret, to kill me this way? Even if I give you permission?" "You are my enemy," said the Arab coolly. "I am going to kill you."

With that, Robert-Houdin picked up an apple on the point of a knife, calm and smiling, and positioned himself in front of the marabout. He told him to shoot. The gun fired, the apple suddenly flew far away, and in its place appeared, on the point of the knife, the marked bullet. This time, the magician did not receive frenetic applause, but quiet disbelief. Shocked, the marabout bowed in front of the man who was his superior, and shouted, "Allah! You are the greatest! You have won and I have lost!"

Let's look at a number of curious differences in the story. In the *Memoirs*, the discussion of the marabout's gun trick was from a conversation with de Neveu, which involved the two men's planning for the show. In this account, Robert-Houdin directly witnessed the gun that wouldn't fire, and this led directly to his demonstration of the Catching a Bullet trick at the theater. The author seemed to mix both tales of the bullet effect from the *Memoirs*, suggesting an extemporaneous challenge from the marabout.

In the newspaper interview, the description of the Light and Heavy Chest was especially brief and did not suggest that the man was shocked at the conclusion of the trick:

> These men prize physical strength. When they found it impossible to lift an object of such a small size, they were terrified, and were convinced that the sorcerer had the power of completely annihilating them, at his whim.

This led directly to the disappearance of the boy, who was, for this particular story, another marabout. Notice that the description implied a sequence of performances.

> "I have the power to reduce you to nothing. If one of you want to try my experiment, I will be glad to make you disappear in smoke." On the appointed day, there was a crowd of people, and a fanatical marabout volunteered himself to the magician.

The marabout supposedly disappeared under the gauze cone, terrifying the audience, so they ran from the theater. A few agreed to return to see what happened to the marabout, where they discovered him and questioned him. He responded that he felt intoxicated, as if he had lost the power to remember. Then the article finished:

Today, the marabouts are all discounted by the natives. On the other hand, the celebrated magician is, for them, an object of admiration.

This bold conclusion in *Le Moniteur Universel* was considerably tempered when the magician wrote his *Memoirs*.

How can we explain the differences? It's possible that the reporter from *Le Moniteur Universel* added emphasis to Robert-Houdin's account, or that Robert-Houdin was recalling the differences from the specific performances. But more than likely, we see evidence of his experiments and adjustments to the story to make the show sound more realistic and more dangerous to his readers.

Robert-Houdin was not brought to Algeria to perform for the marabouts or to challenge them directly. He was brought to demonstrate

An Algerian marabout, photographed just several years after the magician's appearance in Algiers.

French magic for the chieftains, who were influenced by the marabouts. It was a slightly more complicated formula—a duel with someone who wasn't there. De Neveu may have merely intended Robert-Houdin's performance as little more than a magic entertainment.

In his differing accounts, Robert-Houdin sometimes inserted a marabout as someone unexpected and dangerous: the wild-eyed man, making a sudden threat. These scenarios with a marabout were difficult to believe (the man pushing his way through the audience to threaten Robert-Houdin's life, in front of the governor-general) or maybe even impossible to believe (a marabout volunteering to disappear, when that man must have been a confederate of the magician).

His confusion about the marabout may be a telling aspect of his account. Since he never described a marabout in his travelogue of Algeria, and he used them purely as religious bogeymen, we might ask whether Robert-Houdin ever really performed for a marabout or had any interaction with them during his travels.

The adventure led to the overstatements made by later writers, further burnishing the tale in efforts to clarify it. In fact, there was no war to be stopped, no revolution to be subverted, no imminent uprising that was quelled by magic. Describing Robert-Houdin's achievement in this way has been an attempt to argue a negative. He performed his show, and nothing happened.

IN THE EARLIEST YEARS of the twentieth century, as Houdini found success as an escape artist in Europe, he began searching for information and artifacts that pertained to Robert-Houdin's career. Houdini met magicians who had seen him perform and tried to track down Robert-Houdin's children, some of whom were still alive.[43] To his surprise,

Robert-Houdin was not especially remembered, or as highly regarded as . . . well, here's the easiest way to explain it: Houdini was shocked that others didn't share his hero worship.

For his own magic journal, *The Conjurer's Magazine*, Houdini began a series of articles, first titled "Unknown Facts Concerning Robert-Houdin," and then, "Robert-Houdin's Proper Place in the History of Magic," and then, "History Makers in the World of Magic."[44] In 1908, these articles were swept together and assembled into his book, entitled *The Unmasking of Robert-Houdin*.

The Unmasking was filled with original research and important information about Robert-Houdin's predecessors and contemporaries, but the research had been manically diverted to deliver a series of roundhouse punches at the ghostlike French magician. Houdini bitterly criticized the magician for his treatment of other magicians and his exaggerated improvements on previous inventions. He ridiculed the author for his ignorance of magic and even for the careless way he wrote about his own family:

> As a writer of memoirs he is a wretched failure. Whenever he writes of himself, his pen seems fairly to scintillate. Whenever he refers to other magicians of his times, his pen lags and drops on the pages blots which can only emanate only from a narrow, petty, jealous nature. Even when he writes of his own family, this peculiar trait of petty egotism may be read between the lines.[45]

Magicians were shocked by this relentless little volume, from its fancy illustrated cover—a mask being pulled away from a bust of the French magician—to its final pages of text:

> The master magician, unmasked, stands forth in all the hideous nakedness of historical proof, the prince of pilferers. That he might bask for a

few hours in public adulation, he purloined the ideas of magicians long dead and buried, and proclaimed these as the fruits of his own inventive genius. That he might be known to posterity as the king of conjurers, he sold his birthright of manhood and honor for a mere mess of pottage, his "Memoirs," written by the hand of another man, who at his instigation belittled his contemporaries, and juggled facts and truth to further his egotistical, jealous ambitions.[46]

Most frustrating were Houdini's boasts of scholarship. He never noticed that Torrini was a fictional character or that the Algerian adventure may have been exaggerated. And then—we can see this coming—Houdini used his friendship with Torrini to criticize Robert-Houdin's thievery: "Robert-Houdin could not have been ignorant of [Pinetti's version of second sight]," he wrote. "Pinetti, whose tricks were fully described to Robert-Houdin by his old friend Torrini, used the Second Sight mystification with excellent effect."

"If ever an attack backfired," concluded one magic historian, "it was Houdini's onslaught against Robert-Houdin."[47] Houdini's polemic actually served to inoculate Robert-Houdin from decades of serious analysis.

It's clear that Robert-Houdin had filled his *Memoirs* with exaggerations, proudly puffing out his chest. But it was the world of magicians who recklessly pumped their hero full of air, so that he became a sort of parade balloon, put on display or maneuvered down the street for the glory of magic. Houdini was one of those magicians who had inflated Robert-Houdin until he was such a size that he could no longer be contained within impressionable Erich Weiss's imagination. That's when Houdini pulled out a peashooter and took aim.

Houdini's articles and book were not just nasty; they displayed genuine hurt. Houdini sought to settle a score because he had clearly felt wounded by Robert-Houdin and betrayed by his exaggerations. Perhaps Houdini suspected that the idealized show business described in the *Memoirs* never actually existed. Perhaps he feared that his goal in life— achieving renown and respect through magic—had been based on a deception.

The most sensible response to Houdini's book, not surprisingly, was from the grand old man of magic, Professor Louis Hoffmann, who had translated Robert-Houdin's magic books into English, had seen the French magician's son perform in the famous Paris theater, and had analyzed his tricks in the pages of his famous Victorian textbook of magic, *Modern Magic*:

> Unfounded pretensions deserve to be exposed, and if Mr. Houdini had done this, in a fairer and more judicial spirit, we should have nothing but praise for his book, which is in many ways a valuable contribution to magical literature. But he goes much further than this. According to Mr. Houdini, Robert-Houdin was not only an ignoramus as regards to magical history, but he had not mastered even the simplest elements of his craft. The best evidence now available of Robert-Houdin's qualifications as a conjurer is to be found in his *Secrets of Conjuring and Magic*. Robert-Houdin may have had an excessive share of personal vanity; he may have been commercially a bit of a fraud; he may have borrowed other men's ideas and claimed them as his own, but no reader of this book can doubt that the writer was, as a magician, a master of his craft.[48]

It's clear that Robert-Houdin's most famous creations were first used by other performers in slightly different forms: Philippe with an Orange Tree and Pastry Cook; Anderson with an Inexhaustible Bottle; M'Kean, among others, with Second Sight. If Robert-Houdin had explained, in his *Memoirs,* that he had built special apparatus for other magicians, it would have explained his regard for old ideas that could be improved or refined.[49] It would have explained why he felt a proprietary interest in these tricks, claiming them as his own, but didn't complain about their use by other magicians. In the *Memoirs,* he only added to the confusion by minimizing his associations with magicians and repeatedly attempting to distinguish himself in the field.[50]

◯

ALTHOUGH ROBERT-HOUDIN'S achievements now seem hazy and distant, we can still get a sense of those performances. Today, we can still see Robert-Houdin's automata operate. Some have been restored, and some have been accurately reconstructed and performed. They are quaint, charming pieces of machinery that click and whir as they are put through their motions. Often their effects elicit smiles from the audience or gentle laughter for their earnest efforts.

Of course, you might be tempted to think that audiences were less sophisticated and more easily mystified by these mechanical devices in Robert-Houdin's time. Instead, audiences of 1850 were not gullible and would have had a sophisticated appreciation of clockwork automata. They would have understood what these machines were pretending to be. For example, Robert-Houdin did not write about how the Algerians responded to his automata. His Arab audience probably had less appreciation, because they would have been less familiar with the European regard for clockwork amusements.

In watching a re-creation of the famous Orange Tree, we notice that it does not conceal its mechanical nature, nor deceive us with an incredible simulation of nature. It does not bloom. The flowers are pushed from their hiding places with a rustle behind the silk leaves and then disappear again with a snap. The oranges do not swell and change color. The semicircular screens of leaves pivot open, like vertical eyelids, slowly revealing the oranges that have been concealed. Finally, the butterflies do not circle the bush like denizens of a garden. The brass butterflies rattle their metal wings, announcing their presence before they are mechanically pushed up from behind the tree on a track. It is amusing to see a machine simulate the gestures of Mother Nature, using pistons, levers, and wheels.[51]

The Orange Tree was, of course, intended as a magic trick. The machine that apparently produced oranges was the setting, the mise-en-scène, where the borrowed, burned handkerchief was revealed as the last orange opened, so that it could be displayed by the mechanical butterflies. In this way, it echoed the procedure of a number of standard tricks. The borrowed handkerchief was secretly passed to an assistant, who placed it in the tree, between the butterflies, and then brought the tree onto the stage.

Because it worked with pistons, connected with cords to an offstage assistant, it was not an automaton, but it was made to imitate an automaton, to give the appearance that a piece of technology had been charmingly subverted to the cause of magic. If it was amusing, maybe even deliberately mechanical, that was not an insult to its maker. That was his intention.

No reviewers left Robert-Houdin's show claiming that they'd seen an orange tree grow by magic. They claimed they'd seen an automaton orange tree.

This is a great misunderstanding of Robert-Houdin's magic. His best tricks didn't fool his audience with technological secrets. He fooled them with technological presentations.

It's easy to appreciate the distinction if we use a modern example. Today there are a handful of good sleight-of-hand magicians who perform magic using their cell phones or iPads. We can imagine one of these presentations. The magician might take the iPad, open a video, and show a coin on the screen. Shaking the screen, we see the coin "rattle" from side to side, as if it is really being shaken inside the iPad. The magician tips the screen, and the coin apparently rolls down to one edge of the screen. He reaches up with his empty fingertips, grabs for the coin, and it suddenly appears at his fingertips as it disappears from the screen.

We admire the magician's skill; we appreciate the novelty of mixing a bit of technology with sleight of hand. The performance surprises us and makes us laugh. But we don't think that we've seen a coin manufactured by an iPad. The use of technology is an affectation. The hem has been neatly taken up, and the dress is now in fashion.

Here's another example of a presentation that used technology to deceive. In Robert-Houdin's famous Ethereal Suspension, the ether, of course, played no part in the levitation trick. But by assigning the secret to this mysterious new vapor, just then a subject of popular interest in Europe, he made the illusion topical. In Scotland, when the discovery of chloroform became topical, he presented the illusion as Suspension Chloroforeeme.[52]

Now, here's the contrast. Although Robert-Houdin was sometimes credited with being the first magician to use electricity, he was not. From the late eighteenth century, electricity had been exhibited on stages as a scientific novelty and was then used for various experiments and industry. At least two of Robert-Houdin's predecessors, Döbler and Philippe, used electricity in their acts from 1840.[53] We know that he used electricity secretly, concealing its use, not flaunting its presence. For example, he used it for a small electric switch, opening a compartment in a box that was suspended on ribbons. The ribbons concealed the two wires running to the box.[54] He also used electricity to secretly signal his son, with a sort of telegraph key, in an improved, silent version of Second Sight.[55]

Again, in his most interesting use of electricity, the Light and Heavy

Chest, he concealed the electromagnet installed at the front edge of his stage. When Robert-Houdin later described the secret in a book, he admitted that the audience lost interest once the principle became known: "At a later period, when electro-magnetism had become more generally known, I thought it advisable to make an addition to the 'Light and Heavy Chest' in order to throw the public off the scent as to the principle on which the illusion was based." That's why he included the special finale in Paris, using his trick pulley to pull on the rope and lift the man off his feet.

Despite these improvements, the Light and Heavy Chest was not a particular success and was not a regular part of his repertoire.[56] In the *Memoirs*, it was included only in his mention of the Algerian show. In *The Secrets of Stage Conjuring*, he quickly dismissed the electromagnetic part of the trick and its use in Algeria, proudly focusing on his ingenious pulley that completed the trick.

So, we can see the range of ways that Robert-Houdin used technology. He concealed known principles, like electricity, by sewing wires into silk ribbons or hiding an electromagnet beneath the stage. Other principles, like clockwork or ether, were flouted prominently, even when they weren't part of the secret. In these cases, technology became romantic parts of the presentation.

Here's another little thought experiment, an example of a trick that Robert-Houdin did not perform. He could have shown the audience an actual battery and wires, explaining that this was a new type of electricity, even more magical than the sort that had been demonstrated by scientists. He could have told the audience that this particular current could actually transmit a thought, not simply a current. A playing card could have been selected and then shuffled back into the deck of cards before the cards were placed beneath the battery. Then Robert-Houdin could have connected the wires, making a prominent display of the current, so that it rang an electric bell. "I can tell from the tone of the bell that you selected a royal card," he could have said. "In fact, I can do even better than that." Connecting the bell and ringing it again, the bell could spring open, transforming into a large reproduction of the chosen card.

It's a silly trick, but you get the idea. It would have been a very effective way to dress up an ordinary card trick, if the performer wanted to call attention to his utilization of electricity. Why didn't Robert-Houdin do a trick like this? Because by 1845, electricity was no longer glamorous or romantic. It was useful. He concealed its use, so the audience would not suspect it. This sort of card trick would have demonstrated his use of electricity, which may have started the audience thinking about Second Sight, or other tricks in which the electricity was concealed. In other words, we can measure the novelty, or utility, of these principles by how they were being concealed from the audience.

✺

THERE IS A "chicken and egg" problem that presents itself at turning points in history. In this case, we can see that Victorian magic—a burgeoning interest in conjuring that attracted a wide range of creative thought—needed a master and a philosopher. Magicians became successful enough that they needed to erect a statue to someone. Robert-Houdin perfectly suited the bill, but first, magicians needed to overlook the strange qualities of his books and exaggerate the sections that echoed their new sensibilities.

In this way, his contradictions were convenient. He pledged himself to a new magic "divested of all charlatanism" but achieved his triumph in Algeria by appealing to base superstitions, adding importance to his role of a magician. He inspired magicians' textbooks and catalogs of convenient tin boxes, trays, tables, and other apparatus, but offered a battle cry to magicians: "Real sleight of hand must not be the tinman's work but the artist's, and people do not visit the latter to see instruments perform."[57] In fact, the early reviews of Robert-Houdin suggested that audiences did purchase tickets to see the instruments perform.

Although he was cast as the "Father of Modern Magic," Robert-Houdin wasn't actually the origin of modern magic. He inspired the perfect origin myth, and that myth continued to be expanded.

CHAPTER 8

THE GOLDEN AGE

JOSEPH BUATIER DE KOLTA was a slightly awkward, potbellied wizard with thinning hair and the full, dark beard of a tradesman. Of the generation after Robert-Houdin, de Kolta would have horrified the famous French master with his gaucheries on the stage—a boxy tailcoat several sizes too large, dirty shoes, battered props, the mannerisms of a Lyon baker at work at his oven, and a distinct lack of sophisticated humor.

In fact, he was from Caluire-et-Cuire, near Lyon, and had probably been destined to go into his father's business, the silk trade. The family name was Buatier, and the strange addition of de Kolta, a Hungarian name, was a nod to an early Hungarian entrepreneur who had tried to manage his career.[1]

Audiences forgave him. His magic was incredible, inspired, divine. De Kolta seemed to effortlessly reinvent the form, innovating entire categories of conjuring that had not existed before his time—sleight of hand with ivory billiard balls, magic with silk scarves (no doubt inspired by his father), and the production of hundreds of pretty tissue flowers from a paper cone. He invented a way that a small birdcage with a canary inside instantly disappeared at his fingertips. Then he created an illusion in which a lady, seated in a dining chair, could be covered with a large silk shawl, and when the shawl was pulled away, she similarly disappeared in a dazzling split second.

Joseph Buatier de Kolta, the innovative French magician from the late Victorian age.

Maybe one of his most important creations was a technique called Black Art, in which people or objects could be concealed on the stage, right in front of the audience, by using a careful arrangement of lights and black velvet curtains. He was the first to hint at what might be accomplished in a music hall or on a vaudeville stage, if magicians were just given a chance and finally excused from the fussy, proper magic of the earlier generation.[2]

Charles Morritt, one of those later music hall magicians, had known de Kolta early in his career. "Buatier de Kolta was the man responsible for the growth of magic in the popular esteem," Morritt told a group of his fellow magicians. "He it was who first used the word 'illusionist', on a program, and who first produced illusions on a great, modern scale [and] opened up a gold field for magicians."[3]

○

BUT WAS DE KOLTA any less incredible than Johann Nepomuk Hofzinser? This mannered Viennese magician was the opposite of de Kolta: instead of a popularizer, Hofzinser, a contemporary of Robert-Houdin, was a man who reveled in the tiny poetry of magic, the elegant accomplishments of his finely tuned card tricks.

Hofzinser was a professional civil servant and an amateur conjuror. He married Wilhelmine Bergmann, who quickly acquired a repertoire of mind-reading tricks. In 1857, they opened a "salon" (the fashion of the day), a showplace for sophisticated Viennese society and a tiny theater devoted to the couple's deceptions.[4] At this exclusive room, he introduced his sweet, stylized mysteries with ordinary objects. His magic astonished with apparent nonchalance but actually relied on Hofzinser's artistic precision. His presentations artfully involved his audience; for example, when he contemplated the magic of a lady's gaze, he demonstrated how a spectator, just looking away from a card, could apparently make it change its value.

"Card tricks are the poetry of magic," Hofzinser wrote to one of his pupils. "Without poetry, no poet. Without card magic, no conjurer, even if he can do witchcraft."[5] Where de Kolta set off a feeding frenzy of imitators and inspirations, Hofzinser coyly avoided giving information to other magicians. "Have everyone show you everything, but don't show anything to anyone," he advised a friend. "And then always look very amazed and if

*Johann Hofzinser, a specialist in
card magic and a popular society
performer in Vienna.*

possible appear stupid."[6] As a purist, he kept meticulous notes and detailed his routines to his pupils, but for many years his secrets went unexplained. It took magicians decades to fully appreciate the many intricate gimmicks, devices, and poetic routines that had premiered at the Salon Hofzinser.

PROFESSOR JOHN HENRY Pepper provided another counterpoint to Hofzinser, as another man who reinvented the art of conjuring. In 1862, he stepped onstage at the small lecture hall in the London Polytechnic Institute, a popular showplace of scientific marvels, to introduce a short sketch entitled "The Haunted Man." As the audience watched slack-jawed, a three-dimensional, transparent, glowing ghost with a grinning skull and wreathed in a white shroud, slowly appeared to torment an actor on the stage. And then, with a flicker, the ghost disappeared again.[7]

The optical illusion was popularized as Pepper's Ghost. It used a large sheet of transparent glass, fixed in place at a slight angle pointed downward. The glass was invisible to the audience, but it could reflect the image of a ghost that was concealed beneath the stage. The reflected ghost was then superimposed on the actors and the scenery on the stage. This ghostly image attracted long lines that circled the galleries of the Polytechnic and then extended out to the sidewalk.

The Ghost had first been suggested by Henry Dircks, a civil engineer, but it was Professor Pepper who understood how the idea could be fitted into a theater. He wasn't a magician. He was embarrassed that a few spectators were so affected by the Ghost that they thought he might be a Spiritualist. Pepper had been a trained chemist but developed a flair for the theatrical and a knack for scientific demonstrations. That night, in 1862, Pepper intended to stroll onto the stage at the end of his illusion, take his bow, and then meticulously explain the scientific principles, the balance of light and reflection that was responsible for the ghost—that was his usual formula for scientific demonstrations at the Polytechnic. But he perceived the gasps and sensed the wonder exhibited by his audience. "I had previously settled to explain the whole modus operandi on that evening," Pepper later wrote. "I deferred doing so."[8] He realized that the secret of the Ghost was of much more value if it were withheld.

Magicians lionized him, and histories of the art always include this chemist, as if he'd been bestowed an honorary degree in conjuring. Pepper's demonstrations at the Polytechnic—first the Ghost and then a string of amazing reflection illusions in conjunction with inventor Thomas Tobin—introduced the idea of optical conjuring and formed the principles that magicians pushed onto the music hall stages to assure their own successes. Robert-Houdin was a particular fan after he retired;

Professor Pepper's Ghost, a brilliant reflection illusion,
allowed ghosts to share the stage with actors.

the French magician was so impressed by the Ghost that he diagrammed the optics of its secret, interpolated a ghost into a Paris play, and installed a model of Dircks's and Pepper's illusion in his estate in Blois.

⟲

THEN THERE WAS WILJALBA FRIKELL, the German magician who was apparently the first to perform with only a handful of ordinary objects instead of the usual magicians' vases and boxes. It wasn't his plan. Early in his career, Frikell dressed in the fez and embroidered silk vest of a supposed Middle Eastern prince, performing the most fashionable tricks. It was only after a fire, when his stage draperies and apparatus were destroyed, that he was forced to perform magic with a few chairs, a simple table, cards, coins, a handkerchief, a wand . . . and pure, elegant sleight of hand.[9]

Similarly, there was Verbeck, a French magician who had a preference for sleight of hand, found favor in England, and then, managed by

P. T. Barnum, in America. Verbeck spoke only French; his translator, Adolph Guibal, provided his own comedy act by fracturing the words throughout the performance and then adding his own asides. Verbeck's magic was brilliant and witty all by itself; it needed few words to be appreciated. In one of his most distinctive effects, he borrowed a wedding ring from a lady in the audience and then, borrowing a paper program, he crumpled the program into a ball, around the ring. The magician slowly opened the program to show that it had been transformed into a sealed envelope, constructed from the printed page. Inside this envelope was a smaller envelope, and then another, and another. Inside of the tiny, fifth envelope, the magician found her ring.[10]

As he was returning it to the lady, Verbeck was struck with an inspiration and decided to repeat the feat. Again, the ring was pushed into a crumpled program. Again, the ring was discovered within the fifth envelope, this time as the lady opened the envelopes herself. At the end, the magician nonchalantly picked up the scraps of envelopes, squeezed them in his hand, and showed that they'd been returned to the shape of an ordinary program.

HOWEVER, FOR SHEER impact and lasting inspiration, few achieved the success of Ira and William Henry Davenport, who first arrived in England in 1864. The two young men—handsome brothers with dark wavy hair and stern expressions—were born in Buffalo, New York, and had already become successful entertainers in their native America, performing for nine years. But the Civil War had made travel in America difficult, so the Davenports decided to bring their performances to Europe.[11]

Pepper had produced ghosts through purely optical illusions, but the Davenports thrived on controversy. They were not magicians, they insisted, following the formula of some of the first historical deceivers.

Audiences were told that they were mediums. Tying their feats to the controversial new religion of Spiritualism that was raging across America, the Davenports claimed to be representatives of the spirit world. They could summon ghosts to the stage.

The Davenports were tied in place inside of a special wooden cabinet, nearly six feet tall and six feet wide, like a three-door armoire. They faced each other at either side of the cabinet, perched on small wooden shelves. Audience members were invited to the stage to tie them in place. Long ropes were used to lash their ankles in place; the ropes were then pulled up, through holes in the shelves, to pinion each brother's arms behind his back. In this position, there was no doubt that they were held immobile within the cabinet.

The Davenport brothers in their famous Spirit Cabinet.

But as soon as the doors were closed and bolted, an astonishing performance began.

Ropes were heard sweeping through the planks in the seats. The doors were opened just moments later, and the brothers were found unbound. Then the doors were closed briefly, and the brothers were found bound completely again. When the actual séance began, pale hands appeared behind the small windows in the doors of the cabinet, and instruments, left inside the cabinet next to the tied mediums, were heard to play and rattle against the sides of the box. A spectator from the audience, seated in darkness between the two brothers, endured rough treatment by the ghosts—his hair was mussed by invisible hands, his glasses were pulled away, a tambourine was placed on his head, like a hi-hat. The doors were quickly opened. As the light from the stage illuminated the interior, Ira and William Henry were revealed to be sitting placidly, the ropes and knots still undisturbed.

William Fay traveled as their manager. Dr. J. B. Ferguson was the Spiritualist minister and lecturer who introduced their act; it was Ferguson who explained the incredible nature of the performances that the audience was about to witness, and he suggested that real ghosts were at play. The Davenports said almost nothing during their performances, and audiences were naturally puzzled over their roles. Quiet and intense, perhaps they were confidence men, cleverer than the proceedings and above all the controversy. Or perhaps they were somehow dullards in the grip of mysterious supernatural forces, two pawns being pushed to and fro by the spirits.

Newspapers scoffed: they were frauds. Audiences were naturally intrigued and drawn to the shows, but some British crowds challenged them, stormed the stage, drove the mediums from the theater, and even broke up their cabinet into kindling wood. The Davenports quickly earned criticisms from Robert-Houdin (who studied their magic when he was in retirement), John Henry Anderson, and a handful of other magicians, who felt empowered to explain the nature of their imposture and then, in some cases, imitate their performances.

Their topical, controversial performances inspired a number of important innovations within the world of magicians. First, they introduced the idea of a magic cabinet—a box that is closed, and then opened to discover a surprise. In the 1860s, an interesting array of magic boxes and cupboards were devised to make people appear and disappear. Professor Pepper and Thomas Tobin invented some of the best of these cabinet tricks. Second, they popularized the notion of restraint and escape as elements of a modern magic act. Although escape tricks were known elsewhere, in India and in Native American cultures, this represented the popularity of the deception on a stage. And finally, they gave magicians a prominent target for a new twist on magic and a new relevant entertainment—an exposure, as explained by an expert in the field.

◯

A RAY OF SUNLIGHT from a stray blind chanced to illuminate the interior of the Davenports' cabinet for a brief instant when they appeared at a local hall in Cheltenham, England, in 1865. An observant amateur magician and full-time jeweler named John Nevil Maskelyne saw how they had escaped from their ropes and stopped the performance to challenge the imposters. Maskelyne formed a partnership with a friend, George A. Cooke (both were members of a Cheltenham band), and they began their career as magicians and exposers of fraud.[12]

At least, that's the way Maskelyne later told the story. We might be suspicious of the coincidental, fortuitous way that he was called to magic—the same way Robert-Houdin was accidently handed the wrong book. His early career was deliberately modeled after Robert-Houdin's career—Maskelyne was a fan of the *Memoirs*. And so, in 1873, Maskelyne and Cooke ambitiously leased the funny, dusty little theater in Piccadilly, London: Egyptian Hall. Adorned with polychrome sculptures of

Egyptian goddesses and Victorian fantasies of hieroglyphics, Egyptian Hall was already a famous London tourist attraction and had featured many magic shows, including Louis M'Kean and the Mysterious Lady.

Maskelyne exhibited few of the popular attributes of a conjuror; he was a small man with dark hair combed straight back and a brush mustache. He was called "The Chief" by employees. He was neither chatty, nor elegant, nor adept at sleight of hand. Where Robert-Houdin had been a one-man band, Maskelyne quickly became a conductor of magic. He didn't write about magic, philosophize about conjuring, or discuss secrets. In fact, here he differed from Robert-Houdin: he was notoriously old-fashioned about secrecy, which he sternly guarded and exaggerated within a cloud of publicity—he offered a cash challenge if someone could copy his box escape, and he boasted of his insolvable mysteries, like his card-playing

John Nevil Maskelyne, London's famous magician,
with his mechanical man, Psycho.

automaton, Psycho. His success relied on his ability to hire innovative conjurors, forming a sort of repertory company of magicians. Members of the Maskelyne family were swept into the business—most notably his oldest son, Nevil, who was a reticent performer onstage but enjoyed his work as an inventor and a sort of "magician-scientist" in the workshop.

Onstage, the Maskelyne formula was a program of magicians and magical sketches. There would be some elegant conjuring or sleight of hand. Maskelyne's own specialty was plate spinning—his place on the program was usually billed as the "Dancing Delft," in which he kept a number of large plates and basins wobbling on a tabletop. Or he featured automata of his own invention, like Psycho, the supposed clockwork man in a turban who played a card game opposite members of the audience. There would be a variety act, a comedian at a piano, a man who made shadows with his hands, and magic lantern slides. The show included a short comic play: a handful of characters in an amusing setting, to include several illusions in which people appeared, disappeared, or floated in the air.

These magic plays were mostly intended to be commercial, comfortable inventions for John Nevil Maskelyne, Nevil Maskelyne, and George Cooke—who were not especially effective magicians but were amusing actors supporting a strong comedian in the lead part. Their most famous magic playlet, *Will, the Witch and the Watchman*, was a nonsensical story about an escaped gorilla and a magic cabinet. A comedian played the watchman, confused about everything that happened around him. John Nevil Maskelyne often took the part of the butcher, who spoke with a broad Gloucestershire accent, chased the gorilla by brandishing a meat cleaver, and performed the disappearances and reappearances. Several of Maskelyne's plays were farces on Spiritualism—arranged around conniving mediums, silly victims, and a miraculous bit of magic that was, pointedly, more entertaining than what was seen at an average Victorian séance.

The Maskelyne and Cooke Mysteries, "Daily at 3 and 8," found the perfect home and became famous around the world. Their tenancy lasted thirty-one years, until Egyptian Hall was pulled down and they moved the business to a new location. A number of important illusions originated in the Maskelyne workshop and then were premiered on the stage. De Kolta appeared there, and Charles Morritt was a favorite for many years. But maybe the most important magician to set foot on the Egyptian Hall stage was a young man named David Devant, who managed to surprise and impress the taciturn "Chief" himself.

○

HE WAS BORN David Wighton and took the name David Devant when he saw a French painting titled *David devant Goliath*, and he realized that the idea of "David in front" was an especially attractive one. It was also prescient. Devant was twenty-three years old when he joined the Maskelyne shows in 1892, a perfect addition to the company: charming, glib, and adept at sleight of hand in a way that neither John Nevil Maskelyne, nor his son Nevil, could ever be. He was also naturally inventive.[13]

That was how Devant got the job. Maskelyne was looking for a performer and reluctantly agreed to come and see one of Devant's performances in London, including the young magician's latest illusion, in which a male assistant was secured inside an upright cabinet and turned into a woman. Maskelyne must have been impressed, but he left the audition quibbling about the size of Devant's cabinet, asking him to devise something more suitable for the small stage at Egyptian Hall.

We might notice how, from their early meeting, Maskelyne was testing Devant's creative abilities. The young magician suggested a deliberately serious bit of magic, a scene in which an artist dreamed of his dead wife, only to discover that she had miraculously stepped out of a large

*David Devant, a Victorian conjurer who
formed a partnership with John Nevil Maskelyne.*

two-dimensional painting. Devant's ingenious effect, the Artist's Dream, was something unique for Egyptian Hall, and Maskelyne must have realized it, for it was the first play that he decided to present dramatically, not comically. He had it written in blank verse, as if to accentuate the poetry of Devant's magic.[14]

By the 1890s, an amazing thing had happened to magic: the multiplicity of its practitioners and the wide variety of its techniques had gained it respect within the theatrical world.

Here's the best way to explain it. For centuries, magic, like ventriloquism, mesmerism, juggling, and acrobatics, had been solely the purview of specialists: magicians, ventriloquists, mesmerists, jugglers, and acrobats. It was a unique skill, and the purpose of this skill was a performance, an exhibition. You might see it in a town square. You might be tempted to purchase a ticket for a touring show or one in an elegant little theater that advertised its particular specialty.

But after the generation of Robert-Houdin, as magic was redefined, some of the techniques had become publicized and appreciated as works of theater. This became clear in a series of books about stage techniques, published between the 1870s and the 1890s. At that time, elaborate operas and melodramas, which were then the taste in France, England, and America, often called for spectacular scenic effects or fantasies. In many cases, the shows would be written around these sensation effects, for they were the attraction for many audiences. For example, Dion Boucicault, a popular Irish actor and playwright, had a long career by delivering one sensational scene after another, each accompanied by illusionary stage effects. So, in his 1857 play, *The Poor of New York*, Act V featured a realistic fire that roared through a New York tenement. In his 1868 hit, *After Dark*, the audience watched a locomotive rumble across a set of railroad tracks onstage, narrowly missing a victim who had been lashed to the ties.

Audiences were naturally curious about these effects—the intricate special scenery, trapdoors, or imitation fire that provided these illusions—so these books on stagecraft provided answers. Jean-Pierre Moynet's volume, *L'Envers du Théâtre* (*The Theatre Inside Out*), from 1873, began a series of these books. The author was a scenic painter who had worked extensively at the Opéra-Comique, and he explained the intricacies of the theater world: how scenery was painted, how a show was rehearsed and budgeted, and how elaborate sequences like shipwrecks or fires were produced onstage using an array of special effects.[15]

L'Envers du Théâtre was very much a book about the theater, with little that seemed to cross the line into the realm of the magician. Percy Fitzgerald's *The World Behind the Scenes*, from 1881, provided a similar

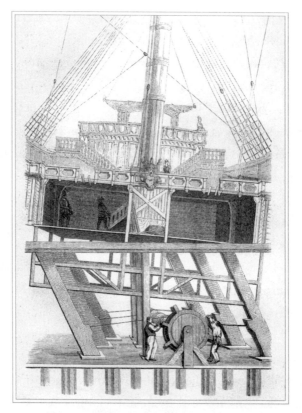

*Elaborate rocking ship scenery for a stage show, a special
effect from a French book on stagecraft.*

mix of backstage gossip and technical information. Fitzgerald, in a chapter titled "Stage Illusions—Mechanism," discussed steam, traps, and animals onstage and included just a brief paragraph on the reflection illusion,
Pepper's Ghost. The author admitted that it had provided some "mild
sensations" years earlier but concluded by listing the impracticalities of
using it in a play.[16]

By 1893, a large French book indicated that magic had become more
highly regarded. *Trucs et Décor* (*Tricks and Scenery*) was written by a different author named Moynet—Georges Moynet. The book was an attempt to update theatrical innovation "for the last quarter of the century,

[as] *L'Envers du Théâtre* had for the mid-century." In *Trucs et Décor*, the author included a chapter on optical illusions, which lingered lovingly on variations of Pepper's Ghost, including the copies in Paris by the French magician Robin and by Robert-Houdin. Moynet then described how this effect had been used, with variations, in stage productions and included the technical details of other magical deceptions.[17]

The American book *Magic, Stage Illusions and Scientific Diversions* (1897) went even further. The book was edited by Albert A. Hopkins and published by Munn and Company, the publisher of *Scientific American*. The book was a compilation about the art of magic; it even had an introduction by Henry Ridgely Evans, the great magic historian, who tied its contents tightly to the traditions of Robert-Houdin, Pepper, de Kolta, Maskelyne and Cooke, and many others. Hopkins's *Magic* was no textbook of tricks but an important, eclectic mix, associating magic with stagecraft, theatrical illusions, trick photography, and optical illusions like de Kolta's Black Art.[18]

Pepper's Ghost was a theatrical effect, an arrangement of scenery, doors, and reflections, to create its apparition. Black Art, similarly, used black velvet scenery and bright, dazzling lighting in a subversive way, to create visual illusions. The next generation of magicians, including David Devant, relied upon these ideas for a number of important tricks; for example, the Artist's Dream, Devant's audition for Maskelyne, used a cleverly disguised black panel, according to de Kolta's principle.

Trucs et Décor, and then *Magic, Stage Illusions and Scientific Diversions*, managed to tightly twist together the worlds of magic and theater, so that they were nearly indistinguishable. By the last years of the nineteenth century, magic was being discussed as a useful discipline, without discussing specific magicians or tricks. Unlike the work of a juggler, a feat of magic could now achieve a life beyond a simple magic show. With that newly found prestige, it meant that magic—not just

magicians—had earned new opportunities to impress audiences. Maskelyne claimed to have been consulted for popular London shows, including deceptions for Sir Henry Irving's dramas.[19] Devant developed magic
routines for actors when the play required it, and for Sir Herbert Beerbohm Tree's 1911 production of *Macbeth*, he created a special illusion
in which the ghost of Banquo appeared standing behind Macbeth's
chair. A magician's journal reported on the effect: "The audience shares
Macbeth's horror in seeing Banquo's ghost with the stone wall of the
banqueting hall showing through it."[20]

THE IDEA OF MAGIC without a magician led to an interesting corollary,
which was quickly exploited by ambitious, commercial producers like
Maskelyne and Cooke. A great piece of conjuring could be franchised
and performed by multiple conjurers at the same time. It was now the
trick, and not the magician, that could be advertised, and the trick that
would attract an audience.

De Kolta's Vanishing Lady premiered in Paris in 1886 and was one of
the first of these marvels. This was the popular illusion in which de Kolta
showed a simple wooden dining chair, placing it in the center of the stage
on a sheet of newspaper, to demonstrate the impossibility of using a trapdoor in the stage. A lady was seated on the chair, and then a large silk
shroud was used to cover her from head to toe. Of course, the nature of
the soft cloth meant that the shape of the lady—her head, shoulders, and
knees—was clearly defined. De Kolta circled the lady, pinning the cloth
behind her head, adjusting the folds on the floor, and smoothing out the
fabric. Then he stopped, standing behind her, and grasped the shroud.
He pulled the cloth away, showing that the lady had suddenly disappeared.[21]

The trick made ingenious use of a trapdoor, in precisely the way that de Kolta supposedly proved to his audience that there was no trapdoor. In fact, the small trap, between the front legs of the chair, was matched with a corresponding flap cut in the newspaper, which was laying on the floor. The idea of pointing out a secret to dispel it, and then boldly using that same secret, was typical of de Kolta's ingenious approach.

The rest of the Vanishing Lady trick depended on a special chair, prepared with wire shapes that could be hinged to the front of the chair and simulate the roundness of the lady's body. Once these shapes were in place, the seat of the chair could be released, allowing the lady to slip down through the stage. As the wooden trapdoor opened, the newspaper trapdoor naturally followed on top. The idea was very simple, but when it was carefully performed, the Vanishing Lady was a sensational surprise. The trick was imitated so quickly that de Kolta had little choice but to franchise its use. Maskelyne made arrangements so that as de Kolta performed it in France, Charles Bertram, a London society entertainer, premiered it in London.

Around this same time, Maskelyne began touring his Egyptian Hall company in towns and cities around London. In the 1890s, Devant was entrusted with the touring company, sent on the road to dutifully supervise the Chief's specialties, while John Nevil and Nevil Maskelyne performed their latest magic in London.[22]

◯

WE CAN SEE that the magic world was changing to Devant's point of view; the evidence is in three books—the important magic volumes written by Professor Hoffmann: *Modern Magic* (1876), *More Magic* (1890), and *Later Magic* (1903).

Modern Magic was the classic textbook of magic, a fat volume packed with dense text and beautiful engravings of trick boxes and containers. In *Modern Magic*, the author had started with the conjuring of the Robert-Houdin era, incorporating the gimcracks and techniques that could be acquired only by hours of dawdling in a magic shop and neatly describing it in a proper "how-to" primer, right down to the standard mindless witter. This is how a magician sounded in *Modern Magic*:

> In an age so enlightened as our own, it is really surprising to see how many popular fallacies spring up from day to day, and are accepted by the public mind as unchangeable laws of nature. Among these fallacies there is one which I propose at once to point out to you and which I flatter myself I shall very easily dispose of. Many people have asserted, and among others, the celebrated Erasmus of Rotterdam, that a material object can only be in one place at a time. Now I maintain, on the contrary, that any object may be in several places at the same moment, and that it is equally possible that it may be nowhere at all.[23]

By his own admission, *Modern Magic* was David Devant's inspiration in magic, and Hoffmann became his hero. *More Magic* was a natural sequel, incorporating the latest inventions and techniques, including some of de Kolta's best tricks. In *More Magic*, we can see the apparatus getting simpler and more elegant—here is Verbeck's trick with the ring and the program; here is de Kolta's Flowers from the Cone or his Vanishing Lady.[24]

Finally, with *Later Magic*, the third and last of the trilogy, the student became the master. The book included a number of Devant's specialties.

Later Magic is an austere book. The illustrations show little clips, bent pieces of metal or wire, a false fingertip, or a tube sewn into a handkerchief. The conjuror's art, by 1903, depended on very few fancy boxes or vases; it now relied on these clever concealed appliances. Devant's tricks were artistically understated. He produced three white handkerchiefs from his bare hands; they seemed to materialize as he rubbed his fingers together. Then he rolled a piece of plain paper into a tube, and passing each handkerchief through the tube, they were changed to three different colors. Hoffmann gave a taste of Devant's patter:

> You'll notice the white handkerchiefs. Not merely white, the most fashionable whites. I'm told this one is "art white." This one is called, "subdued white." This one is called "dirty white." With this paper I make a tube. Nothing in the tube, and nothing concealed in either of these three white handkerchiefs. Oh, yes! I see, there is a tiny little hole concealed in this one—but I expect it was born there. . . . It seems a curious thing, but for a long time past I have been living by conjuring, and now I am going to dye by it. Simply passing the handkerchiefs through this tube will have the effect of changing them into the very latest shades. . . . Here is a nice quiet colour called "autumn green." This again is rather a sweet tint, "faded ginger." This last is exquisite; it is the prettiest pink known—to drapers, and is called "the maiden's blush." [25]

With Devant setting the trends, and Cooke having died in 1901, Egyptian Hall was razed to widen the road several years later. The Maskelynes, father and son, moved the business to St. George's Hall, a larger theater just off Regent Street. In an effort to capitalize on their success, they ambitiously introduced a play, a sort of early science fiction story filled with special effects, based on Lord Bulwer Lytton's novel *The Coming Race*. Maskelyne made Devant the managing partner in 1905, renaming the business Maskelyne and Devant, and Devant thrived at the new theater. In 1911, Devant and Nevil Maskelyne coauthored a book, *Our Magic*, which took on the noble task of finally treating conjuring with respect and carefully analyzing "the art in magic." For the book,

Maskelyne produced an imitation of Aristotle's *Poetics*, defining the terms and suggesting the rules for magicians:

> Magic has received scarcely any attention upon its theoretical side, but has been allowed to drift along the course of progress, as best it might, unaided by the advantages that order and system could bestow. . . . This is where the rising generation [of magicians] lacks understanding, the simple reason being a lack of proper training in the theory and constitution of the art they profess. [26]

There had been no real attempt at understanding magic since Robert-Houdin's basic rules, published almost half a century earlier. Devant wrote the second half of the book, offering some of his best routines as examples and efficiently illustrating the art.

As Orson Welles—a fine magician himself—once said, "If you want a happy ending, that depends, of course, on where you stop your story."

The happy way to tell the story is to explain that Maskelyne and Devant joined forces and brought magic into the twentieth century: St. George's Hall, *The Coming Race, Our Magic.*

⟲

BUT THE STORY isn't that simple, and if the full story is told, it isn't a happy one.

Devant sometimes ignored Maskelyne's traditions and sometimes worked against them. It's easy to see that he chafed under the family's leadership and deliberately pushed the business in different directions. There was an unofficial truce so long as their business was successful—John Nevil and Nevil Maskelyne supervised the London theater, and Devant made good profits by supervising the touring shows. But the first problem was

St. George's Hall, a much larger theater requiring a much larger audience, and the business wobbled.

The Coming Race was an attempt to form a new business. Maskelyne would no longer be a producer of magic shows but would compete with West End productions. But the play quickly failed, and it's difficult to reconstruct just why Maskelyne's *The Coming Race* was such a miscalculation. The special effects must have been impressively mysterious, for we can see how much work John Nevil and Nevil Maskelyne put into the effort. But reviews suggest a simple problem: their play deceived without intriguing. After years in their own theater, the Maskelynes had come to treat a work of theater as a series of magic tricks.

In contrast, when *The Coming Race* opened, David Devant was busy with the Maskelyne touring company, appearing in Edinburgh and performing his own magic as part of the show and charming his audiences. Devant had been treating his series of magic tricks as a work of theater.

By the time John Nevil Maskelyne trudged to Edinburgh to see Devant and complain about his business failure in London, the Chief was desperate. "He appeared very downhearted," Devant reported, "and said he had spent a very large sum on St. George's Hall, and his last hundreds were disappearing. When he saw me, he said he could not go on any further."[27] Devant lent the reserve fund from the provincial company, saved St. George's Hall, and promised to return to London with his new show.

It's easy to see that John Nevil Maskelyne was a proud, stubborn old man, and Devant's quick success with the business may have saved St. George's Hall, but it fostered animosity. His fellow magicians treated him with respect and a certain amount of awe. "A certain nervous diffidence made him difficult to approach. The general attitude of the magic profession," author Will Goldston wrote, "was that of a number of mice watching a sleeping dog."[28] In 1912, he was the only magician selected to appear on the first Royal Command Variety Performance. Magic journals usually singled him out for praise, which the Maskelynes must have found humiliating. For example, in 1912, Goldston joked that St. George's Hall should be renamed "St. David's Hall," to signify the magician's importance.[29] It was a joke, wasn't it?

The Maskelynes and Devant came to disagree more and more over style. By the turn of the century, the modern style was a pure, clean performance of magic, without pretensions or affectations. You could see it in the new music hall magicians, who performed quickly, smartly, and elegantly. Devant dismissed the wheezy old presentations that had been designed to excuse or explain the apparatus, to make their tricks seem important or to occupy time. When Psycho, Maskelyne's card-playing automaton, was put back into service, Devant daringly invented his own modern version of the mystery—clean and sophisticated, without the Victorian obsession with mechanism. Dyno was the name given to a simple carved wooden hand that was examined by the audience and placed inside of a glass case. Mysteriously, the hand moved up and back behind a row of dominoes, pausing to select the correct one to play a game opposite members of the audience. The complicated brass machinery of Psycho—a mechanism that could be secretly operated by air pressure—had occupied John Nevil Maskelyne for years. Devant created Dyno in six weeks. His secret was a single length of black thread.

Although he had written several magic plays for Maskelyne, he was skeptical about their use, describing them pragmatically: "Magical sketches are an excellent means of making one or two illusions go a long way . . . they can also be made to seem important by atmosphere and setting." Devant's plays were not the rattling comic plays of his boss but sharp, dramatic stories. In *The Mascot Moth*, for example, he set the story in colonial India and explained how a native spell, and the appearance of a mysterious moth in human form, suddenly changed the luck of the hero and assured his marriage. In later years, when he toured with his Artist's Dream, Devant went so far as eliminating the blank verse, performing it in pantomime to create a stark, modern impression.[30]

In the front row: from left, David Devant, Nevil Maskelyne,
and John Nevil Maskelyne, the wizards who
formed a partnership and then battled over supremacy.

Although *Our Magic* should have been a landmark publication, it was a deeply flawed book, principally because the authors were then in the middle of myriad disagreements about their business and the nature of their art. The text gave every indication that, outside of a short introduction, they did not collaborate; indeed, that they were not speaking. For example, in the preface, we read:

So far from feeling any reluctance towards letting the general public into the secrets of our procedure, we are most anxious to educate the public in such matters. The point is this. Tricks and dodges are of comparatively

210

small importance in the art of magic. For proof of this, we need only point out one well-known fact, namely that the very best audience a skilled magician can have is one composed entirely of magicians. The reason for this should be self-evident. An audience of magical experts is bound to see the performer's feats in a proper light. Such an audience will very seldom be perplexed by what is exhibited, and will never attach great importance to "how it is done."[31]

This idea, that secrets barely matter and that magic is best appreciated by magicians, was pure Devant and must have felt foreign to his coauthor, Nevil Maskelyne. That point was certainly an anathema to John Nevil Maskelyne, the Chief, who clung to secrecy as the touchstone to his career. Astonishingly, John Nevil Maskelyne, the doyen of British magic who was then at the end of his career, took no part in *Our Magic*; it was as if the fabled Chief crossed his arms and refused to participate in any discussion of magic. In later years, when Devant wrote about his career, his views were clearly at odds with those of Nevil Maskelyne, and he barely concealed his disdain for the Chief's son and his consistently bad judgments.

Nevil Maskelyne's cold, dispassionate analysis of magic—Aristotle's *Poetics* turned to conjuring—was self-important and impressively academic but without a way of addressing the spark that suggested a real artist at work. But even Devant's examples of conjuring were written in a strained, academic manner, as if trying to impress. Devant's earlier, and certainly his later books, show a much more accessible style. Reading *Our Magic* gives a good impression of what conjuring looked like to Edwardian audiences, but Devant's patter, which had once seemed so fresh, was, by 1911, just another passing fashion:

May I close the bag? I do this myself because I do these things so gracefully, don't I? Like an elephant getting off a bicycle on a muddy day. . . .

You really need not be nervous. I've performed this experiment some hundreds of times, and I've killed only one boy. He died, but he was only a very small boy.

The Times Literary Supplement was not impressed. "The time has come to cut out much of the time honored conjurer's jests, which date from the age of the invention of the clown's witticisms," they wrote in their review of the book. "Even children are weary of these dreary conventions."[32]

〇

THE MASKELYNE FAMILY came to resent Devant, and John Nevil Maskelyne particularly hated the modern, music hall nature of the St. George's Hall shows under Devant's direction. He insisted that the shows return to the old formula, emphasizing magic playlets of the leisurely Maskelyne style. In 1914, just as World War I jolted the entertainment business and discouraged audiences, the family succeeded in voting Devant out of the company. It was a particularly bold, foolish move, for Devant was, at that time, a star in the world of magic and responsible for much of the financial stability of St. George's Hall.[33]

Devant was hurt by the rebuff but put all his efforts into a successful music hall career. St. George's Hall struggled precariously under the dis-interested leadership of its "scientist/magician," Nevil Maskelyne. John Nevil Maskelyne died in 1917. Nevil Maskelyne died in 1924. The the-ater passed to the third generation of Maskelynes, who carried on nobly with the support of a number of important London magicians, but they finally closed the business in 1933.

Devant's own career was also cut short, in a very unhappy ending. In 1919, he developed paralysis—it's now evident he suffered from Parkin-son's disease—and he was forced to abandon conjuring. In 1936, reduced by his illness, he authored a magazine article discussing the secrets of his magic, intended to promote an upcoming book about his career. The Magic Circle, England's prestigious club for magicians, promptly cited their rule against exposure and expelled him. His long-held belief that audiences would appreciate conjuring more if they understood some of its principles had been put to the test by the organization that he helped found. *The Sunday Express* explained:

> David Devant, a sixty-nine-year-old, almost completely paralyzed man, yet still the greatest magician the world has ever seen, has just been expelled from the famous Magic Circle, of which he was the "father," [and its first] president. He said, "I am deeply hurt by the action of the Magic Circle, but I am too ill to enter into a controversy. The tricks I exposed were my own, so I did not think I had broken any rule. I owe it to posterity to give the world my secrets before I die. I don't think I shall live much longer."[34]

Was the business still about secrets? Or, after *Our Magic*, was it finally about something else? Despite the initial praise for *Our Magic*, magicians themselves were conflicted about the art and hotly questioned the attitudes of its author. Once the Magic Circle made its loud, public display of their principles, they quietly reinstated David Devant as a member. The club even organized annual shows to the London sanitarium where he was confined, which gave Devant an opportunity to see some of the current magic that he had actively inspired. David Devant died in 1941.[35]

CHAPTER 9

VARIETY

WHAT WENT WRONG in the Golden Age? Why did the combined talents of the Maskelynes and Devant, an inspiring mix of magic as both a commercial venture and as an art, turn sour? Contributing to Maskelyne's difficulties was that his theaters—indeed, John Nevil Maskelyne's entire career—had been haunted by a popular phenomenon that prowled the premises like a mysterious, voracious monster. It altered public tastes. It devoured his best performers. It was music hall.

From the mid–nineteenth century, the music hall was the British version of the variety theater—a weekly mixture of diverting acts: music, comedy, and physical skills. Music hall shows were an ever-shifting kaleidoscope; temporary patterns were weekly broken apart and then reassembled into a different show, at a different theater, for a different audience. Some acts, like a bright shard of golden glass, might provide enough dazzle to attract audiences on their own. For example, there was Vesta Tilley, who arrived dressed in a man's suit and belted out sentimental or patriotic songs.

Or there was Albert Chevalier, who performed as a costermonger and amused his audience with his comic Cockney songs. Other acts provided just flashes of color and texture, twelve minutes at a time—they were responsible for filling out the parade that marched across the stage every evening. Those were the innumerable magicians, jugglers, dancers, strong men, hand-shadow artists, or specialty ("spesh") acts. The halls were noisy, filled with laughter, lager, and smoke. Those early shows were organized by local managers for lo-cal tastes, and they could be attractively rough-and-tumble working-class en-tertainments, without pretension. The pretension came later.[1]

In the United States, with only a slightly different proportion of acts, the tradition started at beer halls and became vaudeville. The origin of the name "vaudeville" is unclear. One poetic theory is that it was derived from the French words *"voix de ville,"* or "voice of the city." The man credited with inventing American vaudeville, Tony Pastor, never used the term be-cause he thought it sounded "sissy" and French. He called it "variety."[2]

Variety shows began to take hold by the 1860s. (Robert-Houdin per-formed his Second Sight trick in Parisian variety theaters in the 1840s.) But the form depended upon a critical mass of talent that could be assem-bled or reassembled. By the 1870s, the halls, the acts, the managers, the agents, the circuits, the theatrical lodgings, and the railroad schedules were all in place, and the profession flourished. It became not only the voice of the city but also the sensibility of modern society.

$\circ$

AS VARIETY SHOWS became more popular, magicians of the Golden Age worked according to a different formula, a sort of "Great Man" show, in which the audiences went to see one magician, one great man who took charge of the evening, was charming, mysterious, or funny, in some particular mixture.

Alexander Herrmann was one of these great men. He was born in Paris to a German family of magicians. His oldest brother, Compars Herrmann, was a contemporary of Robert-Houdin. When he was just a boy, Alexander traveled with his brother, learning the rudiments of conjuring. Starting in 1871, when he was still in his twenties, he made his success with one thousand consecutive nights at the Egyptian Hall, just before Maskelyne and Cooke stepped in as tenants. Herrmann then brought his show to the United States in 1874 and became the country's most highly regarded magician—for several years, he had his own theater on Broadway in New York. He traveled across the country in annual tours until his death in 1896. Herrmann was a slender, goateed man in a swallowtail coat and silk knee britches with black hose: the now-clichéd image of a magician, removing his gloves and waggling his long, thin fingers.[3]

Adelaide Herrmann was his wife and his costar; she had worked in variety as a dancer and with a bicycle act—which was the style for a pretty

Alexander Herrmann was America's
most popular magician at the end of
the nineteenth century.

lady performer in tights. In Herrmann's show, she was featured in dramatic roles, as the floating lady or the heroine in a cremation-and-reappearance illusion. She also was featured in a serpentine dance, in the style of Loie Fuller. Dressed in an enormous gauzy gown, she held poles in her hands to manipulate the folds of fabric in the stage light—swirling to form the shape of an orchid in lavender light; undulating the fabric in red light to simulate an enormous flame.[4]

Herrmann introduced guest performers. One magician, Ali Ben Bey, a mystic in a white robe and turban, strolled onto a dark stage and made people appear and disappear. He wasn't a real Oriental mystery worker, of course. Ali Ben Bey was actually Herrmann's chief assistant, a talented magician named William Robinson, who performed a version of de Kolta's Black Art act.[5]

Upon Herrmann's death, America's next "Great Man" magician was Harry Kellar. Kellar was born in Erie, Pennsylvania, and apprenticed with a traveling magician, the Fakir of Ava, when he was just a boy. Kellar also toured with the Davenport brothers. Later he presented an accurate version of the Davenport brothers' séance and copies of the most popular European magic tricks, especially the inventions of de Kolta and Maskelyne. Kellar made regular trips to Egyptian Hall in London, looking for new material, and begged, borrowed, or stole Maskelyne's and Devant's illusions for his shows. We have evidence of Kellar using all three techniques. For example, he begged for Maskelyne's Will, the Witch and the Watch, borrowed a Devant trick with a ball that rolled up a plank by itself, and stole Maskelyne's most spectacular levitation trick; the theft was arranged when he hired a magician, Paul Valadon, away from Egyptian Hall.[6]

Kellar's wife, Eva, played the cornet and presented a mind-reading act with her husband. Valadon was a German magician who not only provided the secret of the mysterious new levitation but could perform the sort

*Harry Kellar, Herrmann's rival
and successor, diligently brought the
latest marvels to his audience.*

of deft tricks, with cards and billiard balls, that Kellar could never quite master.

Unlike Herrmann, who was known for his effusive personality, bubbly and devilish onstage, Kellar was boldly American without the slightest suggestion of foreign affectations. He was avuncular, meticulous, and direct. He performed wonderful mysteries, giving them careful theatrical presentations that allowed him to comment charmingly on his travels around the world.

A mere magician might entertain you on the street for tossed coins or amuse you at the lodge with card tricks, but a great man traveled from city to city, with a company of assistants and hampers of scenery. He was able to orchestrate an entire show of magic, could hold the attention of the audience for two hours, and had earned his stardom after years of experience.

But with the innovation of vaudeville and music hall, something amazing happened. It was now enough to perform twelve minutes of magic. In fact, it was preferred. Suddenly, not just the great men but now the fashionable, skillful innovators could find success; they invented their careers from bursts of novelty and creativity and were able to become stars. It turned the world of magic upside down.

In 1898, John Nevil Maskelyne received a letter from a young American magician, asking if he could join the Egyptian Hall company. Maskelyne, the impresario, was always careful about accepting new performers; remember how Devant danced to arrange his London audition? Maskelyne wrote a curt reply.

> Dear Sir: I have no room for any addition to my company. I seldom change my artists. Yours very truly, J.N. Maskelyne[7]

Although Maskelyne's letter survived, we don't have the other half of the correspondence. Presumably Harry Houdini had sent him some newspaper clippings of his reviews—this is how it was done, in the days before a photocopier or YouTube links—and these clippings must have been genuinely bewildering to Maskelyne. Houdini was known for getting out of a trunk and was just then beginning to specialize in escapes. But would Maskelyne be interested in these specialties? He had been introduced to magic by watching two Spiritualists escape from their ropes inside of a cabinet, and one of Maskelyne's first successes was escaping from a locked trunk while dressed in a gorilla costume.

At that time, Houdini had been bouncing from circuses to dime museums, the big-city versions of sideshows, doing a sort of young man's version of the "Great Man" act: a few silk tricks, a smashed and restored watch, the production of pigeons from a hat, his trunk trick, and a new idea in which he escaped from police handcuffs. In 1899, he met an agent named Martin Beck who cleverly saw the fashions for vaudeville acts and told Houdini to "cut out all the little magical stuff, it only distracts the audience, and just give a couple of the big thrillers, like the handcuffs and the trunk trick."[8]

The trunk trick had been given a grandiose title by the young Houdini: Metamorphosis. Bess Houdini, Houdini's wife, supervised locking him inside the trunk, then she drew a curtain around it. Within three seconds, Houdini was discovered on the outside of the trunk, and Bess was discovered, in his place, locked inside. But it was the handcuff escape that really allowed Houdini to exhibit his best pugilistic skills. He dared members of the audience, and even challenged the local police, to prevent him from breaking free. Beck booked him on the Orpheum vaudeville circuit, which controlled the bookings for hundreds of theaters across America, and once Houdini proved his value, Beck sent him overseas, where the London music halls had acquired a special taste for quirky, specialist magicians.

The first of these specialists had been another American, Thomas Nelson Downs, in 1899, who was billed as the King of Coins. Downs performed virtually his entire act with a stack of silver half dollars and a derby. For many years, magicians had been presenting a trick called the Aerial Treasury, apparently catching coins in the air and tossing them into a hat. Downs, a sturdy Midwesterner with a dry sense of humor and an arsenal of puns, started with that trick, calling it the Miser's Dream and producing dozens and dozens of coins. Then he manipulated the coins in his hands, like shiny silver jewels in the bright spotlight. The stack of coins was spread across his palm and, with a flick of his fingers, turned over with acrobatic precision, like a row of dominoes.[9]

Howard Thurston, another Midwestern boy, followed a season later at the Palace in London. Thurston did just card tricks. He produced cards from the air, made them disappear again at his fingertips, then caused them to rise up from the pack and through the air to his waiting hand. Then he scaled cards from the stage into the audience, spinning them so that they cut through the space in frightening straight lines, reaching the back row of the balcony or ricocheting off the plasterwork of the boxes.[10]

There was also George Stillwell, who performed with handkerchiefs. Gus Fowler used only watches. Horace Goldin raced through a number of large-scale effects at breakneck speed and without speaking a word. It was around this time that magicians designated their big tricks involving people as "illusions," because many of these deceptions involved the optical illusions pioneered by de Kolta or Pepper. Servais Le Roy, an artistic Belgian magician, appeared in London as the Devil in Evening Clothes, presenting sleight of hand as Mephistopheles himself. P. T. Selbit, a young English magician, performed in dark makeup as Joad Heteb, portraying an Egyptian magician. William Robinson, Herrmann's former assistant, impersonated a Chinese magician named Chung Ling Soo, wearing yellowface and a pastiche of Oriental robes. In 1901, Soo created a sensation in music halls by producing an enormous bowl of water as he stood in the middle of the stage. That, as it happens, was the same Chinese bowl trick that had been performed by Philippe half a century earlier in Paris.[11]

If those acts sounded especially stark or boldly modern, they all paled in comparison to Houdini, who arrived in London in 1900, strode purposefully onto the stage, pulled off his coat, and, in an unmistakable American accent, challenged anyone in his audience to restrain him: lock him up, tie him up, or handcuff him. He was now working as an escape artist. It was a sensation. The act was part dare, part showmanship, part exhibitionism. His early advertising called him "The Weird, Mystifying and Inexplicable . . . Positively the only conjurer in the World Who Strips Stark Naked."[12] That was an exaggeration, of course, but Houdini was certainly known for his special underwater escapes, and his publicity photographs featured the muscular young man daringly posed in bathing trunks.

Was it actually magic? Houdini was an experienced magician, and he had even billed himself as the King of Cards before Thurston claimed cards as his specialty. Houdini turned to escapes, but his publicity always made his feats sound like pure skill and endurance—his incredible study as a locksmith or his muscular training—and minimized the feeling of magic.

Whatever people made of it, however, it certainly worked. Houdini's 1900 trip to London was his first opportunity to visit Egyptian Hall for one of their famous matinee performances. He was no longer an unknown job applicant but a music hall star, now as unobtainable as he'd been misunderstood by Maskelyne. Houdini watched the hieroglyphic-painted curtain raise and the famous John Nevil Maskelyne spin soup plates. He saw David Devant perform handkerchief tricks. There were animated photos, shown with the new motion picture projector, accompanied by the Hall's organ. The show finished with *My Twin Spirit*, a wheezy, knock-about comic sketch about a funny Spiritualist, written by Nevil Maskelyne. People appeared and disappeared. An upright piano rolled about the stage, chasing characters as if it was possessed, and then the piano floated in the air.[13]

Houdini didn't record his impression of Maskelyne and Cooke's show, but it's hard to imagine more of a contrast, and a more significant nexus, than the twenty-seven-year-old Harry Houdini sitting in the creaking wooden seats at Maskelyne's sweetly Victorian little theater. More than likely, he was disillusioned. After all, that first European tour was the one where Houdini resolved to research his hero, Robert-Houdin, and began the quest that ultimately led to *The Unmasking of Robert-Houdin*.

○

YOU WILL HAVE NOTICED the designation of "Great Man." Although there were a few successful woman magicians, magic seldom offered opportunities for the "Great Woman."

Adelaide Herrmann provided the exception to the rule. Alexander Herrmann had been a bon vivant through his career; when he died unexpectedly in 1896, there wasn't much money left. Adelaide was forced to go back on the stage to earn a living. She worked with another Herrmann, Alexander's nephew Leon Herrmann, who was brought from Europe to continue the family tradition. But when they argued and broke up the partnership, Adelaide discovered that she didn't actually need another Herrmann. As far as the public was concerned, she had become the star of the Herrmann family.[14]

Adelaide Herrmann, Alexander's
widow, was a popular vaudeville star.

In 1899, an agent named Murdock asked if she'd accept a job in a small theater in Chicago. She was surprised to be considered for vaudeville, and she quibbled about the size of the stage and what she'd require for her tricks, but Murdock told her, "I don't care what you do in the way of an act; all I want is a name." To her credit, she didn't scrimp on the act and always went out of her way to give audiences their money's worth. Her fifteen-minute vaudeville premiere earned the sorts of reviews that would have been the envy of any stage professional:

> Madame Herrmann arrives handsomer than ever, as graceful and intel-
> ligent, and gives wings to her faultless taste.... She does not speak in her
> entire act, but her pantomime is captivating. She wears a costume of her
> own design.[15]

Adelaide Herrmann had a successful career for almost thirty years and established herself as the "Great Woman" magician. She performed sleight-of-hand manipulation; supervised a troupe of assistants, an array of birds and rabbits, and a stage full of apparatus tricks; took part in dramatic illusions; and presided over her performances like an elegant, classically trained actress—playing a Japanese princess, Cleopatra, or a distaff version of the Louis XV–era mystic, Cagliostro. She enlarged her show, and worked in vaudeville and music hall throughout America and Europe. In an article about her career, she explained:

> I do not wish to stand alone on the unique fact that I am the only presti-
> digitatrice on the stage today. I shall not be content until I am recognized
> by the public as a leader in my profession, and entirely irrespective of the
> question of sex. I am but continuing the traditions of the Herrmann fam-
> ily. My short experience has already taught me that I am practically alone
> in a big field.[16]

In 1926, a New York warehouse fire destroyed much of her apparatus and put an end to her career. She died in 1932 at the age of seventy-nine, still famously elegant and renowned among magicians as the Queen of Magic.

Today there are many talented female magicians, and it's a source of embarrassment that they are still scrambling for a foothold in the profession. The roles of the witch, sibyl, or enchantress have been well-established in mythology for centuries and should have transferred directly to the theater, just as Madame Herrmann's notable success should have led to imitators: a procession of women in magic. Instead, during her vaudeville career, a very different model took hold, and magicians' assistants were suddenly portrayed in a puzzling new way. Magic assigned a specific role to women.

NOW IS A GOOD TIME to consider the assistants. Ladies were not always the subjects of magic illusions—or more to the point, the victims of magic illusions. That cliché of the shapely female assistant, impaled with swords or endangered by blades, was not from the Victorian age, but a much later creation. As a practical matter, it could only happen after showgirls and the abbreviated costumes that showgirls wore were introduced. Victorian magicians often worked with male assistants or a son, like Jean-Eugène and Emile Robert-Houdin. Female assistants, like Harry Kellar's wife, Eva, appeared dressed in nineteenth-century clothing, and nineteenth-century sensibilities prevailed: it was impractical to have a lady crouch on a table or squeeze herself into a box. In general, audiences did not wish to see ladies being made uncomfortable onstage. One exception to that rule was Colonel Stodare, one of the Egyptian Hall magicians who preceded Maskelyne, who performed a trick where a lady entered a wide rectangular basket, and the basket was pierced with swords—her cries for mercy were an effective part of the act.[17]

Many assistants—male or female—did jobs as difficult, and used skills as demanding, as the magicians. This was the case in the Second

Sight act, where spoken code conveyed the information from the magician to the assistant—"And now, quickly, this object. What am I holding? Tell me. Now." Similarly, Robert-Houdin's son played an important part in the Ethereal Suspension, as the effect of the levitation was due to his acting skills and his experience with the special metal harness that allowed him to be apparently suspended in space. Bess Houdini was getting into the trunk—using exactly the same set of skills as her husband—just seconds after Houdini was getting out. It's a magical version of a popular quote about Ginger Rogers: she did everything that Fred Astaire did, but backward, and in high heels.

Still, it was uncommon for the assistant to be credited with the same skills as the magician. This may have been a holdover from an old cliché, that a magician's subjects were capable of wonders because they had supposedly been enchanted or controlled in some magical way by the magician. It's easy to see how this may have been an especially effective theatrical conceit when people read minds or floated in the air.

P. T. Selbit, the British magician who started his career with the Egyptian act, had developed a precise set of skills for music hall and vaudeville. He was wildly inventive and commercially cold-hearted. His 1910 success was a trick called Spirit Paintings, in which pictures materialized on blank canvases. Selbit toured with the trick and then franchised it, sending out fellow magicians to blanket the vaudeville circuits under the company name of Selbit Limited. It was a way to quash imitators by beating them to the marketplace.[18] (Houdini cleverly did the same thing, after his success as an escape artist was secured, when he put his brother to work with a "rival" escape act.)

Selbit was always poised for the next music hall hit. In 1914, he had one with Walking through a Brick Wall, a trick in which his lady assistant went from one side of a solid brick wall to the other; the wall was built by a team of bricklayers during the performance. The trick was later the subject of some controversy when it was featured by Houdini in New York City.

Then, in 1920, Selbit had an especially good idea. Or, more than likely, he remembered a good idea that had been described in Robert-Houdin's *Memoirs*. He showed a coffin-shaped wooden crate, just big enough for a person. A lady assistant was roped inside the box, and it was laid across a wooden trestle. Then, using a long crosscut saw, the box, and presumably the lady inside, were dramatically sawed into halves.

Selbit auditioned Sawing through a Girl (his original title; later it was popularly called Sawing a Woman in Half) at the Maskelyne theater, one morning in December 1920. By then, John Nevil Maskelyne had died, Devant had retired, and Nevil Maskelyne was running the theater. Nevil watched Selbit's trick and quickly turned it down. Over a career of spectacularly bad choices and misinformed ideas, this may have been Nevil's very worst. But agents from the Moss Empire music halls were also present that morning, and they quickly signed Selbit's new illusion. It was an instant success with the public, first in England, and then again when he brought it to America and franchised it around the world. It inspired imitations, variations, and sensational publicity stunts—a runaway hit that Selbit struggled to control through his magicians at Selbit Limited.[19]

To this day, it's difficult to understand the wild success of Sawing a Woman in Half. On some level, it was just another illusion, even one that had been described in a book fifty years earlier. But it was not only a unique hit with the public; it also established a specific fashion in magic. The illusion was a thinly disguised act of torture—indeed, an act of murder—presented within a conjuring act.

Significantly, the success of this illusion, in 1921, happened to perfectly correspond with a new fashion in popular culture, portraying the woman as the victim. This can be clearly seen in motion picture serials, which presented weekly episodes ending in cliffhangers: the lady tied to

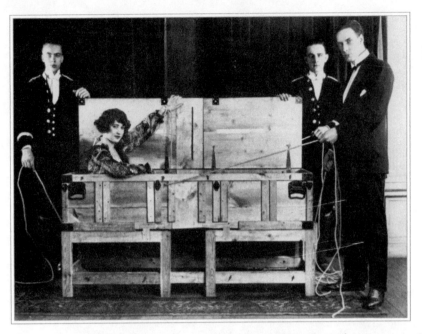

P.T. Selbit, right, and his novel illusion of Sawing through a Lady.

railroad tracks or threatened by a buzz saw, only to be saved by her hero in the opening minutes of the next installment. When these sensational scenes were first created, in stage melodramas from the 1860s to the 1890s, there was no set formula; often a man was imperiled and a woman saved him. By the time of film serials, from 1915 to 1920, however, the roles had been firmly established, and the woman was the victim. In Britain and the United States, these years perfectly corresponded to increasingly violent protests by women's groups, demanding the right to vote.

There's no coincidence. As part of his advertising campaign, Selbit publicly challenged Sylvia Pankhurst, the famous suffragette who had organized protest marches in London, to come to his stage and be sawn in half. Although Selbit's publicity campaign may have been intended as funny, it now seems unpleasantly prejudiced. By 1920, the suffragette movement was desperate and frighteningly disruptive, sometimes resulting in smashed windows, explosives, and riots in the streets. Women were regularly imprisoned, where they began hunger strikes, and the suffragette marches often resulted in bloody confrontations.[20]

When the illusion was first presented in the United States, just months after Selbit's premiere, it was imitated by Horace Goldin. Hearing of its success, Goldin hurriedly arranged a performance at a magicians dinner at the McAlpin Hotel in New York, using a bellboy from the hotel as the victim. In the spirit of Nevil Maskelyne's missed opportunity, sawing a man in half meant almost nothing, especially to a group of magicians. Once Goldin made the correction, putting a pretty damsel beneath the saw, the public became interested, and his illusion was quickly franchised across the Keith vaudeville circuit.

Selbit followed up with a series of similar illusions: Destroying a Girl, Growing a Girl, the Elastic Girl (in which she was stretched, as in a torture rack), the Indestructible Girl (spikes through the lady), Crushing a Woman (seemingly flattened), Through the Eye of a Needle (a lady pulled through a small hole), and the Girl without a Middle (originally performed with a man, and then adjusted to a lady, who was divided into three pieces). Goldin tried, too, just a year later with Tearing a Woman Apart, which was a variation of an earlier trick that had been performed with a man.[21]

It's now become popular to portray Selbit and Goldin as simple misogynists, exploiting the public's dissatisfaction with women's roles, but that's not fair. It seems that the magicians never quite understood the monstrous, all-consuming public interest that they had unleashed. Selbit in particular seemed mystified by his quick success, but he was too commercial to pass up an opportunity. That's why he tried to repeat the formula with similar illusions. Over the years, he invented dozens of important deceptions, and just a handful of his ideas indulged in this sort of torture.

By the mid-1920s, the new cliché of the endangered magician's assistant was firmly established in the mind of the public. Assistants were no longer costars of the show; they were the nameless, faceless victims in sensational little dramas. They smiled sweetly, often inanely, as a torture was applied, and then smiled even more as they took their bow alongside the magician and walked offstage.

The Queen of Magic, Adelaide Herrmann, happened to be a guest at that historic dinner at the McAlpin Hotel, sitting at the main table on the first night that Goldin demonstrated that he could saw someone in half. We don't have a record of her thoughts about the new illusion, but it's impossible to imagine the costar of Alexander Herrmann's great show, the elegant Adelaide, who had played almost every role necessary in a magic show, would ever have demeaned herself by portraying a bit of theatrical lumber.[22]

○

THOMAS NELSON DOWNS and Howard Thurston, two of the earliest American sensations in vaudeville and music hall, turned their backs on these forms. Both returned to America and put together large illusion shows, attempting to offer the next "Great Man" performances. Downs's show was a flop. But based on the success of his card act, Thurston assembled an impressive show that traveled the world. When he returned to America, he was named Harry Kellar's successor in 1908. Thurston's show became a colorful, popular stage spectacle that toured the country for decades—a performance full of costumes, scenery, and showgirls. Thurston made a horse disappear and then, several seasons later, made the latest model of automobile vanish within a puff of smoke. Sawing a Woman in Half—indeed, a number of Selbit's subsequent tortures—found a home in Thurston's show, alongside tricks from the previous generation, like Kellar's Spirit Cabinet and the levitation he purloined from Egyptian Hall.

*Howard Thurston, who became famous as a card manipulator,
later became America's great magician.*

Houdini was always a creature of vaudeville, and he never had a reason to leave it. His greatest sensations were his escapes, presented on vaudeville stages. In 1914, he attempted to put together a full magic show. It wasn't a success, but just as his career had been built on challenges, his very best magic was designed around superlatives. He performed a version of Walking Through a Brick Wall and instinctively turned it into a sensation by going through the wall himself—there was no doubt that Houdini was the one with the magical powers, not an assistant. In 1918, Houdini performed a colossal wonder in New York, making a full-size elephant disappear. On his last tour, in 1925, Houdini finally achieved his own "Great Man" show, in a production that combined magic, escapes, and a dramatic lecture on the frauds of Spiritualism. Houdini died in 1926, when he was just fifty-two years old. He was the victim of a ruptured appendix, which may have been exacerbated by a blow to his torso—a fan heard that Houdini could tighten his muscles and withstand any punch, and Houdini accepted the challenge.[23]

☽

THERE WAS ONE more trend that paralleled vaudeville, a fashion that could never quite be ignored. When Harry Houdini first watched a show at Egyptian Hall, he saw a series of "animated photographs," or motion pictures. At that time, it was a popular novelty. Within years, motion pictures had become another monster, snapping its teeth at magicians.

The inclusion of animated photographs at Egyptian Hall wasn't an accident. Magicians were tightly tied to the origins of film. In 1896, David Devant saw the first British exhibition of motion pictures by the French inventors, the Lumière brothers. When he read of the invention of a rival motion picture camera, he raced across London to meet the inventor, Robert Paul, and secure one of the devices for Egyptian Hall. The link between magic and film seemed natural: many magicians like Devant were skilled at shadowgraphy (hand shadows simulating animals or celebrity profiles). Egyptian Hall regularly closed their programs with magic lantern shows. These consisted of projected still images, painted slides with dissolving views (one scene that changed into another), and trick slides that involved moving or shifting images. Devant himself was comfortable with these showy novelties, and valued the popular magic lantern performances at Egyptian Hall. The moving picture was, to a magician like Devant, simply the latest magic lantern—the latest trick.[24]

When he heard about Devant's transaction, John Nevil Maskelyne scoffed at his junior partner. He was convinced that motion pictures would be "a nine days wonder," which was probably the worst judgment that the Chief ever made. Nevil Maskelyne was interested in the invention only in his attempt to build an improved model. In 1896, Egyptian Hall became famous as London's first permanent motion picture theater. The Paul projector was still in use nearly twenty years later, and Nevil Maskelyne's machine, an amateur effort that occupied his time in the workshop, was never put into service.

Across the channel, a French magician named Georges Méliès was then the young manager of the Theatre Robert-Houdin in Paris, which had been moved to the Boulevard des Italiens and was a quaintly nostalgic tourist attraction. Although Méliès had never seen Robert-Houdin perform, as manager of the theater, he used many of Robert-Houdin's automata and apparatus in his shows. In 1895, he saw a demonstration of the Lumière brothers' motion picture camera and attempted to purchase one, to add to his shows. When they wouldn't sell, he purchased a Paul camera through his fellow magician, David Devant.[25]

According to legend, it was Méliès who made an important discovery in the autumn of 1896. He had set his camera on a tripod and was filming a street scene in Paris—the earliest motion picture demonstrations consisted almost solely of these short slice-of-life scenes—when his camera temporarily jammed. Méliès fixed the problem and continued turning the crank on the camera. When the strip of film was developed and viewed, Méliès was surprised to see a vehicle on the street suddenly transform into another.

A later generation would call this mistake a "jump cut," but Méliès recognized how such a cut, carefully arranged, made real magic. The early Méliès trick films have all the trappings of a magic show: the scenery, the assistants, the stage draperies, the magician's tables, and the trick cabinets. But instead of using the devices that had been installed at the Theatre Robert-Houdin, Méliès utilized his cuts to accomplish a new and miraculous type of magic.[26]

Méliès was a good magician but an inspired designer and painter. He produced beautiful scenery for his films that today impress us as fanciful and theatrical. His early films still dazzle with their weird, magical atmosphere—some strange hybrid of a theater production that had been captured on celluloid. The filmmaker himself often took a prominent role, and he is recognizable as the old-fashioned magician in the black goatee who gestures wildly and circles the magic with the exaggerated steps of a dancing master, drawing our attention to his split-second miracles.

Devant made similar trick films. He is a solid, sunny presence as he presides over his magic show, now with the herky-jerky surprises of the early cinema. Other magicians followed suit, eager to add motion pictures to their acts. Carl Hertz, an established music hall magician, became a popular film exhibitor. J. Stuart Blackton and Albert E. Smith, young performers at the start of their careers, made the jump to become film producers. By 1918, Houdini starred in his first Hollywood serial, *The Master Mystery*, which enshrined his daring escapes and allowed him to save his heroine, according to the same formula that would be explored by P. T. Selbit on the vaudeville stage.

As music hall and vaudeville were dying—and performers were shocked to watch the symptoms develop through the 1920s—a number of critics attributed the problem to a system that had gotten too large and sophisticated for its audience. "Vaudeville had been dressed to kill, and it committed suicide," as one magician and critic explained the problem.[27] Instead of appealing to local audiences, instead of being tailored to specific tastes, the vaudeville circuits had established systems and routes that homogenized performances across the country. This was how Horace Goldin franchised his Sawing in Half illusion among five magicians, fanning out across America to deliver the product as quickly as possible. When Selbit arrived in American vaudeville months later, with his own Sawing in Half, he franchised it among seven more magicians.

The theory about vaudeville's demise sounded interesting, but the nature of popular culture is to be standardized. As for vaudeville, it almost certainly wasn't about taste; it was about finances. When motion pictures—the elaborate Hollywood versions, not the tricky European versions—finally supplanted vaudeville and killed variety theaters, audiences were perfectly happy to be given the same experience around the world: the same laughs when Charlie Chaplin stumbled; the same gasps when Douglas Fairbanks dueled; the same sighs, in the same proportions, when Mary Pickford dabbed at her tears.

Houdini found some success in serials and features, the escape artist who apparently performed his own stunts. Thurston made an attempt at a supernatural movie, with a story well-suited to magic. But he was frustrated by the efforts. Filmmakers seemed to quickly understand that they no longer needed magicians. "Whenever I approached the picture people on an idea," Thurston told an interviewer, "they explained, politely but firmly, that personally I was a swell fellow . . . but they could do better tricks with their cameras than I could ever hope to do with magic."[28]

Whether they were "great men" or deft, skillful innovators, a wizard depended on your undivided attention and interest. Real magic depended upon the fantasy of a particular experience, a particular moment in time when the stars aligned and incredible things happened. Audiences had to be there to witness David Devant turn a painting into a real person; to watch Houdini make an elephant disappear; or to listen to Thurston intone the whispered spell that made a princess float in the air. When audiences were happy to have imitation wizards, confined to little strips of celluloid, duplicated, and sent around the world in tin canisters, there was no need for the real thing.

◡

FILMS TOLD STORIES better than magicians ever had. When magicians finally started analyzing what they did, they had to decide upon the nature of magic. Was it a theatrical art? Was it accomplished through a combination of plot and visuals? In other words, was the presentation of magic really supposed to be, "Let me tell you a story"?

Or was magic a display of skill? Was it an opportunity to see a particularly adept performer or a particularly ingenious performer, part challenge and part demonstration? Was the presentation of magic as simple as "I can do this"?

Magicians seem to have known, instinctively, what they were supposed to reply, and Maskelyne and Devant did their best to answer the question. Magic is a work of art; magic is a piece of theater. The magician is actually an actor playing the part of a magician—even Nevil Maskelyne quoted Robert-Houdin to prove his point.

But this can't be right, can it? If it were true, our magicians would be our great actors; our shows would be histrionic re-creations of Merlin, or Cagliostro, or Hecate; the scripts would be poetic versions of their spells, followed by even more acting to pretend that something magical had occurred. It's grand to consider that Robert-Houdin's acting would have been enough for his audiences, but it wasn't. He became popular because he exhibited some very good tricks.

The panoply of vaudeville demonstrated that many of the most effective magicians were those who boldly presented their skills onstage—who didn't hide behind costumes, or roles, or imagined fantasies, or make excuses for their props, or tell stories about what they were about to do. So, magicians like Devant or Thurston may have perceived that it was artistic to tell a story, but such transparent fantasies could make magic feel contrived. Howard Thurston talked about the "ancient Hindu prayer cage," as it was being attached to cables and swung over the audience—it was an oversize, satin-covered cabinet, adorned with elaborate gold carvings and silk tassels—because it was considered artistic to explain such an odd prop. Thurston had an Indian princess, Iasia, enter the cabinet and, after it had been raised to the dome of the auditorium, he fired a pistol. The gimmicky cabinet fell open, and the princess had disappeared.[29]

In contrast, a performer like Houdini achieved his success with a completely different approach: "I can do this." In 1913, he introduced a new marvel, the Chinese Water Torture Cell, a vertical glass tank of water built with oversize brass hinges, locks, and mahogany ankle stocks, so that the escape artist could be perilously suspended in the water, upside down.

Harry Houdini, in rehearsal (no water),
and his famous Water Torture Cell escape.

What was a Chinese Water Torture Cell? It was one of the flashiest, most gimmicky pieces of apparatus that had ever been put on a stage. Obviously purpose-built for Houdini, there was no reason to trust a single plank, lock, or hinge that had been used in the construction. Houdini didn't offer an excuse or a story. He didn't explain. The Chinese Water Torture Cell made perfect sense, simply because Houdini was using it to show you what he could do.

When magicians really needed to impress, they were always willing to abandon their stories and appeal to stark, simple mystery. Sleight-of-hand magicians certainly worked on this level: "I can do this." But the past masters of such direct presentations were the mind-reading acts. They were always immune from theatrical fantasies or stories, because they guaranteed to intrigue audiences by being challenging and a little too easy to believe. However, that directness, that believability, continued to be a problem.

ႍ

CHAPTER 10

THOUGHT
TRANSMISSIONS

ONE OF THE PIONEERS of early film was George Albert Smith. He was, according to one film producer, "the father of the British film industry."[1] He created some of the earliest special effects and invented Kinemacolor, the first commercial color film process. He also developed continuity-editing techniques. By using different points of view, he conveyed to the audience what the character in the film was looking at. In other words, he helped the viewer enter the mind of someone else. This, as it happens, was something in which Smith had experience. Before he became a film pioneer, he was a key figure in some of the earliest experiments in "thought transference."

Like his friend and colleague, George Méliès, Smith had a background in magic. In the 1880s, he and his partner, Douglas Blackburn, performed a version of Second Sight. Blackburn claimed that the duo had psychic powers, and this attracted the attention of the Society for Psychical Research (SPR). The SPR had just been founded, and the purpose of the society was the scientific study of psychic phenomena. Members of the SPR began a series of experiments in thought transference, with Blackburn and Smith as their subjects.

During the experiments, Blackburn concentrated on names, numbers, colors, and drawings, and he transmitted his thoughts to Smith. Smith managed to receive the thoughts and, while some suspected that the pair used a secret code, the experiments were deemed a success. They became part of the growing body of evidence for the reality of thought transference, which was in the process of being given a new name: telepathy.

It was only one episode in the ongoing story of how mind-reading performances were taken seriously. Victorian audiences understood that magic was an illusion. When, in the middle of a magic show, a stage conjuror performed a Second Sight routine, they generally understood that this was not a demonstration of psychic powers. However, extended demonstrations of mind-reading were more ambiguous. Performers made more extravagant claims, the public wondered if they were real, and scientists often became involved. And the Blackburn and Smith episode, like so many others, ended in controversy.

〇

VICTORIAN SCIENTISTS had been keen to explain seemingly supernatural phenomena. When Spiritualism had appeared in the mid–nineteenth century, visitors to séances had reported that, when they placed their fingers on top of a table, the table began to move. It seemed to move in response to questions that they had in mind. For some, this was evidence of communication from spirits. However, the English physiologist W. B. Carpenter revealed the secret. He called it "ideo-motor action." When people placed their fingers on top of the table and then imagined it moving, they were unconsciously causing it to move. Michael Faraday conducted an experiment to show how this could happen. He placed a board on top of a table, and people placed their fingers on top of the board. As a result, the board moved, not the table. Later, Ouija boards would appear, which relied on ideomotor action.

Over the following decades, a variety of new phenomena appeared, and scientists did their best to explain them. Some dismissed it all as trickery, while others provided psychological explanations. One of these explanations was that, without the aid of spirits or other supernatural powers, we can know what others are thinking. This seemed more plausible to scientists than spirit communications. The mind remained a mysterious phenomenon and was about to be the subject of a new science called psychology. The idea that in some sense, we can know what others are thinking, did not seem such a strange idea.

But what does it mean when we say that we can know what others are thinking? We can tell from what they say and do. We might pick up on more subtle clues, in their faces or in their body language. We might be able to spot a lie and may suspect a hidden agenda. There is, however, a limit to this. After all, we can never be sure, and we frequently get it wrong. So, to what extent can we know what others are thinking?

Where do the limits of mind-reading lie? At what point does normal mind-reading become paranormal or even impossible? This has not been obvious. Indeed, it has been a rather gray area that has attracted some shadowy characters, who often worked blindfolded or out of sight yet managed to keep their audiences in the dark.

〇

IN OCTOBER 1874, J. Randall Brown was tested at Yale. This was not an exam. It was an experiment in thought-reading. Brown held one end of a wire that was 210 feet long. The wire stretched down to the basement, then back up to the lecture room where he stood. At the other end of the wire was Professor William Henry Brewer of Yale's Sheffield Scientific School. As he held on to his end of the wire, Professor Brewer concentrated on a hammer that was lying on a blackboard in the room. After a few minutes, Brown walked over and picked up the hammer. It appeared as if Brewer's thought had been transmitted through the wire.

It was, admittedly, an odd experiment. However, it was an attempt to determine the limits of thought-reading. After all, J. Randall Brown had already performed a variety of thought-reading feats. His typical performance went something like this: He asked a volunteer to hide a small object somewhere in a building. Brown was then blindfolded. When the volunteer returned, Brown took him by the hand and led him through the building. A few minutes later, though nothing was said, Brown located the object.

J. Randall Brown could "read thoughts,"
but not without physical contact.

This seemed impossible, but the American neurologist George Beard revealed the secret. He called it "muscle-reading." It relied on having physical contact with the person who knew the location of the object. Brown was picking up on subtle, unconscious cues about its location by constantly testing the movements of the person. In this way, the person unconsciously let Brown know where the object was, by subtly resisting the wrong direction and by moving more easily toward it. It was, like ideomotor action, a case of unconscious movement.

However, Brown had then come up with more impressive feats, which avoided direct contact with the volunteer. He sometimes asked another person, who did not know the location of the object, to act as a link between him and the volunteer. At other times, he and the volunteer held either end of a handkerchief, or a walking stick, or a short wire. But this did not prevent him from "muscle-reading." As long as he had some kind of indirect contact with the volunteer that allowed him to pick up on his ease of movement, Brown could succeed.

This was why the test at Yale was conducted using a long wire. A short wire could be used in "muscle-reading," but one that was 210 feet long seemed to rule out the possibility. "I would stake my reputation upon the genuineness of the phenomena," declared the astronomer C. S. Lyman, who was present at the Yale experiments. "The theory of unconscious muscular action is entirely opposed to the facts observed."[2]

Brown went to greater lengths in order to make it seem impossible. When scientists said that they knew his method, he gave a demonstration that appeared to exclude the use of that method. That is how to demonstrate the impossible. Consider the possible explanations and where their limits lie. Then go further by doing something that cannot be accounted for by these explanations. Identify the boundary of possibility, then cross it. This is what makes it magic. But it is also what makes it paranormal or supernatural: it is beyond what we think of as normal or natural.

In the case of magic, the audience knows that it is an illusion. Conjurors were clear that this was the case, but many performers were not so clear. They claimed to have psychic or supernatural powers. They pretended that their magic was real. Many people believed them, but many people did not. For all of Brown's efforts, George Beard remained unconvinced and dismissed them as "conjuring tricks." He explained how some of it could be done, but he did not know how all of it was done. He guessed that a confederate might have been involved, but he did not really know this. This is what prevents it from being viewed as paranormal or supernatural: it can always be attributed to trickery, in which case, anything is possible.

This, you might say, is the difference between belief and disbelief. A believer sees something that seems impossible and concludes that it is real. A disbeliever sees the same thing and assumes that it is not. At some point, scientists become involved in an attempt to settle the matter. They conduct experiments in controlled conditions in order to rule out the possibility of trickery. But whether the test succeeds or fails, it does not settle the matter. If the test succeeds, then disbelievers claim that the subject somehow managed to cheat. Or perhaps it was merely a fluke. If the test fails, then believers claim that the conditions were not conducive to the phenomena. Or perhaps the subject had a bad day. And so the debate continues to this day, with each side repeating the same old arguments, which seem so convincing at the time. Meanwhile, as the controversy has continued, some performers have spotted opportunities to make a reputation and a living.

Brown was one of these performers. He was tested by several scientists, and the results were mixed, at best. At the Western Union Office in Philadelphia, he attempted to read the thoughts of a telegraph operator in New York. The operator in New York held on to the wire and was asked to think of a number. Meanwhile, in Philadelphia, Brown held on to the wire and concentrated. He wrote down the number 37. A request for confirmation was requested. When the reply arrived, however, it was not what anyone had predicted. Apparently, there had been a technical problem, and it read: "Battery put on the wire by mistake. Sorry."[3]

The impossible is never easy, of course, but then, it did not particularly matter. The publicity was what really mattered. In the world of popular mind-reading, scientific validity is unimportant. Success is measured in box-office receipts. When Brown arrived in town, he gave private demonstrations so that he could obtain publicity. He then gave a large public demonstration so that he could make some money. When he played Chickering Hall in New York, he made almost $1,000 in one night. The attention of science brought free press coverage, not all of which was positive. Nevertheless, he found that he could manage the hostility of disbelievers by pretending to be a disbeliever himself. He portrayed himself as an exposer of Spiritualism and joined the growing bandwagon of conjurors who pretended to do what mediums did. Later, when attention began to fade, he pretended to be a genuine medium. It may have seemed inconsistent, but it was not. It was entirely consistent with his primary aim, which was to make a living.

For all that has been said about fraudulent psychics—and an extraordinary amount of things have been said—one of the things that is often forgotten is their need to make a living. People who pretend to have special powers do so for a number of reasons, but many end up in that strangest of careers because it provides an opportunity. Most famous mediums and psychics, like most conjurors, came from humble roots. Demonstrating extraordinary powers was not only a way to get attention but also a means of getting by. An initial pretense that provoked others to look at you with greater interest might lead to a chance to make some money, when money was hard to come by. Before long, you had the attention of well-off but not necessarily well-informed strangers. They thought that you might provide an answer to their own problems, which were not material. A lie, once started, was difficult to stop, while money and recognition were always welcome. Deception, like the desire for wealth and fame, became a habit.

SINCE THE FOX SISTERS, many young women had become successful spirit mediums. And, as Brown was being tested by American scientists, several of them were being tested in England. The key scientific figure was the chemist William Crookes, a Fellow of the Royal Society. Crookes had already tested Daniel Home, the most impressive of all the spirit mediums, and concluded from these experiments that he had discovered a new "psychic" force. Edward Cox, who had endorsed George Goble, had been present at these experiments and suggested the term "psychic." The word was meant to denote a new natural force, rather than a supernatural power. This placed it within the realm of science, which deals with the natural, not the supernatural. Crookes then went on to test several young women who had become successful mediums.

One of these was the quite remarkable Annie Eva Fay. Fay had begun conducting séances at the age of eighteen in rural Ohio in exchange for a modest fee and a meal. She had then developed a new "spirit cabinet" act, which was better than that of the Davenports. Her cabinet was a semicircular screen with a curtain at the front, raised several inches from the floor. Her wrists were tied behind her back and a cotton bandage was wrapped around her neck, then fixed to the back of the cabinet. Her ankles were tied together with a cord that extended outside the cabinet and was held by a member of the audience. When the curtain was closed, she was out of sight, but the audience could see her feet below it, still secure and stationary. Nevertheless, from behind the curtain, strange noises were heard. Bells rang, tambourines shook, harmonicas and flutes were played. When the curtain was opened, a glass of water had been mysteriously drunk, and figures had been cut out of paper.

Annie Eva Fay, the mindreader and medium,
also known as the "Indescribable Phenomenon."

The Ohio press soon hailed Fay as the "most remarkable phenomenon of the present age" and the "greatest wonder of the century."[4] She had success in New York and Boston, until her secrets were exposed by a fellow medium in the *Boston Herald*. She then sailed to Britain, and by the time she arrived in London, her reputation preceded her. She was, for some, the most impressive of mediums. For others, she was a remarkable conjuror. Either way, the *Morning Post* noted, this was "extraordinary and incomprehensible entertainment."[5]

She quickly attracted the attention of William Crookes, who wished to experiment with her. In 1875, he conducted a test that was supposed to establish the truth of the matter. The reality of Fay's phenomena, like those of the Davenports, was based on the assumption that her movements were restricted. However, as everyone knew by then, mediums who were tied up could escape. So Crookes decided to employ technology, instead of textiles, to restrict her movement. During the experiment, she held brass handles connected to a wire, so that she completed an electrical circuit. If she let go of either handle, the current would drop, and this would be revealed on a galvanometer that he was watching. Crookes reckoned that the electrical current running through the wire provided "absolute certainty" that her hands were not free, despite her being unseen behind a curtain. And so, like Brown and Professor Brewer at Yale just a few months earlier, a wire provided the necessary connection.

Crookes invited both believers and disbelievers to observe. They included William Huggins, another Fellow of the Royal Society, and Francis Galton, a well-known polymath and cousin of Charles Darwin. During the experiment, they saw a "spirit hand" appear through a gap in the curtain. While Fay was still sitting at the desk, according to the galvanometer reading, the "spirit hand" passed books through the curtain to several of the observers. Galton was handed a book on travel, which he himself had written. Huggins and Edward Cox, who was also there, were each handed books that they had written. The editor of *The Spiritualist* was handed a copy of his own periodical. Fay, we are told, had not known precisely who would be there. It seemed as if she had been able to pick up information about those who were present.[6]

Needless to say, the galvanometer experiment was disputed at the time and has been ever since. But those who were there could not explain what happened. Fay returned home to the United States with a letter from Crookes stating that he was a believer. Her agent, Washington Irving Bishop, decided to make the most of it. "Mr Bishop begs respectfully to state that Miss Fay, the celebrated spiritual-physical medium," he announced in an advert in the *New York Herald*, "as to the genuineness of her manifestations, is indorsed [*sic*] by William Crookes, F.R.S. and other members of the Royal Society."[7]

A few months later, however, Bishop fell out with Fay and published an exposé of her act in the *Daily Graphic* entitled: "The greatest humbug yet: how Professor Crook's [*sic*] 'gifted and wonderful' medium, Annie Eva Fay, performs her tricks."[8] Bishop then began to perform the Fay act, followed by an explanation of how she did it, along with the feats of other mediums, such as the Davenport brothers. He then saw a performance of J. Randall Brown and quickly realized its potential. He came to Britain, where muscle-reading was then unknown, billing himself as the "world's first mind reader." When he arrived in London, he met with W. B. Carpenter and presented himself as a fellow debunker of Spiritualism. He also performed some thought-reading feats, and Carpenter was impressed. He described Bishop's skills as "of great value to the Physiologist and the Psychologist."[9]

This led to investigations by some of the most eminent psychological scientists of the time, such as George Romanes and Francis Galton, which were reported in *Nature,* the *Lancet,* and the *British Medical Journal*. In the process, Bishop tried to confuse the matter by making a variety of claims and trying to use a variety of methods. He claimed that he read minds, or thoughts, or bodies, or that he did not know what he was doing. At some point, he claimed that he could read the thoughts of people without physical contact. This was tried, and he succeeded. It was tried again, and he failed. The success was dismissed as an "accident."[10]

In his report, Romanes accused Carpenter of making a mountain out of a molehill. To Romanes, there was nothing remarkable going on.

Bishop was "guided by the indications unconsciously given through the muscles of his subjects—differential pressure playing the part of the words 'hot' and 'cold' in the childish game which these words signify." It was merely "an ordinary drawing-room amusement." Carpenter, the great debunker of Spiritualism, "the great opponent of all humbug," had recommended Bishop to the attention of scientists, and "the result is to endow the powers which were afterwards exhibited with a fictitious degree of importance in the eyes of the public."[11]

Carpenter then tried to defend his endorsement and, in the process, presented Bishop as having more impressive powers. He pointed to Bishop's "power of naming words and numbers previously written and sealed up in private." This, he noted, Bishop had "repeatedly performed in the presence of distinguished medical and scientific men in the United States . . . and, also before a like assemblage in Edinburgh." Carpenter thought that this was genuine and that the secret lay in Bishop's "acute recognition of indications unconsciously given" by the person who knew what was written on the paper.[12]

What Carpenter did not realize was that this had nothing to do with psychology: it was a trick. Bishop had indeed asked someone to write something down on a slip of paper, placed it inside an envelope, and then revealed what was written down. However, before it had gone into the envelope, he had switched the piece of paper, then read it when nobody was looking. He explained elsewhere that this was the method, "that he had not let the audience see him do so, but he could never have told the name if he had not examined the paper beforehand."[13] In other words, it was neither mind-reading nor muscle-reading. It was simply reading.[14]

As the skeptics squabbled over what to believe, Bishop profited. He performed around Britain, presenting himself as an anti-Spiritualist and offering to perform for charitable causes. He asked only for expenses to be paid but then took the bulk of the money. He relied on respectable

Washington Irving Bishop reveals a message inside an envelope to a blindfolded volunteer.

folk being too embarrassed to admit that they had been scammed, and if he was accused, then he simply denied it. On one occasion, he was challenged to read the serial number of a banknote, in conditions that ruled out muscle-reading. He first agreed, then refused, then announced that he would perform the feat onstage and donate the proceeds to Victoria Hospital. In front of a packed house, he performed the feat in a way that clearly did not rule out muscle-reading. He then declared that he had won the challenge and walked off with £300 in box-office receipts. After deducting "expenses," he offered Victoria Hospital a donation of £19.[15]

Meanwhile, Bishop continued to be debated in scientific circles. One letter to *Nature* dismissed Bishop's feats as "tricks" and "legerdemain." If not, then "Dr Carpenter must invent a name for Mr Bishop's new power."[16] Another letter, from William Barrett, made a distinction between the muscle-reading of Bishop and noncontact mind-reading that he had observed elsewhere.[17] The latter, he thought, were genuine phenomena, because they were not due to muscle-reading. Barrett, a physicist, had already proposed the founding of a new society to investigate such phenomena. The following year, he was one of the founding members of the Society for Psychical Research. In the first paper of the *Proceedings* of the SPR, Barrett again distinguished between contact mind-reading and noncontact mind-reading. It was the latter that would be given the new label of telepathy.

This was the primary focus of the early SPR, which included some eminent members. It included Fellows of the Royal Society, such as Alfred Russel Wallace, J. J. Thomson, Lord Rayleigh, and Oliver Lodge. It included John Ruskin, Lord Alfred Tennyson, and Charles Dodgson (Lewis Carroll). It included past and future prime ministers William Gladstone and Arthur Balfour. It attracted the great and good because this was a profoundly important matter. It was nothing short of an attempt to show that there was more to the world than merely physical matter. This was, according to Gladstone, the "most important work being done in the world."

Such lofty ambitions, however, had to be grounded in a more mundane reality. It began in experiments with individuals who seemed to be able to read minds. The primary point about telepathy was that it involved communication across space. SPR investigators were interested in demonstrations that involved no physical contact between the "agent" and the "recipient." This was why they investigated the mind-reading skills of George Smith and Douglas Blackburn. Blackburn and Smith appeared to transmit thoughts without physical contact.

Several years later, however, Blackburn confessed that they had used a code. The Blackburn confession was reported in the press and greeted by believers and disbelievers with, respectively, disbelief and belief. Blackburn claimed that the experiments involving himself and Smith had been a deliberate fraud. Smith publicly denied this and dismissed it as a "tissue of errors." William Barrett expressed his faith in Smith and his disbelief in Blackburn. But nobody who did not already believe in telepathy found this convincing. And many who did believe in telepathy regarded the whole affair as embarrassing.

〇

IN HINDSIGHT, of course, it is easy to wonder how scholars and scientists could have been so gullible. But the SPR investigators were suspicious and conducted a series of tests in different conditions. Some suspected a code was involved, while others thought that this had been ruled out. They attempted to rule out trickery, of course, but they also came to know the people they tested and felt that they could be trusted. They were open to the possibility of telepathy, of course, but then why was that such an implausible idea? After all, there were many scientists who believed that thoughts could be transmitted, in one way or other.

There were psychologists and physiologists who thought that mental abilities were transmitted through evolution and that mental illness was a physical disease, which could be biologically inherited. There were biologists studying how physical diseases could be transmitted through the air and psychologists who reckoned that thoughts might also be contagious. Gustave Le Bon, for example, who famously wrote about the madness of the crowd, described how the collective mind of the group appeared to be guided by mysterious forces.

There was also a rather fuzzy boundary between transmission of sound and transmission of thoughts.[18] Physicists publicly exhibited the transmission of sound through the air, using tuning forks and flames. In a similar way, Barrett thought that the brain might be agitated by a distant mental disturbance, like a tuning fork or a flame. Since the 1860s, the Atlantic telegraph had demonstrated that people could communicate across vast distances. The telephone showed that, by relying on the sympathetic communication between one form of energy and another, voices could be heard. For some, the mind was like a telephone exchange. Alexander Graham Bell went to séances and speculated about telepathy.

The potential of electromagnetism also suggested all kinds of possibilities. A few years later, William Crookes, who made some controversial claims, suggested that electromagnetic waves might be used in wireless telegraphy. At the time, some people were skeptical about that. Other pioneers of radio, such as Oliver Lodge and Thomas Edison, found telepathy and spirit communication quite plausible. Many scientists were skeptical, of course, but what was possible—and what was not—remained a matter of scientific debate. All of this meant that demonstrations of mind-reading could be a serious topic for scientists. And this, for performers of mind-reading, provided an opportunity to tap into the scientific controversy.

However, they played by different rules. The value of scientific controversy to them was not in the science but in the controversy. Consistency, therefore, was neither necessary nor profitable. Bishop worked with Fay, and then debunked her. He denounced the false claims of Spiritualist mediums as he made false claims about his own abilities. He made a variety of contradictory claims about what he did and what he could do, so that it was near impossible to pin him down. And when someone made a specific accusation about what he had said or done, he denied it. It was a dishonest but effective strategy, which continues to be used to this day.

Meanwhile, others could benefit, too. Conjurors who made no such claims could nevertheless gain publicity by denouncing such claims. John Nevil Maskelyne, who had begun his career by debunking the Davenport brothers, debunked Annie Eva Fay. He also engaged in a battle with Bishop, denouncing him as "a cheat and an impostor." Bishop responded by accusing Maskelyne of being "devoid of honorable instincts," and promised to hold him "criminally liable and make Justice punish him for his villainous conduct."[19] Maskelyne then sued Bishop for libel and was awarded £500 in damages. Of course, he did not receive a penny. Bishop had left the country.

When he returned to the United States, Bishop continued to attract attention. His methods were often exposed in the press, along with details of his personal life. He was, by all accounts, an eccentric man who married and divorced several times and was suspected of drug and alcohol abuse. He was also prone to cataleptic states and could fall into a coma that closely resembled death, though he remained fully conscious throughout. In 1889, during a performance in New York, he collapsed and fell into a coma. Doctors pronounced him dead, and an autopsy was performed just a few hours later. His brain was removed, and it was, it seems, a perfectly ordinary brain. However, a coroner's jury felt that the doctors had "acted in some haste," and later, they found themselves on trial for "illegal dissection."[20] The jury was unable to reach a verdict, and historians since have wondered whether, as his brain was being removed, Bishop was dead or alive.

○

BROWN, BISHOP, BLACKBURN, and Smith could, in a sense, read minds. But this was not telepathy. There was nothing "psychic" going on, since they relied on a mixture of psychological techniques and legerdemain. This made it difficult for those who wished to explain what was going on. Those who had expertise in psychology did not have expertise in magic. They might think that they were watching a psychological technique, which was beyond what was thought to be psychologically possible, when it actually relied on trickery. The fact was that, if they wanted to demonstrate that nothing psychic was going on, then they needed expertise in magic.

This mattered at the end of the nineteenth century, when the new science of psychology emerged. At the time, "psychic" and "psychological" were terms that were often used interchangeably. As a result, the new discipline of psychology was often confused with psychical research. It did not help that William James, the most eminent of American psychologists, was a supporter of psychical research. He was aware that mediums and psychics cheated, of course, but that was not the point. As far as he was concerned, it only mattered if one was genuine. After all, we used to think that there were no black swans, until we discovered one. We have also observed countless black crows, but this does not make a white crow impossible. As far as James was concerned, a genuine psychic was like a white crow. One merely had to find one.

However, most psychologists were eager to separate psychology from psychical research. And so they did their best to draw some boundaries between the two. They went out of their way to debunk psychic and supernatural phenomena. They investigated psychics and dismissed them as frauds. They came up with psychological explanations for what was going on. And, in an attempt to become experts in deception, they began to study the psychology of magic.

Some of the most prominent early psychologists in Europe and America wrote about magic. They conducted experiments with famous conjurors and attempted to reveal their secrets. In 1893, Alfred Binet invited five of France's most eminent conjurors to his laboratory in Paris. He used new chronophotographic apparatus to allow him to view some sleight-of-hand tricks at slow speed. This, for Binet, was a successful separation of brute sensation from mental interpretation.[21] This hardly explained how magic worked, but one of the conjurors present found it interesting. His name was Georges Méliès, and he would make practical use of this distinction when he invented the first special effects in early cinema.

Joseph Jastrow, who established one of the first psychology departments in America, conducted experiments with Alexander Herrmann and Harry Kellar. He claimed that "the influence of special kinds of occupation and training upon the delicacy, range and quickness of sensory, motor and mental powers is an important and interesting problem." For this reason, "psychological tests made upon virtuosi are desirable." He therefore employed a range of psychophysical tests that he thought "to be related to the processes upon which their dexterity depends" and which he felt "most likely to yield definite results." As it turned out, he was wrong on both counts.

Jastrow compared the two wizards in terms of tactile sensibility, such as point discrimination (both were below average), weight discrimination (both were below average), and length discrimination by touch (Kellar was below average, and Herrmann average). In tests of visual perception, they were unable to divide lines equally or to judge lengths any better than others. In a test using the "form alphabet" (in which the subject had ninety seconds to identify as many instances of a chosen symbol in a long string of symbols), Kellar was average and Herrmann "did not fully comprehend what was wanted." Both did manage to excel in rapidity of movement of finger and forearm and in reaction time to visual and tactile stimuli. However, when the response involved some kind of discrimination, they were again below average. Jastrow conceded that the experiments "suggest no very decided conclusions."[22]

The pioneer of social psychology, Norman Triplett, also conducted experiments. One was based on an illusion used by conjurors. A demonstrator who was sitting behind a desk in a schoolroom threw a tennis ball (though he found it worked equally well with an apple or a silver dollar) about three feet in the air and caught it. He threw it a second time, slightly higher, and caught it again. He then secretly dropped the ball on his lap and mimed throwing it a third time. When asked what happened, nearly half the pupils (40 percent of the boys and 60 percent of the girls) reported that they saw the ball go up and disappear. On the gender difference, Triplett observed that "illusions of fancy and tendency to hallucinations, are more frequent in females. Pliny tells us that women are the best subjects for magical experiments, and Bodin estimated the proportion of witches to wizards at not less than fifty to one."[23]

For the most part, however, psychologists merely read what conjurors wrote and repeated it in psychological language. They paraphrased, usually without credit, Robert-Houdin and Professor Hoffmann. They attempted to make some meaningful distinctions and to discover some psychological laws. Binet was confident that conjuring could be explained according to psychological laws, "of which he [the conjuror] no doubt knows nothing, and which he has never heard explained."[24] But Binet struggled to explain the connection between psychological laws and conjuring tricks. He claimed, for example, that there was a difference between "positive" and "negative" illusions, but Triplett discovered that such a division "would have no practical value."[25]

Psychologists revealed very little, but it did not particularly matter. They studied magic because it was interesting and because they found it useful. They were not interested in the experience of magic, which was an obvious psychological topic. They did not study magic because they wanted to understand the experience of wonder. Their interest in magic was as a deception. Like Reginald Scot and Sir John Forbes, they cited magic as something that was natural but appeared to be supernatural. It was part of the continuing battle against the very idea of real magic. And it once again reinforced the view that magic, rather than being a source of wonder, was merely a deception.

⟡

MEANWHILE, MIND-READERS CONTINUED to play with the boundaries of illusion and reality. They often did it tongue-in-cheek, but they found it hard to resist the public's appetite for genuine mystery. And, while magic provided wonder, it was not particularly mysterious, since everyone saw it as merely a trick. They might wonder about how it was done, but they understood that it relied on deception. Mind-reading, on the other hand, was always more mysterious.

S. S. Baldwin, after all, was obviously an entertainer. He presented *An Hour in Laughter Land* and *The Funniest Show on Earth*. He dressed in robes and wore a turban, calling himself the White Mahatma. He demonstrated pseudo-Spiritualist feats and revealed how they were done. He wrote a book entitled *Spirit Mediums Exposed* in 1879, which revealed the methods of mediums, such as the Davenports and Annie Eva Fay. He also published a book, *The Secrets of Mahatma Land Explained* (1895), that exposed the secrets of Indian magic. He even, on occasion, revealed how some of his own tricks were done.

Nevertheless, for all the secrets that he revealed, he remained a mystery. His main feature was the Question and Answer act, of which he was a pioneer. This began with the audience writing down questions on pieces of paper, folding them up, and putting them in their pockets. The act consisted of Baldwin's wife, who was onstage, supposedly in a trance and apparently psychic, providing answers to these questions. While the show was clearly light entertainment, it was far from obvious that the Question and Answer act was merely trickery.

As one reviewer put it, this part of the show was "not funny, but it causes a feeling of deep interest and mystery, that is almost tinged with awe." "We do not profess to know how the results are achieved," declared another, "but we can state that the manifestation is devoid of trickery." "We are willing to admit that it may be by the exercise of some natural yet unknown power," stated yet another, "but we certainly can't admit it was mind reading. . . . It is a question well worth the attention of scientific men."[26] And what was this "natural yet unknown power," which was not "mind reading," yet was "well worth the attention of scientific men"? That remained a mystery.

S. S. Baldwin, the White Mahatma,
also known as The King of Laugh-land, but
his Question and Answer act was "not funny."

Baldwin exploited this mystery to the full. He claimed no supernatural powers, but at times, he claimed that he did not use trickery. His audiences did not know if what he did was real, or for that matter, if it *was* real, then precisely what was real about it. And it worked. He performed sellout shows around the world, in Milwaukee and Melbourne, Southampton and South Africa, Indianapolis and India. He briefly worked with Thurston and was admired by Kellar and Houdini. However, as they knew themselves, the life of a showman was precarious. At the end of his career, he was in San Francisco, providing clairvoyant readings for a pittance.

⟲

BY THE TURN of the twentieth century, there were various forms of mind-reading. Brown was still performing muscle-reading, though his career was in decline. By then a growing number of performers had appeared who covered their eyes and found hidden objects while holding the hands of strangers. The most successful was Bishop's former assistant, Stuart Cumberland, who managed to earn a fortune while making similarly ambiguous claims. When asked to assist in the discovery of Jack the Ripper, for example, he first admitted that there was nothing that he could do but later claimed to have had a dream in which the killer's identity had been revealed.[27]

The secrets of muscle-reading had been widely exposed, but when performed well, it continued to work. For those who understood the basic principle, it remained a remarkable feat. For those still unaware of the secret, it appeared to be impossible. The two-person code act continued to flourish. The possibility of using a code had been suspected and discussed in newspapers in the days of M'Kean, the "double-sighted Scotch phenomenon." But it continued to work, so long as performers did things that went beyond the imagined limits of a code. The Zancigs, for example, were a husband and wife from Denmark who imaginatively billed themselves as "Two minds with but a single thought." They developed such a sophisticated code that, even though a code was suspected, it nevertheless seemed impossible, and some were convinced it was telepathy.

Meanwhile, the Question and Answer act was taken to a new level by the extraordinary Alexander, the Man Who Knows. Alexander was a former fake Spiritualist medium who mixed traditional stage magic with his featured Question and Answer act. One of the strategies that made it so convincing was that he used a variety of different methods, all of which he cannily excluded by listing them in his program:

Mr Alexander desires especially to call the attention of the audience to the fact that in these demonstrations he uses no confederates, no codes, no waxed pads to write upon, no exchange of your questions, thereby permitting the same to be transferred to some dressing room to an assistant to be transmitted to him via a telephone line.... These are some of the methods resorted to by alleged performers, irresponsible, aspiring charlatans, pure and simple, who have copied Alexander's billing matter verbatim, and have endeavored to imitate him in the smaller houses.[28]

Alexander, the Man Who Knows, wearing his extravagant stage costume and posing by his 1924 Buick.

The secrets were out there, but it did not prevent the audience from being astounded. It did not matter if they had read about the secrets of muscle-reading, codes, or other means of surreptitiously discovering information. What mattered was that, as they were watching, what they were watching seemed impossible. After all, everyone knows that a conjuror uses sleight of hand and gimmicked props. But if the sleights are invisible and the props look innocent, then it still seems impossible. However, when mind-reading seems impossible, people wonder if it might be real. There are at least two reasons for this.

First, performers often pretend that some of the things that they do are real. Alexander, like others before him, played both sides of the boundary between illusion and reality. On the one hand, he was "a hater of imitators and fakers who pose as seers and soothsayers." On the other hand, he sold astrological forecasts and Ouija boards and claimed in the press that he could predict the future. He even claimed that he predicted a theater fire, despite the fact that it destroyed all the equipment in his show. When making astrological predictions, he disclaimed any "supernatural" abilities, yet billed his demonstrations as the result of "psychic powers" that were "science baffling."[29] In other words, Alexander exploited the ongoing ambiguity surrounding the mysterious powers of the mind.

Later, he presented himself as "the world's foremost psychologist" and sold a mail-order course called *The Inner Secrets of Psychology*, which promised to "UNLOCK the door to unlimited POWERS," including clairvoyance and telepathy. His brother, who performed a similar act, presented "psychic lectures and dream interpretations," billed himself as "The Master Psychologist," and included in his advertising a quote from Edison that attributed his powers to "a supersensitive brain." He also published a monthly periodical, *The Master Mind*, devoted to "applied psychology," which defined "the science of Psychology" as "the study of the human mind," and described Senator Warren Harding (then president-elect) as "a true Psychologist."[30]

All of this was possible because people struggled to distinguish between the psychological and the psychic. This is the second reason why mind-reading was often seen as real. The public did not know where the boundary between possible and impossible lay. Even those who tried to clear things up could make things fuzzier. For example, Hugo Münsterberg, director of the psychology laboratory at Harvard, once investigated a girl with "x-ray vision." He concluded that "nothing mysterious, nothing supernatural" was going on. It was, instead, an example of "unusual, supernormal sensitiveness together with this abnormal power to receive the signs without their coming at once to consciousness . . . under conditions under which ordinary persons would neither see nor hear them." On reading this, the *New York Times* reported that "Dr Munsterberg scouts the theory that she is possessed of what is known as 'X-ray vision' . . . while admitting the girl possesses unusual psychic powers."[31]

In the world of mind-reading, it has rarely been clear what is real or what is possible. Mind-readers exploited this ambiguity, but they did not create it. They saw an opportunity and took it. Their priority was not the truth but rather a much more practical matter. They were in the business of entertainment, and they wished to make a living from it. They pretended, and they obfuscated. At times, they simply lied. It was not the deception of the conjuror but a different kind of deception. They played by different rules, and the audience did not understand the rules. They did not realize that they were being deceived, and they did not know what was possible.

By the early twentieth century, of course, the boundaries of possibility had shifted further. The public were now familiar with things that their ancestors would have thought were impossible. Magical images could be seen in moving pictures, and distant voices were being transmitted through a telephone wire. What else might be possible?

◌

As Marconi was developing his wireless telegraph, skeptics expressed doubts about the security of the information. They worried about its vulnerability to interference. Or perhaps worse, that the messages might be tapped, and the content of the transmissions revealed to others. This problem became worse in 1902, when Marconi succeeded in sending the first long-distance wireless telegraphic messages, 750 miles across land and sea. It was reported that the messages had been tapped, which proved the lack of secrecy in long-distance wireless telegraphy. The man who hacked into the Marconi system was Nevil Maskelyne, the magician and the son of John Nevil Maskelyne.[32]

The Marconi Company denounced Maskelyne's revelations as a deception. In an attempt to prove the conjuror wrong, Marconi's assistant announced that there would be a public demonstration of long-distance wireless telegraphy at the Royal Institution in London. As far as Maskelyne was concerned, this was an "opportunity too good to be missed." He installed an induction coil in Egyptian Hall, which was just around the corner from the Royal Institution, and prepared to interfere with the demonstration. As the audience awaited a message from Marconi, another message arrived in Morse code. When translated, it read as follows: "There was a young fellow of Italy, who diddled the public quite prettily."[33]

It was Maskelyne, of course, proving in rhyme that Marconi's system was not secure. But it was a rather minor setback. Wireless telegraphy was used extensively for naval communication during World War I and, by the 1920s, the first commercial radio programs appeared. They transmitted news and weather reports, played music, and covered sporting events. They were hardly an ideal medium for magic, of course, which relied overwhelmingly on vision. But some performers saw the potential.

In the early days of commercial radio, astrologers such as Rajah Raboid and Dr. Korda RaMayne were popular. They used Indian pseudonyms and fake credentials in a bid to seem mysterious but reliable. Listeners sent in questions to the station and heard the answers over the air. Both Rajah Raboid (whose real name was Ray Boyd) and Dr. Korda RaMayne (whose real name was Bob) also performed live.[34] Like Baldwin and Alexander, they wore turbans in their posters and when they were onstage. They exploited the image of the mystic East, both in their names and in their costumes. But radio offered a much closer connection to the audience. Rather than talk to a large crowd, a performer could talk to individuals in the comfort of their own homes. The radio mind-reader could reach into their personal world and get inside their heads.

○

IN 1929, "the world's strangest experiment in telepathy" was conducted. Joseph Dunninger transmitted his thoughts to the American public from the New York headquarters of the National Broadcasting Company. He told NBC listeners that he was thinking of the name of an American president, a three-digit number, and a drawing of a simple geometrical figure. He was thinking of Lincoln, the number 379, and a simple drawing of a house. But his listeners did not know this. He concentrated for a few seconds and asked his listeners to write into the station to report what they received. In the following week, more than two thousand letters were received. Most of them got at least one of them right. In Pittsburgh, it seems, they received the images more clearly than in Kansas City. However, listeners in St. Louis were more

Joseph Dunninger transmits his thoughts via radio.

accurate than listeners in Detroit. On the basis of this, Dunninger concluded that "the effects of distance seem erratic."[35]

The results had little meaning, but the experience would have been new. Thousands of individuals participated across the country, but they participated as individuals. They did not know who else was listening or who was thinking the same thing as them. They could not see Dunninger, but they could hear him, as if he were speaking directly to them. They could imagine that he was sending his thoughts out directly to them. It was a personal connection that would have been impossible in the theater. Radio may have been no good for magic, but it was the ideal medium for transmitting thoughts through the ether. Dunninger did his best to make the connection. "No one is positive by exactly what means radio waves reach the listener," he explained, "and perhaps in its rays will be found a clue to the understanding of what telepathy is." William Crookes and other early psychical researchers might have agreed.

However, the once-novel technology of wireless telegraphy was no longer as mysterious as it used to be. Everyone was now familiar with the radio, and they knew what it was for. By now, the medium of radio had become a medium of entertainment. Of course, it reported news and sports and other factual events. But the gap between fact and fiction—most of the time, at least—was clear. When Orson Welles, another magician and filmmaker, narrated *War of the Worlds* in 1938, there were reports of widespread panic that the Martians had invaded. However, it now seems that this panic was nothing like the reports suggested. In short, in this supposed blurring of fact and fiction, few were really fooled.[36]

By the 1940s, mind-reading on radio remained mysterious and entertaining, but psychical researchers did not believe it for a moment. Maurice Fogel, an English magician who billed himself as "the world's greatest mind reader," managed to arrange a transatlantic "experiment" with J. B. Rhine, the founder of parapsychology. Rhine dismissed the test as meaningless and Fogel as a showman. However, it garnered enormous publicity for Fogel, who gave the clear impression that he was telepathic. When three million radio listeners heard Fogel on the BBC, he was asked by a journalist if he could really read minds. Fogel replied, "I do not claim any supernatural powers. All I say is that I am able to read people's minds with my own methods." The journalist, unmoved by the air of mystery, discovered some of Fogel's methods and exposed them in a national newspaper.[37]

A few months later, a larger controversy erupted over the Piddingtons. Sydney and Lesley Piddington were a successful telepathy act from Australia, booked to perform on a BBC radio series. The Piddingtons were equally mysterious about their powers: their slogan was "You are the judge." Indeed, they tried to keep it lighthearted. Sydney told the press that his wife "could read an average of seventy per cent of my thoughts when I am deliberately transmitting—and a disturbingly high percentage of my thoughts when I am not trying." The producer, however, claimed that it was telepathy. During the shows, Sydney sent thoughts to Lesley when she was in a series of seemingly secure locations. She appeared to read minds while submerged in a diving bell, as she was flying at cruising altitude, and when under guard at the Tower of London.

The public were captivated, but the SPR was still unimpressed. They explained that "[t]he conditions in which the broadcasts have taken place lend themselves to the employment of codes of various kinds, confederates, and mechanical aids, and anyone with knowledge of the methods of illusionists can recognise . . . the manner in which many of the effects could have been achieved." Nevertheless, despite their disbelief, members of the SPR did not know how it was done. The same journalist who had exposed Fogel's earlier methods did not know how it was done. Even magicians struggled to explain how the Piddingtons did what they did.[38]

But knowing the secrets did not matter. They did not need to know how it was done to assume that it was not real. Magicians and skeptical journalists naturally assumed that it was a trick. Even psychical researchers, who believed that telepathy was real, did not believe that *this* was real. It was, once again, a matter of context. Radio was no longer a mysterious medium that might be tied to telepathy. It was now a familiar mode of entertainment, and these programs were not to be taken seriously. Psychical researchers saw them in much the same way as they saw a magic show. It was a piece of fiction, which was designed for entertainment, not for scientific assessment. And, of course, it did not matter that some people could fake telepathy. What mattered was that other people, in a different context, could do it for real.

This is the true line between belief and disbelief. Nobody believes that everything is real. Everyone believes that something can be faked. The believer is merely someone who thinks that, on at least one occasion, it has been real. As William James said, for white crows to be possible, there only needs to be one white crow. This is why debunking has not succeeded in converting believers to nonbelievers. It does not matter how many mediums are accused, exposed, even caught in the act of cheating. A believer merely needs to believe that there is at least one white crow out there. And nobody, not even the most eager of skeptics, has managed to see every crow.

This is also how mind-readers could expose psychics as frauds while claiming to have psychic powers themselves. The public wanted to see the secrets of fraudulent psychics exposed. But this did not prevent them from believing that some psychics might be real, and they wanted to see them, too. Some were convinced, and some were not, but most remained uncertain. They did not know, and could not have known, what was real and what was possible. It was simply not clear where "psychology" ended and "psychic" phenomena began. After all, even skeptical psychologists such as Münsterberg had publicly stated that some individuals possessed an "abnormal power." In any case, psychologists continued to disagree about the possibility of mind-reading. In the 1930s, when parapsychologists began to talk about "extrasensory perception," most psychologists were open to the possibility.[39] Meanwhile, psychologists themselves claimed to know what people were thinking, and some would speak of "mind-reading" as a perfectly normal form of empathy. The public might be forgiven for thinking that, when it came to reading minds, there was probably "something" to it.

As the mystery of mind-reading survived, protected by a fog of ambiguity, the wonder of radio dissipated in the familiarity of the everyday. Wireless telegraphy, once unimaginable, was now a consumer product. What had seemed impossible not so long ago was now taken for granted. When wonder depends on novelty, it quickly dies, because novelties cannot last long. However, when wonder depends on mystery, it lasts at least until the mystery is solved. And mind-reading continued to be mysterious because when people spoke of reading minds, they referred to reading muscles, or thoughts, or facial expressions, or body language. They spoke of it in academic psychology, popular psychology, and parapsychology. It remained mysterious because when people spoke of mind-reading, they meant different things. They still do, which is why, if someone asks, "Is mind-reading possible?" then the correct answer is, "Yes and no; it depends upon what you mean."

Mind-readers, of course, were deliberately vague, not only to increase the mystery but also to avoid accountability. They implied but were rarely explicit, and when they were explicit, they were seldom clear. Dunninger famously said that he did not read minds; he read thoughts. It was one of those distinctions that explained nothing but gave the illusion of detail. It suggested that he was not making such an extraordinary claim. At other times, however, he simply said that he read minds. Indeed, at various times, he took a number of positions. As a friend of Houdini, he was a fellow debunker of some things but not of others. He wrote several books—or rather he had them ghost-written—which debunked the spirits. He challenged psychics to do anything that he could not duplicate by deception. Meanwhile, he claimed that he could read thoughts, without resorting to deception. "There is no illusion," he explained. It is "not the jugglery of the mountebank."[40]

Dunninger knew all about illusions and jugglery. He had begun as a conjuror, performing sleight of hand, and had even dabbled in escapology. But his real success had come when he transferred from magic into mind-reading. He became a household name by sending his thoughts into households via radio. Having exploited the wireless transmission of sounds, he moved into a new medium: the wireless transmission of sound and vision. By the mid-1950s, most American households had a television, and they could see Dunninger on it. They could now not only hear his voice but also see his piercing eyes staring through the camera lens, reaching into their living rooms and into their minds. He also performed some visual magic, since this was a visual medium.

The new medium, of course, was an opportunity for magicians to reach a larger audience. But they would need to figure out how magic could work on television. The public knew that magic was a deception, but they also knew about special effects. For magic to work on television, there would need to be new rules. Meanwhile, ongoing technological advances were making it harder to astonish. Dunninger, the master mind-reader, knew this. "With the wonders of the radio, the miraculous achievement of sending pictures by wireless, and the evergrowing achievements of the seemingly impossible," he wrote, "it is difficult for the conjuror to keep up with the times." "[T]he tricks of the magician of the future," he pointed out, "must be still more sensational."[41]

ᘒᘒᘒᘒᘒ

CHAPTER 11

BEFORE YOUR EYES

GUY JARRETT WAS an acerbically honest illusion inventor and Broadway property man who worked with many of the world's finest magicians throughout the 1920s. He'd seen great magicians. He'd seen terrible magicians. By the end of vaudeville, he wrote about magic by giving full voice to the frustrations he'd seen throughout his career and magicians' lack of insight. Jarrett wrote:

> Have our magicians had any training or direction in the art of magic? Have they stage presence, or can they act? No, they have not. They just got hold of a bunch of tricks, and walked out on the stage. Magic, which is one of the arts, and one of the best entertainments for the great intelligent public, has suffered terribly. In fact, it has been murdered.[1]

As Jarrett explained, the end of vaudeville had produced a group of magicians who were barely qualified to entertain audiences. A man named Dr. Harlan Tarbell helped magicians weather the storm. In 1926, he introduced the Tarbell System, a comprehensive correspondence course in magic, from his Chicago offices.[2] The timing was right. Vaudeville was winding down, but there was still an appetite for magic shows at parties and clubs, if the magicians were knowledgeable or talented enough to deftly adapt their shows to their audiences. Tarbell endeavored to teach magic by covering all the categories. Unlike Hoffmann's *Modern Magic*, which had seemed obsessed with the Victorian knickknacks that adorned a conjuring show, the Tarbell System focused on simple, efficient tricks with ordinary objects like cards, coins, ropes, balls, and envelopes. As the course swelled, month after month, it gave every impression that not only were the tricks limitless but the opportunities for magicians were similarly infinite.

Dr. Harlan Tarbell was the perfect instructor, a sort of wellspring of positive thinking. Originally, the course was to be produced by Houdini and sold under his famous name, but Houdini's busy schedule prevented his involvement. Tarbell was a talented part-time magician, part-time artist, and part-time naprapath (hence the designation of "Doctor"). By most accounts, he was a slightly dull, slightly corny Midwesterner.[3] But history has proven that he was the right man for the job; he had infinite patience in explaining the tricks, writing out patter with safe, middle-of-the-road appeal, and illustrating the entire course with neat line drawings. His one hundred lessons were later gathered together into a series of books, *The Tarbell Course in Magic*.

As part of the expanded course, Tarbell's Lesson 34 consisted of "Routining a Magic Show," by analyzing the structure of performances.

> Showmen know the importance of opening and closing a program—they must be right, if nothing else. Audiences will forgive a lot if you make a good appearance in the beginning and wind up with a whirlwind finish.[4]

Magic's great teacher was Harlan Tarbell,
the author of The Tarbell Course in Magic.

Not surprisingly, Tarbell's examples demonstrated the value of small magic. Alexander Herrmann's famously graceful opening consisted of "removing his white gloves and causing them to vanish in the air." Thurston's elaborate show similarly depended on the magician establishing his skill through his card tricks. After a fast, colorful opening number filled with dancing girls and large-scale tricks, Thurston stepped forward, "talked intimately to his audience and occupied the stage alone with his card manipulations, finally blending into a full stage with his famous rising cards."

Later in the same volume, Tarbell offered lessons on "Intimate Magic," explaining to his students that "the tricks that one may do impromptu, among friends, at the bar, club, et cetera, occupy an important place in the magician's repertoire."[5] A good magician was always prepared to do something, he suggested, pointing out how magicians like Herrmann and Houdini prided themselves on their ability to perform wonderful tricks at the drop of a hat.

⟲

PREVIOUS GENERATIONS HAD never bothered to designate certain tricks as "intimate," certain tricks as "stand-up," or "stage," or even "illusions." In the generation of Reginald Scot, magicians performed whatever they needed to perform to attract attention and make money. The cups and balls were good, because the metal cups made a lot of noise, attracting attention, and could be tossed into a bag and carried to the next street corner. Robert-Houdin felt no need to suggest that small sleight-of-hand tricks were necessary, placed in a particular spot in a program, to establish the magician's bona fides. Wasn't every good trick an "intimate" trick?

The first twenty-seven pages of a 1936 catalog from Thayer Magic Manufacturing Company, at that time one of America's most popular magic suppliers, were devoted to "Pocket, Parlor and Close Up Magic." Magicians could buy tricks like Wizzo, a cut and restored string, for fifty cents. Or the Sponge Ball trick, three soft rubber balls that appear in the spectator's hand, for twenty-five cents. Or the Demon Snapper trick, a little wooden plunger that snapped back in its holder, but when someone else tried to make it snap, it wouldn't work. That was twenty-five cents in "ordinary grade" and fifty cents for stained wood, "in beautiful superior grade."[6]

The tricks were tiny and insignificant, the things that you'd show friends in an attempt to get them to buy you a beer. But they were not intended as tricks for kids; they were appealing mysteries that you held at your fingertips. In the 1930s, they were exerting a powerful gravitational force upon magicians. As magic found fewer and fewer opportunities on a stage or in a nightclub, avid magicians stuffed their pockets with these little tricks—coins, cards, or sponge balls—and began innovating.

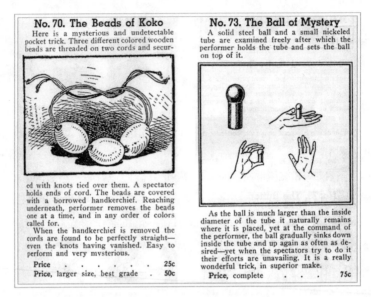

No. 70. The Beads of Koko

Here is a mysterious and undetectable pocket trick. Three different colored wooden beads are threaded on two cords and secur-

ed with knots tied over them. A spectator holds ends of cord. The beads are covered with a borrowed handkerchief. Reaching underneath, performer removes the beads one at a time, and in any order of colors called for.

When the handkerchief is removed the cords are found to be perfectly straight— even the knots having vanished. Easy to perform and very mysterious.

Price 25c

Price, larger size, best grade . 50c

No. 73. The Ball of Mystery

A solid steel ball and a small nickeled tube are examined freely after which the performer holds the tube and sets the ball on top of it.

As the ball is much larger than the inside diameter of the tube it naturally remains where it is placed, yet at the command of the performer, the ball gradually sinks down inside the tube and up again as often as desired—yet when the spectators try to do it their efforts are unavailing. It is a really wonderful trick, in superior make.

Price, complete . . . 75c

Thayer Magic in Los Angeles offered an array of close-up tricks.

It wasn't very different from the way that Robert-Houdin had surreptitiously learned the craft a century earlier, his hands jammed inside the pockets of his coat, manipulating little cork balls or palming coins.

CLOSE-UP MAGIC WAS slowly being refined and redefined into something important. The movement had really started around the end of the nineteenth century, when a handful of magicians began to devote efforts to intimate tricks—treating them not as amateur mysteries or barroom gags, but as serious art. In Great Britain, it was G. W. Hunter, a music hall comedian who became a master of tricks that he could carry in his pockets.[7] In the United States, it was Dr. James William Elliott, who had trained as a medical doctor from Boston but whose avocation was card magic. Elliott was a magnificent failure at business, "the most successful failure," one of his admirers quipped. "If he went into the undertaking business, nobody would have died."[8] But sitting at a card table, Elliott was something of a genius. He was also a famous perfectionist. He would rent a room in a quiet part of town that he kept empty except for a table and a single chair. This was for his daily magic rehearsal, and he committed endless hours to his work at sleight of hand.[9]

James William Elliott, the distinguished
card manipulator, set the trend for
a generation of magicians.

Elliott swapped card moves with Houdini, dazzled the New York magicians, and may have taught Thurston the fundamental maneuvers that became his groundbreaking music hall act. Elliott's earnest work gained many admirers, including a young man from Canada named David Verner, who became famous among magicians as Dai Vernon. When he arrived in New York, young Vernon couldn't resist showing off his skills, so he found Elliott just where he was told he'd find him, in the back room of Clyde Powers's magic shop, on Forty-Second Street in New York, working on card sleights. "Be natural," Elliott offered, insisting that this simple advice was his most valuable suggestion.[10] Vernon came to personify the advice, acquiring the reputation for pure, elegant card magic. He handled the cards with such a light, innocent touch that the magic seemed to happen by itself.

Vernon was a tall, lean, brash young man from Ottawa, who had been emboldened by a careful reading of a magic book and his own experiments with the tricks that he learned from that book. *The Expert at the Card Table*, by S. W. Erdnase, was published in 1902 and advertised by a Chicago magic shop.[11] In later years, it was sold by gambling supply dealers. Vernon was surprised that New York magicians had paid so little attention to Erdnase, as the Canadian had considered that book to be his Bible. He had studied the contents religiously.

Erdnase was, the book's introduction suggested, a former gambler who wrote the book because he now "needs the money":

> In offering this book to the public the writer uses no sophistry as an excuse for its existence. The hypocritical cant of reformed (?) gamblers, or whining, mealy-mouthed pretensions of piety, are not foisted as a justification for imparting the knowledge it contains.[12]

It was a small book, packed with line drawings of hands holding cards and densely written to explain essential sleight-of-hand maneuvers. Unlike other books, which rehashed the same moves over and over again, Erdnase included some of his own particular moves. Gamblers tended to dismiss the book as mere magic tricks—virtually worthless to them. Magicians, on the other hand, regarded the author as obsessed with gambling maneuvers—the actual tricks were just variations on classics and pushed to the back of the book, seemingly less important than Erdnase's moves. As Erdnase introduced the magic section: "Acquiring the art is in itself a most fascinating pastime, and the student will need no further incentive the moment the least progress is made."[13]

Somewhere between the publication of Erdnase's book, its advertisement in magic journals, and the book's final discount, ignominious wholesale, and cheap republications, the author quietly slipped out a side door. Magicians read the book, attempted some of the moves, and shrugged over its contents, but they never bothered to find Mr. Erdnase. Years later, it became apparent that the author's name was a ruse: if the letters were reversed, it formed E. S. Andrews.

Erdnase, or Andrews, has remained one of the great literary mysteries in the field of magic. Who was he? The book was so carefully crafted, so obsessively individualistic and well-written, that it seemed impossible that the author hadn't left a trail or turned up at a magician's meeting to display his skills and take credit for his work. Magicians like Vernon naturally assumed that the references to gambling were the key to the mystery. Erdnase seemed to be a particularly attractive model because he was not part of their world. The first chapter was deliberately filled with the swaggering slang of the confidence man:

> We betray no confidences in publishing this book, having only ourselves to thank for what we know. Our tuition was received in the cold school of experience. We started in with the trusting nature of a fledgling, and a calm assurance born of overweening faith in our own potency. We bucked the tiger voluntarily, and censure no one for the inevitable result. A self-satisfied unlicked cub with a fairly fat bank roll was too good a thing to be passed up.[14]

It's now apparent, in careful analysis of Erdnase's skills, that he was much more of a magician than a gambler. His style seems to have been a clever literary device to mythologize his story. Whether Erdnase came from the world of gamblers or not, he inspired Vernon's paradigm—analyzing card sleights so that they could withstand the cold, hard scrutiny of the poker table.

Why did no one ever identify Erdnase? And what successful magician has refused to take a single bow? Researchers have found several interesting candidates, including a murderous gambler named Milton Franklin Andrews, a Chicago-based E. S. Andrews who was close to the original printer, and a curious Montana writer and mining engineer named W. E. Sanders (here, the name would have been a true anagram).[15]

It's unfortunate that Vernon went to New York rather than traveling to Chicago to track down the mysterious author, while the trail was still warm. For better or worse, Erdnase's slender green-bound book has now acquired the status of true gospel: the mysterious origin, the persecuted author, the message of the true believer. And, of course, there has been a

The Canadian magician Dai Vernon
influenced magicians with his natural,
subtle use of sleight of hand.

century of misinterpretation, selective reading, and confusion—which has ensured its status as a holy book.

Vernon was the first disciple, and in his hands, close-up magic found new respect among magicians: "be natural." Maneuvers were no longer just described; they were analyzed, studied, refined, and improved. The Pass, a centuries-old move used to secretly shift a card from the center of the deck to the top, had been applied over and over again by Victorian magicians, like a blunt-force tool. But following the philosophy of Erdnase and Vernon, a skillful magician might learn many different versions of the Pass, select them and fine-tune them to suit a particular situation. Other close-up magicians and friends of Vernon, like Cardini, Dr. Jacob Daley, Francis Carlyle, and Ross Bertram, worked their magic at a table—it was no longer about slapping someone on the back and cadging a beer. As far as magicians were concerned, close-up had become the new frontier of magic.

WE FIND OBVIOUS close-up magic in Scot, Decremps, and Robert-Houdin. A fine Victorian textbook on magic, Edwin Sachs's *Sleight of Hand*, is filled with tricks we'd now call close-up magic. Several vaudeville magicians performed deliberately tiny tricks onstage, making a point of their simplicity.

For example, there was Emil Jarrow, who began his career as a vaudeville strong man but became a comedian and magician. In his act, a nickel, held in a spectator's hand, changed places with a penny, which Jarrow held in his own hand. He also made a handful of loose tobacco disappear, as he cupped the tobacco between his palms. Jarrow's tricks were much too small to be seen in big vaudeville theaters, but he depended upon the reactions of the spectators, who had been brought onstage to watch closely.[16]

Similarly, a Stockholm-born magician, Nate Leipzig, made a specialty of small tricks in vaudeville. He invited a handful of spectators to the stage and performed card tricks. For example, Leipzig showed how the aces, cut into the middle of the cards, quickly jumped to the face of the pack. Maybe Leipzig's most famous feat was his manipulation of a single silver dollar, rolling it over his knuckles, from finger to finger, and then back to the top of his fist again—just as if the coin were tumbling down a flight of stairs. Audiences could barely see the flicker of the silver coin as it tumbled, so Leipzig's act included a motion picture screen and a short segment of film, showing the magician's flourish in close-up and then again in slow motion.[17]

The term "close-up" was a sign of the newfound respect. Unlike the pocket tricks of the previous generation or small tricks turned into big tricks on a stage, close-up signified a performance style. Often the audience sat at a table, with the magician at the opposite side. The tabletop was the stage. The magician's hands, the playing cards, coins, and sponge balls were the cast.

We can understand the change of focus by comparing presentations of the cups and balls. From its medieval days, with a magician at the fairground, the trick was performed by standing behind a tall table, with oversize tin cups. The magician did his best to attract an audience from far away and gesticulated to make the trick look as big as possible. But when Dai Vernon performed the cups and balls, the spectators sat at his elbows, and Vernon hunched over the table, unassumingly narrating the trick as if it were a conversation. The cups were simple and squat; the balls were small and delicate. The props were handled in delicate, precise motions at the fingertips—carefully confining the action to the tabletop.[18]

The popularity of close-up magic turned the art upside-down. Avid amateurs became as influential as professionals. New techniques could be tried and tested quickly, in informal settings; experience gave way to experimentation. The nature of close-up magic is that it never had a proper "golden age," nor a vaudeville or music hall experience. It didn't always need to be polished in front of audiences and turned into a commodity. It wasn't franchised or standardized.

Instead, close-up magic was developed by a handful of performers working in small cliques, each group with their own distinct characteristics. In Chicago, close-up magic focused on bars and restaurants, performed by Matt Schulien or Frank Everhart. In New York, it grew out of performances at clubs or on cruise ships, as personified by Vernon or S. Leo Horowitz. In Los Angeles, it formed its own club, the Magic Castle, enshrining close-up within its own tiny theater.[19] Magicians shared their work with colleagues in books and lectures, or later, videotapes and DVDs.

This fashion corresponded perfectly with the rise of video—the newest medium that had to wrestle with entertainment, in all its forms. It should have been a simple transition to television. "On television, a mouse is as big as an elephant," British magician and television consultant Ali Bongo used to explain.[20] But for some reason, magic had a particularly challenging time finding its way in front of the television camera.

○

THE FACT THAT television was watched in your home meant that the earliest television programs were built around trust. The least threatening, friendliest hosts were given the jobs. The trustworthy newsmen rose to the top. The least adorned, most direct entertainments seemed to be the most appealing: a camera was turned on, pointed at the end of a studio, and a small review show or variety program was marched from one side of the screen to the other.

Unlike the Edwardian's fascination for early cinema—the Méliès and Devant special effects that made a crowd of people gasp—television was held in a tight rein by networks and government agencies. It was not supposed to be magical or unexpected. When Milbourne Christopher, a New York magician, went in front of television cameras in the late 1950s and early 1960s, it was with a television-size production of the "Great Man" show—the tuxedo, the dancing girls, the wooden boxes.[21]

When a young Dallas magician named Mark Wilson proposed a family magic series for television in the late 1950s, the television executives gave him a list of reasons why it couldn't possibly work. Wilson later recalled:

> First, they thought viewers would think the magic was done with trick photography. Second, they felt magic would only be enjoyed by children. And third, they said, "What are you going to do for your second show?" None of them realized the variety that [is] magic.[22]

Mark Wilson premiered a Saturday morning series, *The Magic Land of Alakazam.* His television shows were made believable by having a live studio audience watching, along with the viewers, and by not cutting from one camera to another during a trick—in other words, demonstrating that the magic was not accomplished through editing. In the first few decades of television, a network's Standards and Practices (S&P) executives were always on hand to supervise the honesty of the shows—if it was represented as magic, performed for a live audience, the S&P representative made sure there was no extra trickery. Unlike magicians' early work in film, magicians could only become successful on television by denying special effects and treating the medium as perfectly ordinary and invisible.

In the 1960s, a Chicago magician named Don Alan appeared regularly on network television shows, including *The Tonight Show* and *The Ed Sullivan Show.* It wasn't the sort of magic that television viewers had ever seen before. Ed Sullivan introduced the magician and then sauntered over to the stage and took a seat at a card table, opposite Don Alan. Alan used a metal cup, a deck of cards, and a handkerchief to perform amazing close-up magic—one astonishment after another—accompanied by his funny, self-effacing rat-a-tat banter.[23]

And then, in 1975, a different kind of magic special appeared, with a different kind of magician. A Canadian performer, Doug Henning, had just made a hit in Broadway's *The Magic Show* the year before. His first television special was live, and he performed an hour of spectacularly varied magic.

Doug Henning created a new approach
to magic in the 1970s, combining
styles of magic for television.

The show began with the camera in extreme close-up on his empty hand—a hand actually larger than life. Henning closed his fingers and then opened them, showing a nickel. In a way that never could have been possible in vaudeville, the camera quickly moved back, and Henning presented a series of impressively large tricks; he even magically produced a full-size tiger from a small, square wooden box. Then, with the cameras moving close again, Henning sat at a table and demonstrated several close-up routines. As a student of magic, he had studied with Dai Vernon and Slydini, another expert at close-up magic. At the end of the show, Henning, in a bathing suit, was lifted by his ankles and lowered into a tank of water, performing a white-knuckle re-creation of Houdini's Water Torture Cell Escape.[24]

Doug Henning demonstrated how, in the television age, an hour of magic could now combine a wide range of stage marvels: escapes, sleight-of-hand, and even tiny close-up magic. As Mark Wilson had expressed it, this was "the variety that [is] magic." During that hour, Henning even managed to redefine the "Great Man" role. A slight, unassuming young man, still in his twenties, Henning had long brown hair and a fuzzy mustache; he dressed in a T-shirt, jeans, and tennis shoes. His iconoclastic, breezy style suggested that he experienced the same sort of wonder that he elicited from his audiences.

These television innovations worked both ways. When Doug Henning took his magic show on the road, from theater to theater, he performed a special section of close-up magic. He sat cross-legged on the stage as a video camera was pointed at his hands. Two large video projectors were rolled on from the wings. With his hands shown on the screens, Henning presented sleight of hand. It was a nice twist on Nate Leipzig's vaudeville act from almost fifty years earlier.

For his second annual television special, Doug Henning made an elephant disappear. For the third, he walked through a brick wall, another Houdini specialty. The pace of bigger and bigger tricks seemed to set a trend for magic specials. David Copperfield, an artistic young magician with his own magic specials, was known for his dramatic illusions woven around sweet or sentimental stories. On his annual television shows, he made an automobile disappear one year, and a small jet plane disappear the following year. Then, in 1984, during a videotaped performance, Copperfield presented the most famous illusion of his career.

The magician had erected a stage at the base of the Statue of Liberty in New York, and he introduced a small audience that had been to the island to watch the trick. A large curtain was raised, temporarily concealing the Statue from the camera's point of view. The curtain lowered, and the Statue was gone. Other cameras cut to different viewpoints, including an overhead, helicopter view of the empty ground. Copperfield reversed the procedure. The curtain went up and came down again. The famous Statue was once again back in place, on top of its pedestal overlooking the East River.[25]

Was it a trick, or was it merely a special effect? Magicians insisted that, strictly speaking, the techniques used were not camera tricks. They were the same basic secrets that would work in stage shows—but now they had been applied to the frame of a camera and to the needs of television. Just as a "mouse is as big as an elephant," the lens of the camera could frame both Copperfield and the enormous Statue, as if they were about the same size. In this way, the famous Lady Liberty could take the place of one of de Kolta's famous disappearing ladies.

The race for bigger and bigger tricks continued, to the delight of network executives. Copperfield returned in following years, levitating and flying over the Grand Canyon, walking through the Great Wall of China, making a train car disappear, and escaping from an imploding building. These epic feats—which felt more like movie special effects than magic tricks—began a perilous debate among magicians. What was honest, and what was dishonest, in the world of deception? Was the use of certain secrets unfair, and how could anyone really evaluate their unfairness, so long as they remained secret?

Most important, should magic be in competition with movie special effects? After all, Méliès had cleverly innovated a new style of trick

David Copperfield specialized in artistic
illusions and larger-than-life television effects.

photography, but his films were old-fashioned once the cinema came of age. The Maskelynes pioneered short plays built around magic tricks, but they stumbled with *The Coming Race*, when they tried to compete with West End plays. Magicians couldn't risk going one step too far and then earning the mistrust or dismissive remarks from their audience: "Oh, those must just be camera tricks." As one experienced television magician said, shaking his head over David Copperfield's latest production, "When the camera cut to that overhead view, the patch of ground where the Statue of Liberty had just been, Godzilla's foot should have come down on top of it all."[26]

WHAT WERE THE RULES? Some people don't like magic, because they don't enjoy being fooled. But this is usually the result of having seen a magician who just made them feel foolish. If the magician does his job, the audience knows that they are being deceived. They don't mind being deceived. They understand that this is the game. They simply don't want to feel cheated.

If the show is live, before your very eyes, the game is relatively simple. But if the camera becomes part of the deception, the game can feel rigged.

Robert-Houdin realized that the audience and the magician can be on the same side—a game that's being played together, not in opposition. He explained it this way in his *Memoirs:*

> The ordinary man only sees in conjuring tricks a challenge offered to his intelligence, and hence representations of sleight of hand become to him a combat in which he determines on conquering. . . . Well, whatever he may say to distract my attention, my eyes shall not leave his hand, and the trick cannot be done without my finding out how he manages it. . . . The clever man, on the contrary, when he visits a conjuring performance, only goes to enjoy the illusions, and, far from offering the performer the slightest obstacle, he is the first to aid him. . . . He knows, too, that these amusing deceptions cannot injure his reputation as an intelligent man, and hence he . . . allows himself to be easily put off the right scent.[27]

When David Copperfield took his show to theaters, he had a new way of using television. At one spot in the show, as he was about to take a break, he lowered a screen and used a video projector to show the audience an exciting episode from his career, the night he made the Statue of Liberty disappear. His audiences, much like Robert-Houdin's clever spectators, were willing to watch a videotaped trick. They oohed and aahed, and then, at the conclusion, they applauded as Copperfield walked back onstage. The audience seemed to implicitly understand that he had done a trick for a television show, using his deceptions specifically for that situation. No reviewer expressed disappointment that David Copperfield, the master of epic magic, failed to make the entire theater disappear for that performance. The audience understood the rules of the game.

⟲

THE SUCCESS OF TELEVISION magic invited renewed interest. In the 1980s, Doug Henning and David Copperfield regularly appeared in Las Vegas. Harry Blackstone Jr., the son of Harry Blackstone and a grand, tuxedo-clad performer of the old school, brought his magic review show to Broadway. In Las Vegas, Siegfried and Roy, two German magicians, became famous for a dazzling combination of magic and wild animals; a breathtaking array of lions and tigers were magically produced and then paraded across the stage.

Inevitably, there weren't enough "great men" to go around. Magic shows, onstage and on television, offered review shows, starring multiple magicians—one short act after another. It was the old vaudeville formula, a clever way for producers to hedge their bets. Overall, a multiplicity of magicians has never made the product better. Based on the fantasy that there is one person, special or skilled enough, to bring you these wonders, a second magician—or a third, or a tenth—simply dilute the product and muddle the fantasy. The tricks, and the acts, start looking similar or indistinguishable, a terrible fate for something that's supposed to produce wonder.

By the turn of the new millennium, Ricky Jay, another student of Dai Vernon, had brought close-up magic off-Broadway in a David Mamet–directed show.[28] It was stark and engaging and promised skill instead of production value, with a mix of card magic and crooked gambling. David Blaine created his own "magical/messianic" point of view in numerous television specials, by starkly performing close-up magic in unexpected settings. Then, refreshingly, Blaine allowed the camera to watch the audience's astonishment, and let their reactions speak for themselves.

It was Blaine's inspiration that changed the designation of close-up magic to street magic, how it's now described in magic catalogs or online shops. It's still close-up, of course, but now with the suggestion of a hip, urban audience. Curiously, "street magic" is a term that Reginald Scot might have easily understood. Blaine's physical endurance stunts were the sorts of things Robert-Houdin encountered in Algeria, and his dangerous, challenging tricks recall the heyday of Houdini in vaudeville. "Fashions often revert, but to be popular they modify," the American author Charles Fort explained. "Come unto me, and maybe I'll make you stylish. It is quite possible to touch up beliefs that are now considered dowdy, and restore them to fashionableness."[29]

○

OF COURSE, it was only in the good old days of television that executives from Standards and Practices promised the quality of a magic special. In the new era of cable television and YouTube videos, magicians seem to have fewer standards and spend far less time practicing. Judicious video editing can solve a world of problems, and shadows, mirrors, and wires can be economically painted out of the frame to make the magic look flawless. Several years ago, a young Chinese magician circulated a video of himself on the internet, producing an enormous loaf of bread from his empty hand, as he sat in a restaurant. It was a simple result of trick photography. But when he was accused of this sort of fakery, he bolstered his claim as a real magician by producing a behind-the-scenes video documentary in which he showed the meticulous planning, the special mirrors, and the elaborate restaurant set that were supposedly the secrets behind his trick.[30] All those "secrets" were another deception. It was still a camera trick, of course, and had been accomplished by a digital artist at a computer. Video deceptions could now be used, in ways that could only have been appreciated by Lewis Carroll, to chase other video deceptions down the rabbit hole.

Magic and video have been combined in rather dubious ways. Maybe the most dishonest trends in video magic are the "one-second" or "two-second" tricks that fill sites like YouTube or advertise the wares of magic dealers. Fast, flashy tricks are perfect for a camera or for an amateur to practice in front of a mirror. For an actual audience, there's very little need for a one-second trick, any more than there's a need for a one-second song. Most people would define that as screaming.

In a purely old-fashioned way, magic is always best when audiences watch it live, and the magic occurs before one's eyes. Film, video, and the internet all provide barriers to the experience that, at best, may generate some new magic fans who will go out in search of a real magic show. The short videos on the internet provide very convenient ways to watch tricks. It turns out that they are awful ways to experience magic. That's not a surprise. We might say the same thing about opera, or ballet, or almost any performance art. Attracting and charming an audience can be two distinctly different experiences.

◯

IN *OUR MAGIC* from 1911, Nevil Maskelyne addressed styles.

> The modern tendency is towards specialization. There are performers who pride themselves upon being exponents of pure sleight-of-hand, and nothing else. What, after all, do such claims amount to? Nothing whatever! There is no such thing as a pure sleight-of-hand performer. Or, if there may be, may the gods have pity on him.[31]

More than a century after Nevil Maskelyne, the latest fashion offered by magicians is, again, pure sleight of hand. Just a deck of cards or a few coins. This simplicity can imply a certain self-important refinement, as if a pencil line guarantees quality but oil paints are just too complicated to be considered art.

An audience might be suspicious about the affection of skill, in the middle of a very deceptive art. Robert-Houdin wrote about the danger of showing off. When he displayed his flourishes to Torrini—the flashy shuffles and riffles that demonstrated the skill of his hands—the old magician doubted the value of these boastful displays:

> After such a brilliant exhibition, the spectator will only see in your tricks the result of dexterity, while, by affecting a good deal of simplicity, you [will] produce a [seemingly] supernatural effect, and pass for a real sorcery.[32]

Instead, many magicians use sleight of hand and then desperately want audiences to realize that it's sleight of hand. If an audience tells themselves, with some satisfaction, that the magician they're watching is a master of pure sleight of hand, that magician has probably done something wrong. As Erdnase advised, "Conceal, as far as possible, the possession of digital ability, and leave the company still guessing how it is done."[33] Some magicians flaunt skill for its own sake, and there is sometimes a level of deception even in this sort of demonstration. Magicians have long valued flourishes or secret maneuvers that look like much harder maneuvers— promising certain skills, like false dealing or false shuffling, and then using a bit of simpler trickery to simulate these moves. In other words, they cheat at cheating. The artist Banksy explained the phenomenon: "Become good at cheating, and you never need to become good at anything else."

Pure skill can be a genuine aspiration offstage, but it can also be a pose onstage. Audiences may delude themselves about the skills they are observing; they can also delude themselves that stage illusions, or magic with apparatus, look more effortless so they must be less refined or require less skill. "Stage illusions which can be presented without the aid of some considerable amount of manipulative ability represent a class of inventions yet to be produced," Nevil Maskelyne wrote.[34] Many fine artists draw with pencils and also paint with oils.

☉

NOT SURPRISINGLY, some of the most interesting work in magic is not the result of television specials, or Las Vegas spectacles, or YouTube channels. Around the world, hundreds of magicians—magicians you haven't heard of—understand their history and adapt the traditions or deliberately ignore them. They might not be stars. They're experimenters. It's just these sorts of experiments that will inevitably pull and push magic in front of new audiences. They are examples. They represent branches of an art that continues to bud and flower.

For instance, British-born Will Houstoun earned his doctorate in literature, film, and theater from Essex University with a thesis on the works of Professor Hoffmann, the great magic writer and teacher from the late Victorian age.[35] Houstoun's perspective on Hoffmann has given him a unique way of looking at magic. "Hoffmann was unique in trying to write about magic in a significant way, not 'how it's done' but 'how to do it.' His books took beginners and provided the information to make them competent magicians. He also felt that an understanding of magic, of trickery and theatricality, was useful to many professions."

The success of Hoffmann's books firmly rooted many magic traditions in the Victorian age. "Hoffmann inspired additional books, magicians, and magic clubs, which continued for many years, perpetuating both good and bad traditions. For example, one of Hoffmann's legacies is the prevalence of the male magician, because his work defined magic as a boy's interest instead of a girl's."

For his own performances, Houstoun has focused on performing close-up and in small theaters, combining his tricks with the history of the art—part lecture, part show. "It allows me to talk about magic in a broader way, to tell audiences that there are a lot of different things that magic has meant to people, and a lot of different things that magicians have been." It naturally suggests a different performance style, as well. Houstoun is tall and quiet, with a reassuring whisper of a voice and a slightly academic manner. "Rather than that fantasy, 'When I snap my fingers, this happens . . .' I can make it all reasonably authentic by talking about a magician who accomplished miracles, and recreate those tricks for the audience." This apparent "outside looking in" quality gives a uniquely theatrical, and apparently nontheatrical feeling, to the performance.

Is it really a magic show? It's less a lecture than you'd think, and Houstoun's tricks always come across as surprisingly bright, entertaining, and modern. "Every trick I perform is something that would be perfectly good without the story. Something I'd be happy to do in a pub. Both the tricks and the stories are strong in their own right, but both are stronger together, more significant together."

So, the notoriously old, simple Ball and Vase trick, described by Hoffmann, has long since been reduced to children's magic sets. But during Houstoun's performance, it becomes an astonishing sleight-of-hand mystery. He also performs the cups and balls, with a presentation inspired by Matthew Buchinger, the famous eighteenth-century dwarf performer. Nate Leipzig, the vaudeville sleight-of-hand artist, suggested a surprising card trick: a deck is randomly shuffled by the audience but manages to arrange itself perfectly, in a predetermined order. Performed by Will

Houstoun, the feat successfully demonstrates Erdnase's ideal, concealing every element of skill and producing an effortless, miraculous effect.

"Magic is important," he explains. "But magicians have, over the years, been afraid to say it that way. Too often, they feel embarrassed by the tricks, so they will talk about different subjects, important subjects, trying to tie magic to those subjects."

Houstoun has found a different emphasis. "I find it more interesting to talk about magic as its own art, with its own history. There's nothing wrong with tricks," he explains. "The tricks are fine, and when the context in which they were developed and performed is unearthed, audiences understand that magic is a much bigger, richer, subject than they may have realized."

◯

ALBA WAS BORN in Argentina and had never actually seen a magic show, but she asked her mother for magic lessons when, at fifteen, she had heard about a school of magic in Buenos Aires. "It was run by the widow of David Bamberg, who performed as a Chinese magician, Fu Manchu."[36] The Bambergs were a European family of magicians that spanned several generations; David Bamberg, performing as Fu Manchu, became a star in South America during the mid-1900s. Not unexpectedly, Alba was the only girl in the class, and she was encouraged by her teacher to create a magic act with "ladylike" things, like flowers or silk scarves. "So, of course, that made me never want to do those sorts of tricks," she recalls with a laugh.

She realized, very early, that the tradition of magic is a boys' club: "I'm sorry to say it, but that's just the way magic has been for many years. That shouldn't be. In literature, in drama, women are often the magical creatures. Magic belongs to women. But tricks belong to men. Too often, that's how audiences end up seeing it, as tricks."

Alba developed her own style with close-up and sleight-of-hand magic; she's focused on her interaction with the audience and emphasizes her warm, irreverent sense of humor. "Magicians have the reputation of lying to people, or of treating them dismissively. Of course, there always is a deception involved, a lie. That might be something simple, like hiding the coin in your hand. But that's just the technique. Everything else can be truthful—in fact, for me everything else has to be truthful. That's what invites a shared experience," she says.

That honesty, Alba feels, is often amplified during a close-up show, where the audience is just inches away. "The audience will talk to me, they'll tell me what they're thinking. That's important. That's part of the formula. Sometimes people tell me, before I start, that they don't like magic. That's one of the best things I can hear," she says, "because I know what that means. I know how to make a connection with that person. I've learned that magic doesn't happen in my hands, it happens in their brains. So I can't simply show them something. I need to earn their trust, so they are willing to engage in the performance."

Now her shows use very simple props, like cards, or ropes, or even a length of thread, which is torn to bits and then restored into a single piece. The result is a perfectly theatrical experience that vibrates and hums with a disarmingly "nontheatrical" nonchalance. As she engages her audience on the contradictions of everyday life, the magic is introduced with a wry smile, and the impossibilities begin. Maybe that's what always makes her performance feel so special, like a little bit of real magic has just crept into our lives.

"The process of sharing a mystery with people, of being vulnerable, of being surprised together, is a very powerful experience," Alba says. "People always underestimate that feeling. It's a feeling that magic does better than anything else. I believe that's the moment that magic hints at some-thing deeper, when it becomes an art."

⟲

ALEX RAMON HAS turned the "Great Man" model on its ear. That was the formula in which the magician would take the role of masterful entertainer to bring you the latest wonders. The magician would dazzle with sleight of hand, make you laugh, make you gasp, and deftly steer your attention through a fast-moving array of illusions.

Reconfigured and reimagined, that artifact from theatrical history—the magic show—can be stripped completely of its Victorian fashions, nightclub gaucheries, or supernatural affectations. Ramon's show suc-ceeded with a contemporary approach for a masterful magician—a conju-ror who is completely in control but disarmingly youthful and nonchalant. Once the formula is dusted clean, once it loses its pretensions, it shines and surprises. It's an inspiration to see it in action with a modern audience and to see how magic becomes neatly, effortlessly contemporary.

Ramon's process wasn't quite effortless, but he had a head start. When he was still in his twenties, his success as a touring magician earned him the job as the only ringmaster-magician in the history of the Ringling Broth-ers, Barnum & Bailey Circus, "The Greatest Show on Earth." For two years, he was seen by more than four million people in more than eight hundred shows, in arenas seating audiences of more than ten thousand.

"That experience was amazing for me, because in the circus, the props are huge, the cast is enormous, and my magic had to be performed on a gigantic scale,"[37] he said. For example, his opening illusion was making an elephant disappear, in the middle of the arena floor: "It teaches you a lot about magic, about an audience's perceptions. Robert-Houdin wrote about 'the eye,' and how a good magician captures and controls the eye of the audience. It's really the same principle, for ten thousand people watching an elephant, or for ten, watching a coin. You get a sense of what draws their attention, their focus."

After the circus, he assembled a show by scaling down the props but emphasizing the magic; he's specialized in new, original ideas that don't feel like standard tricks. "You learn that magic depends on challenging people and entertaining them at the same time," he explained. "It's not like special effects in a movie. It's not just about spectacle, or doing the most impossible thing. A magician uses an intellectual process—an audience thinking about something, wondering about something—to get to an emotional response. That's a really unique process, and it only works if you have a feeling for your audience.

"As a performing art, magic hasn't become old-fashioned. The idea of making someone float in the air is as relevant today as it was hundreds of years ago, if the performance is relevant for the audience." Ramon presented the levitation as a visualization of music—a person who seems suspended upon sound waves, floating between oversize concert speakers, and then apparently wafted from one side to the other, as the speakers are twisted and tilted on the stage. In other illusions, the objects of his magic might be an iPad, an old-fashioned lightbulb, or a cardboard box full of mixtapes.

"I don't think that the use of technology changes the magic," Ramon said. "I use objects that are familiar to the audience, bits of everyday technology. Those sorts of objects are also highly charged; everyone feels that those things are a little magical, a little romantic. They might sense that they've been taking them for granted. They are perfect subjects for magic, because they connect with all of us, and suggest perfectly magical stories."

○

A YOUNG FRENCH MAGICIAN, Yann Frisch, electrified audiences and won awards with a fantasy he called *Baltass*. It was an act that was impossible to classify, a reconfiguration of magic combining old traditions with startling new techniques. It felt a little bit like a close-up act being performed on the stage; it reminded audiences of the ancient cups and balls cliché, but the magic became overwhelming, with a staccato series of breathtaking surprises.

Frisch is not your typical magician. In *Baltass*, he played the part of a man tormented by the magic around him. His skills quickly gave the impression that the audience had been trapped inside his dream—perhaps it was his nightmare—of unexpected, frustrating, endless transformations of the commonplace objects that were now haunting him like characters in a play.

It was a funny, ingenious way of accentuating magic by playing against magic, creating a fantasy and using Frisch's talents for traditional clowning, mime, juggling, and sleight of hand. "I see opportunities to combine these disciplines," Frisch explained. "The juggling and the clowning are at the service of the magic. The juggling gives me a pause, a breath, in the routine, but it also changes the rhythm of the performance, which helps me accomplish the magic. At the same time, magic gives me opportunities for clowning; it gives me inspirations for reactions. There's an intuitive way that these disciplines help each other."[38]

For Frisch, the history of magic points to opportunities. "We can read *Our Magic*, and it feels like it was written just yesterday. That's not really because Maskelyne and Devant were ahead of their times, it's because we're still in the same place, still asking the same questions as magicians. That's a shame. We need to be asking new questions, not because we expect answers but because those new questions will invite new ideas," he said.

Frisch is part of a recent movement in French magic, a group called Magie Nouvelle, with its founders, anthropologist Valentine Losseau and stage directors Raphaël Navarro and Clément Debailleul. Magie Nouvelle has become a way of reimagining the art without Robert-Houdin's devotion to polite fashions. "Magic starts from one idea, that everything is possible, that everything is imaginable." In developing their ideas, these magicians set their goal as a sort of "radicality." "I feel that we magicians are often too deliberate, too careful as students," Frisch explained. "Magic often has to struggle to be insolent, crazy. If the nature of magic is the impossible, it should encourage radicality, shouldn't it?"

Their results are inspiring. The magic is amazing, and the human interactions with the magic create something truly astonishing, whether those reactions are deliberately dreamlike and dispassionate or comically frantic and desperate. The magician is no longer an actor playing the part of a magician but an actor playing the part of the enchanted. By exploring how human beings encounter magic—as victims, protagonists, witnesses, or masters—magicians are no longer confined to simply waving the wand. They now open the door to imaginary forces and become swept up in the storm.

"An audience has become used to watching a man put a woman in a box and cut it into several parts," Frisch explained, discussing the traditional formula. "No one expects any discussion, any personal expression, through this act, which is really strange. It's innocuous, isn't it? In magic, it's often been enough to just be amazing. I think that's laziness, which is dangerous for the art. We have nothing to lose by being more audacious."

◯

THE REAL APPEAL of close-up magic is not that it's closer to art, or closer to technique, but that it's closer to magic. By the nature of its intimate setting, it feels less like a performance, more like an experimental laboratory—a magician's jazz riff rather than a magician's concert. The idea of sitting close to a magician, watching small marvels performed for a handful of people, has always been a novelty. There are no distractions from costumes, or lights, or, in many cases, elaborate patter. At a table, the magic is performed for magic's sake.

That's certainly why magicians came to love it, because it always felt immediate and exciting. If the show felt a little rough around the edges or experimental, it was sometimes possible to perceive the stitches that held the trick together, to sense the construction of the mystery. And that can actually add to the appreciation.

This is one of the paradoxes in magic: sometimes the methods are more impressive than the effects. When the magician and author Henry Hay was a boy, he was fortunate to study with Thomas Nelson Downs, the retired vaudeville magician. Downs instructed him on some of his finest close-up coin tricks. During those lessons, Hay perfectly experienced the magician's quandary, realizing a clandestine thrill, that Downs's secret techniques were even better than the tricks. Hay explained:

> The work of people like Downs can be more astounding if you know how they do it than if you don't. For instance, when he made sixty coins disappear from his closed fist, it was merely a diverting illogicality; but if you knew that they disappeared because he had noiselessly palmed the whole stack in the innocent hand, so carelessly spread against his knee, that approached the incredible.[39]

It's that insider's knowledge, the love of secrets themselves, that has inspired some of our greatest magicians—unapologetically and unashamedly. As the mysterious Mr. Erdnase wrote, "acquiring the art is, in itself, a most fascinating pastime." For the great magicians, they needed no excuses. It was unnecessary for anyone to tell them it was art. They just kept their heads down, working on new tricks, in search of new secrets.

One way or another, it's the secrets, and sometimes even the secrets about secrets, that managed to make the difference.

CHAPTER 12

THE REAL SECRETS
OF MAGIC

THERE ARE DIFFERENT types of secrets. There are things that we know that we do not know. But there are also things that we do not realize that we do not know. There are, as Donald Rumsfeld put it, "known unknowns" and "unknown unknowns." It is rather ironic that this now-famous description of secrets came from a secretary of defense. A "secretary," after all, was originally a person who was entrusted with keeping secrets. Nevertheless, it is a useful distinction.

To put it another way, there are questions for which we do not have answers, but there are also questions that we simply do not ask. The former questions, the ones that we ask, are the ones that occupy our minds. They irk us, because we are aware that there is something that we do not know. Some of these are profound questions, about who we are and how we should act, about the nature of life and death. These profound questions have incomplete answers, and so they continue to concern us. Other questions have straightforward answers, and someone else knows what they are. They irk, because we do not know the answers, but we know that they are out there. These answers are usually matters of fact: a name, a number, a place, a date, the first this, the biggest that, how does it work, is it true or false? We answer those questions by asking other people or by doing a little research. Today, we simply look on our phones. And then the irk ends.

The most irksome of all is when someone lets us know that they know something that we do not. A moment ago, we did not care, but now we want to know. We feel that we are missing out. Someone alludes to a piece of gossip, and now we wish to hear it. A crossword puzzle teases us with cryptic clues, and we try to work it out. Perhaps we do work it out, and we feel satisfied for a moment. We did not know that, and now we do. And then we move on to other things. But until then, it remains a secret, which is not merely something that we do not know and wish to know. A secret is something that someone else knows, which they will not tell us. And that, indeed, is irksome.

The secrets of magic are usually imagined to be this type of secret. They are thought to be the hidden methods that magicians use. The magician knows them, but we do not, and the magician will not tell us. If we wish to satisfy our curiosity, then we can investigate, and today it is easier than ever. We can look online, and there will be a website or video that explains it all. A masked magician, or a novice on YouTube, will reveal how it is done. They do this for the same reason that people gather gossip. It is a way of appearing knowledgeable, by discovering and revealing the secrets of others. And when they tell us how the trick is done, then our curiosity is satisfied. We did not know that, and now we do, and then we move on to other things.

But these are not the real secrets of magic. These are pieces of gossip. They are the answers to a crossword puzzle that we have failed to solve ourselves. The real secrets of magic are not the hidden methods, which we know are out there. They are behind the questions that we do not ask, because we take the answers for granted. They are in the places that we do not look, because they do not concern us. We pass them by without a thought and do not realize what we are missing.

◯

THERE IS ALWAYS more going on than we think. There are, in fact, countless magic tricks. Here are the main types: Things appear or disappear, or change into something else. Something is destroyed and then put back together, or mysteriously travels from one place to another. Solid penetrates solid. Things float in the air, minds are read, and the future is predicted. These are the main types of magic tricks, but there are innumerable examples of each. They involve an endless variety of animals, minerals, and vegetables, with birds and beasts, gold and silver, flowers, fruit, and the occasional potato.

Think of an object, any object, and chances are that a magician at some point has made it disappear, or float in the air, or has found a selected playing card inside it. Think of a card, or a name, or a number, and you can be sure that a magician at some point has predicted that someone would think of it. And for every type of trick, and for every trick with every object, there are a variety of ways to do it. There are endless versions and variations, by different performers at different times, for different audiences in different spaces. Some are better than others, of course, and while anything is possible, not everything has been done. Nevertheless, there are far more than you think. And yet, when people think of magic, they usually think of one trick in particular.

It used to be the cups and balls. For most of history, this was the best-known trick. Until the eighteenth century, this was part of the stereotypical image of the magician. It was the image of the traveling street performer, who performed outdoors and passed a hat. In the nineteenth century, the stereotype was replaced with the image of the modern gentleman, dressed in respectable evening clothes, performing onstage for a theater audience. By the start of the twentieth century, a new stereotypical trick had appeared. It is still this trick, more than any other, that is associated with the magician: producing a rabbit from a hat. This is a little odd because, as it happens, it was not a particularly common trick. As you may have noticed, we have barely mentioned it. Throughout the nineteenth century, conjurors performed a variety of tricks with rabbits and hats, but relatively few produced a rabbit out of a hat.[1] Even at the end of the century, when it became more popular, it was not a feature attraction. David Devant, for whom "the production of a rabbit was an art," only used it as an occasional opener.[2]

Nevertheless, the rabbit from the hat became the classic symbol of the conjuror. It began to be used as a metaphor in sports, business, and politics, for something that was hard to believe or seemed to be impossible. When he was president of the Board of Trade, Winston Churchill was accused of producing statistics in support of his claims, "much in the same way as a conjurer produces a rabbit from a top hat."[3] When the Brooklyn Dodgers played the Giants, Zack Wheat, the Dodgers left fielder, "made a catch ... like a magician pulls a rabbit out of a hat."[4] During the Depression, President Hoover was expected "to pull a rabbit out of a hat," and when Franklin D. Roosevelt introduced the New Deal, his use of deficit spending was compared to "a magician pulling a rabbit out of a hat."[5]

By then, the top hat was already going out of fashion, and magicians were talking about it as an outdated trick.[6] By then, however, it had been fixed in the public imagination as what magicians did. And so performers who did not wear top hats nevertheless displayed top hats, and then produced rabbits from them. Audiences, who did not wear top hats, found this perfectly normal, because they thought that this was what a magician did. A trick that had been a tiny part of the conjuring repertoire came to represent the whole.

This is the power of the stereotype. It gives the illusion of representing the whole, when it does nothing of the kind. It can be a useful shorthand, but it is deceptive. Sometimes it is simply inaccurate, but almost always, it is misleading. It provides, at best, a narrow view. This is not what magic is, but it is, in part, how magic works. Magic depends on the fact that we make generalizations without realizing that we do. We see a fraction of what is going on and think that we know what is going on. We see a part of something and think that we have seen it all. We take a narrow view and we miss the bigger picture.

☉

HOW IS IT DONE? That is the obvious question, and most people think that it is about the methods, whether they take the form of hidden moves or gimmicked props. They think that, if they know the method, then they will not be fooled. However, as we shall now reveal, this is simply untrue.

There are many types of methods, but here are the main types. Objects are concealed from view before they appear and after they disappear. They are surreptitiously switched and secretly smuggled from one place to another. They appear to be there when they are not, or they appear to be something that they are not, and sometimes there is a duplicate object that nobody knows about. A choice can be forced, information can be secretly discovered, and, when it is not, the impression can be given that it was known all along. Any object can be concealed, substituted, smuggled, simulated, disguised, or duplicated, and any piece of information can be forced, discovered, or revealed as if known. For each of these, there are an endless number of ways in which it might be done, with a given object or piece of information, depending on the circumstances.[7] There is no magician, alive or dead, who has ever known all the possibilities.

But even if you know of the method, it does not really matter. After all, many methods have become common knowledge, but they are still used. Since ancient Greece, audiences have known that magicians rely on sleight of hand. Reginald Scot revealed how objects were palmed and how a juggler pretended to convey them from one hand into another. A variety of palms, passes, secret loads, and false shuffles have been revealed over the centuries. Magicians have continued to use them, however, because they have learned to do them better. It does not matter if you know about palming, only that you think that the palm is empty. It does not matter if you know about false shuffles, only that you are convinced that the cards are mixed.

The same goes for other well-known methods, such as trapdoors, mirrors, and wires. Trapdoors onstage were immediately suspected, because they were known to be used in theater. As it happens, they were rarely used in magic, since cutting a trap on a stage was often impractical, particularly during a short run. However, whether they were used or not, they were nevertheless suspected. So, when Robert-Houdin produced a wealth of objects from his magic portfolio, he placed the portfolio on sawhorses so that the audience could see a gap between the portfolio and the stage floor. When Johann de Kolta performed the Vanishing Lady, he placed a newspaper below the chair so that anyone suspecting a trapdoor would then dismiss that possibility. Since the nineteenth century, mirrors have been used for certain illusions. However, by the 1880s, conjurors were going out of their way to show that they did not use mirrors by displaying the apparatus to the audience or by inviting people onstage to inspect it.[8] In the case of a levitation, magicians naturally assumed that wires would be suspected. So they passed hoops around the floating body, to demonstrate that there were no wires. Meanwhile, they found other ways to continue to use trapdoors, mirrors, and wires.

And then there is, perhaps, the worst-kept secret in magic: magicians hide things up their sleeves. Before the era of modern magic, audiences knew that it was common for conjurors to hide things "up their sleeves."[9] By the time of Robert-Houdin, it was a "popular belief," which he did his best to dispel. With few exceptions, he explained, "the sleeves have nothing to do with the disappearance of any article." After all, he persisted, if the conjuror had a ball or some coins up his sleeve, "what trouble he would have to keep them there! He would be obliged constantly to keep his arm in an upward position." Nevertheless, he still used his sleeves to make objects appear and disappear.[10]

The fact that audiences knew about sleeves was addressed in various ways. Bosco performed with bare arms, which "enhanced the magical effect of the feats." However, some thought that this "detracted from the elegance of their personal appearance." Robert-Houdin, more modestly, recommended "drawing back the coat-sleeve a little."[11] By the 1870s, however, conjurors were openly rolling up their sleeves. "I tuck up my sleeves," one pointed out, "so that nothing passes *that* way."[12] Magicians continued to pull up their sleeves, but they also continued to hide things up their sleeves. Before too long, they found a way to turn the problem into an advantage. They began to use the action of pulling up their sleeves as a method in itself by ditching or stealing an object in the process of pulling up their sleeves.[13] They used their sleeves at the very same time as they were demonstrating that they were not, by using them in a different way than the audience suspected.

It does not matter if you know of the method. Audiences have always known, to some extent, how magic tricks are done. But they have not known, as they were watching, what was going on. This is because magicians have been creative. They have created slightly different methods or different versions of existing methods. They have discovered ways to show that a method is not being used, even when it is being used. They have exploited the fact that audiences often suspect a certain method might be used, and have used this to direct their audience's eyes and minds away from the method being used. We wonder if it might go up the sleeve, and so they show us that it does not go up the sleeve. Meanwhile, it goes somewhere else. Magic relies on the fact that we focus on the areas that concern us. In doing so, we do not think about what is going on elsewhere. We do not realize what we are missing.

MAGIC, THEN, is not a simple deception. It is, in fact, a unique form of deception. Other forms of deception work because you do not realize that you are being deceived. After all, if you know that someone is lying, then you will not believe them. In magic, however, the audience knows that they are being deceived, but still they believe what they see. They do not believe in magic, but they do believe what they see.

After all, this is not a play, where the audience willingly suspends their disbelief. When they watch a play, they temporarily allow themselves to believe in the characters and plot. But for magic to work, they need to believe that what they see is real. They do not believe that an object really disappears, but they need to believe, really believe, that now it is there, and now it is not. They do not believe that the magician really flies, but they need to believe that he is in the air, and that nothing is holding him up. If Peter Pan flies above the stage and the audience ignores the wires, then that is a willing suspension of disbelief. If David Copperfield flies above the stage, then the audience actively looks for the wires. They become convinced that there are none. That is magic. If the presence of wires is not ruled out, then it does not seem impossible. That is why a hoop is passed around the floating person.

The audience will naturally wonder how the trick is done. That is the obvious question. But they cannot *know* how it is done, or it will not seem impossible. And the purpose of magic is not merely to deceive; it is to demonstrate the seemingly impossible. Deception is a means to an end. Nevil Maskelyne once wrote: "To most people, the secret of any magical presentation means simply how it is done. A more erroneous view has never been conceived." Nevertheless, Maskelyne knew that the audience would wonder how the trick is done. He understood that if someone floats in the air, then wires will be suspected, and if the audience thinks it is done by wires, then it will not seem impossible. So Maskelyne came up with the idea of passing a hoop around the floating person, so that the audience would not think that this was how it was done.

It does not matter if you know of the method. What matters is that, as you are watching, you do not think that it is being used. We know that people sometimes lie, but still we are deceived. We are aware of the method, but it still fools us, because it is done in a convincing way. This is why we can reveal some secrets. We can tell you that there are palms, passes, secret loads, and false shuffles. We can tell you that objects can be concealed, substituted, smuggled, simulated, disguised, or duplicated, and that a piece of information can be forced, discovered, or revealed as if known. We can tell you this because it does not matter. These kinds of methods have been revealed for centuries, but all of them still work, if they are used in a convincing way. They can still be employed in ways that are neither detected nor suspected. The audience will not realize what they are missing.

The kind of exposure that is problematic is the gratuitous exposure of the masked magician, or of the novice on YouTube. They perform a trick, which was invented by someone else, and do not perform it well. And then they expose the "secret," as someone might reveal a piece of gossip. They give the impression that magic is nothing more than an irksome puzzle. They completely miss the point of magic, because magic is not a puzzle. Puzzles are supposed to be figured out. That is the purpose of puzzles. The purpose of magic is the seemingly impossible. The methods are merely tools of the trade, and these can be used in different ways. A novice may perform a trick, then show you how it is done. But an experienced magician can then show you the same trick, and it will seem impossible.

This has always been the case, and it remains the case today. Penn and Teller have revealed a few secrets, for example, but if you see them live, then what you see will seem impossible. When they perform magic, they do it in a way that assumes that certain methods are suspected. Sometimes they even tell you how the trick is done. When Teller makes a ball float in the air, this is introduced by Penn as a trick that is done with a piece of thread. However, the ball then floats in the air in ways that the audience cannot imagine could be achieved with a piece of thread. The audience is told how it is done, but it nevertheless seems impossible.

The real secrets of magic are not the hidden methods, which we know are there, and which we would like to know. They are in the details of the performance. We do not discover them because we tend to look in the obvious places, ask the more obvious questions, and settle too easily for the answers that we are given. We wonder what the secret is, and we are told that it is a hidden move or a gimmicked prop. And we settle for that, because it satisfies our immediate curiosity. But if we wish to be more curious, then we need to ask different questions. Why does it work? Why does it matter? Then we might realize what we are missing.

✿

So why does it work, and why does it matter? Magic works by exploiting the limits of what we can see and how we think. We are surrounded by an endless amount of information, which bombards our eyes and minds. We do not notice everything, and we cannot question everything. So our attention has to be selective, and we need to take certain things for granted. We look at one thing rather than another, and we think about things, up to a point. These are the things that occupy our minds, and beyond these lie the secrets of magic. They are in the spaces that we do not see, because we do not look at them. They are in the thoughts that do not cross our minds, because we take them for granted.

Now you see it; now you don't. Now you see *these words*, and now, right now, you don't. The words are in italics, and they are right before your eyes. However, you do not see them right now because you are looking at these words. Perhaps you have glanced back at them in the past few seconds, but now, *at this very moment*, you do not see them.

Nevertheless, you know they are there, because you saw them a moment ago. So, here is a miracle: they have disappeared!

Now, at that moment, when you looked back, they were there. However, what happened was this: they vanished when you were not looking, then reappeared just before you looked back. We know what you're thinking: it did not really happen. You are a skeptical person, and we respect that. But here is the thing. No matter how ridiculous the idea may seem—that the words disappear when not being looked at and reappear when being looked at—you cannot rule it out by observation. You need to assume that, when things are out of sight, they do not really disappear.

This is how we look at the world. We see bits and pieces, and then assume that everything else is as it should be. However, things are rarely as they appear. It may seem as if you are looking at this page, but not really: only these words, and now these ones, a tiny fraction of your view. That is why, though it is right before your eyes, right now, you do not see your thumb at the edge of the page . . . now you see it; now you don't!

It is now common knowledge that our perception is narrow and that we notice far less than we think. It is one more flaw to be added to our long list of psychological shortcomings. For more than a century, psychologists have been pointing out how our minds get things wrong. Our memories are unreliable. We believe in things that are not true. We fail to notice the most obvious things that happen right in front of us. We are biased in every imaginable way, and our brains are hardwired to deceive us. Quite frankly, it makes you wonder how we manage to get anything done.

And yet we manage rather well. We can dress ourselves and feed ourselves. We can walk down the street without falling over and cross the road without getting knocked down. We are not bad at paying attention. In fact, we are very good at it. We attend to one thing rather than another, because we cannot attend to everything at once. And, as we focus on what we think matters, we miss what we think does not. This is mainstream psychology now, but magicians have known it for centuries.

The conjuror has always known how easily our attention can be directed. This is how they have made a living, by regularly exploiting this. They make a particular area seem interesting, then do the dirty deed elsewhere. And everyone in the audience knows this, too, but it does not make any difference. The tricks still work because we cannot resist being attracted to what seems interesting in the world around us.

We are drawn to the novel aspects of our view, just as we are attracted to news and gossip. We notice if a friend has grown a beard or is wearing a new dress, particularly if it is the same person. The novel attracts our attention. If a conjuror spreads playing cards on the table, and the cards are facedown, but one is faceup, our attention is immediately drawn to that card. It does not fit with the rest of the view, and so it is odd in that particular context. There is nothing essentially odd about it. We would just as easily be drawn to one facedown card in a spread of faceup cards. We are simply presented with a view, form a sense of what is normal within it, and then notice what does not seem to fit.

And if it were normal in our society for a man with a beard to wear a dress, then we would not give him a second glance. We notice him because he seems weird, in our view, because we are not used to that sort of thing. Like a picture that is level when others hang askew. Like a jockey— or a basketball player—of average height. Like a person who sits when others stand or stands while those around her sit. They stick out not because they are inherently odd but because they are not in line with their surroundings.

This is also why we notice what is not there. Life proceeds, everything seems normal, then suddenly we   that something is missing. The surrounding context leads us to interpret nothing as a lack of something. That is why we feel that something is missing: no word becomes a missing word. Without this context, we would not notice. After all, an entire sentence has been deleted from this paragraph, but it is unnecessary to the reading of the paragraph, and so you do not notice. The missing piece of a jigsaw puzzle declares its absence loudly, but nobody notices the absence of a jigsaw puzzle.

We notice what is odd, according to the situation, and notice only the absence of something when we expect it to be there. Nobody thinks of the boiler until it breaks. Nobody notices a telephone not ringing until an important call is expected. And then the ongoing silence feels as loud as that of an unexpected call, and we seek an explanation for this nonevent, by wondering if our watch is correct or if the phone is working.

This is how we see things, whether they are there or not, based on what seems normal (in our view), and what we expect to be there. This is how the magician deceives, by making what is visible seem normal and by concealing nothing that might be missed. Magic depends on the fact that we do not see things as they really are. We notice only a fraction of what is before our very eyes, and what we notice depends on a range of hidden assumptions and expectations. Magic relies on the unseen, the unsuspected, and the unexpected. The unseen is beyond our view, the unsuspected is beyond our doubt, and the unexpected is, of course, beyond our expectations. When we see a magic trick, when something happens that appears to be impossible, we are forced to realize the limits of our views, our doubts, and our expectations.

This is what magic reveals to us, if we pay attention. When we encounter the seemingly impossible, we are reminded that there are things beyond what we see and what we take for granted. Magic demonstrates, if only for a moment, that our view is simply inadequate. The real secret, however, is to realize that this is not a momentary lapse. Every day, we experience the world from a restricted point of view, directed by ways of thinking that we do not realize are there.

This is not a problem. It is simply the way we have evolved as a species and learned to engage with the world since birth. The point is not that we are flawed; that should go without saying. The point is that the world is a more magical place than we generally think. There is a hidden world inhabited by what we cannot see and do not suspect. There is a secret world beyond the questions that we ask. If we choose to ask other questions, if it occurs to us to ask them, then we become aware of so much more. If we step back, so that we have a wider perspective, then we will see the bigger picture.

✺

SUCH LOFTY AMBITIONS, however, need to be grounded in a more mundane reality. After all, at the end of the day, is it not simply a trick?

This is the enormous gap between how magic is seen and what it might be. We have seen how, in ancient Greece, magic tricks were compared to a paradox. This, for Socrates, was a source of wonder. But the story of magic, for the most part, has not been a story of wonder. It has been a story of people who struggled to make a living, as the world became increasingly filled with other kinds of wonders. It has been a story of how magic became a weapon in the fight against witchcraft, Spiritualism, and psychic phenomena. It was used by debunkers as a way of showing that magic was not real: it was merely a trick, and you have been fooled. But the very idea of real magic was something profoundly meaningful. A trick, on the other hand, was not profound. The magic of conjurors was compared to real magic and suffered by comparison.

Magicians had to make a living, and they made it as entertainers. Their priority was neither philosophy nor art; it was the bottom line. They did what they could to attract a paying audience, and sometimes they blurred the truth. They managed to astonish a public that was becoming increasingly difficult to astonish. They succeeded in this, but their primary focus was on making a living as entertainers. And so they included a host of other curiosities and entertainments, which helped to sell tickets. If the audience paid and felt satisfied, then that was what really mattered. Even if they were not always fooled, the show could still be entertaining. The audience could leave, satisfied that they had managed to figure out some of the tricks. Sometimes magicians revealed how their tricks were done and cashed in on the public fascination with secrets. This may have been necessary to make a living, in a world that regarded magic as a trick.

But magic is not what magicians do. It is only part of what magicians do. Magicians tell stories, make witty remarks, and display remarkable objects and skills. They put on a show, with music and lights. They often do things that are not really magic, such as juggling, shadowgraphy, fire-eating, and escapes. These may be impressive, but unless they seem impossible, then they are not magic. However, at particular moments in the show, something impossible happens. In an instant, something appears or disappears, or transforms into something else. Now you see it; now you don't. Now it is this; now it is that. Occasionally, it lasts a little longer. He is floating, but nothing is holding him up. He is still floating, and I cannot see any wires. But magic cannot happen too often, and it cannot last for too long, or else it begins to seem possible. At some point, the audience is no longer astonished, because astonishment is not a lasting emotion.

And when astonishment fades, what is left? There is, of course, the obvious question: how is it done? This is the secret that the magician will not tell us, and that can be irksome. But there is also something more mysterious, behind the questions that we do not ask. They are about the things that we do not look at, and which we take for granted. They are about the things that do not concern us. But they should.

〇

MAGICIANS HAVE TRIED to make magic relevant by tapping into contemporary concerns. They exploited the interest in mesmerism and Spiritualism, presented seemingly novel technologies, and even tried to be politically topical. Magicians continue to seek a place within a wider context. Some present themselves as experts on confidence tricks or cheating at cards. Some pretend to be psychological experts who can read your facial expressions. Some draw on the tradition of the shaman and talk of the power of transformation. And magic certainly has something to say about deception, psychology, and metaphor. But the reason why magic matters is more fundamental than this.

Magicians have taken the things that we thought were impossible and discovered how they can be done. They have provided us with a particular kind of wonder, which allows us to experience the impossible without believing that it is real.[14] The methods of magicians have been revealed for centuries, but magic has survived. The audience has learned that new things are possible, and magicians have adapted to this. It has all been part of an ongoing interaction between performer and audience. It has evolved over time, because what we think is possible has changed over time.

We discovered the power of electricity and invented film, radio, and television. We circumnavigated the Earth and went to the moon. Yet magic has continued to astonish audiences. It shows us—it does not simply tell us; it actually shows us—that we do not know what is possible. We do not really know what is going on. We know only what we can see through the narrow window of our limited experience, and we cannot even be sure about that.

Magic should challenge our sense of certainty and encourage genuine curiosity. It should make us more curious, beyond the obvious question of how it is done. It should make us ask less obvious questions about the things that do not irk. They have become a familiar part of the background, and so we no longer notice them. We pass them by without a thought and do not realize what we are missing. When we circumnavigated the Earth and went to the moon, we thought this was extraordinary. Not anymore. It does not even cross our minds. But we still need a genuine sense of wonder. We need to step back from those things that immediately concern us to see the bigger picture. We need to be reminded not to take extraordinary things for granted.

ACKNOWLEDGMENTS

The authors would like to thank our agent, Jim Fitzgerald of the James Fitzgerald Agency, and our editors, Mitch Horowitz and Heather Brennan at TarcherPerigee, for their understanding and support of our interest in this ancient and often neglected art. Even better, for the encouragement that a new look at magic history might find new readers.

We would also like to thank the Arts and Humanities Research Council (UK), who provided support for the "Magical Thinking" project from which the idea for this collaboration emerged. To our friends and fellow historians and collectors, who have supported us with open files, answered questions, and suggested ideas, we are truly grateful. Our thanks to David Britland, Mike Caveney, David Copperfield, Eddie Dawes, John Forrester, John Gaughan, David Hibbard, Will Houstoun, Ricky Jay, Bill Kalush, Todd Karr, Ian Keable, Peter Lane, Patricia Magicia, Paul and Nicole Mandrex, Max Maven, Pietro Micheli, Stephen Minch, James Smith, Pierre Taillefer, Steffen Taut, and Barry Wiley.

And, of course, to Claudia and Frankie, who know things that shall never be revealed.

NOTES

CHAPTER 1: ORIGIN MYTHS

1 Miriam Lichtheim, *Ancient Egyptian Literature*. Vol. 1, *The Old and Middle Kingdoms* (Berkeley: University of California Press, 1973), 217–20; R. B. Parkinson, *The Tale of Sinuhe, and Other Ancient Egyptian Poems, 1940–1640 BC* (Oxford: Oxford University Press, 1997), 102–27. The story is set in the Fourth Dynasty (c. 2500 BCE), at the time of King Khufu, also known as Cheops, the builder of the great pyramid at Giza.

2 Sidney W. Clarke, *The Annals of Conjuring* (New York: Magico Magazine, 1983), 22. This book was based on articles first published in the 1920s.

3 For example: Will Dexter, *This Is Magic: Secrets of the Conjurers Craft* (London: Arco Publications Limited, 1958), 4; Edwin A. Dawes, *The Great Illusionists* (Secaucus, NJ: Chatwell Books, 1979), 14; Henry Gordon, *Henry Gordon's World of Magic* (Toronto: Stoddart Publishing Co. Limited, 1989), 52; Edwin. A. Dawes and Arthur Setterington, *The Book of Magic* (Leicester, UK: Admiral, 1986), 16.

4 Thomas Frost, *The Lives of the Conjurors* (London: Tinsley Brothers, 1876), 2.

5 Henry Ridgely Evans, "Introduction: The Mysteries of Modern Magic," in Albert A. Hopkins, *Magic, Stage Illusions and Scientific Diversions,* (New York: Munn & Co., 1898), 1.

6 Thomas Ady, *A Candle in the Dark* (London: Printed for Robert Ibbitson, 1655), 31.

7 John Webster, *The Displaying of Supposed Witchcraft* (London, 1676), 154–55.

8 Joseph Glanvill, *Saducismus Triumphatus* (London: J. Collins, 1681), 39–43.

9 This is also the view of Steffen Taut, who has done more extensive research on the topic.

10 E. T. Kirby, "The Shamanistic Origins of Popular Entertainment," *The Drama Review* 18, no. 1 (March 1974): 5–15; Rogan Taylor, *The Death and Resurrection Show: From Shaman to Superstar* (London: Anthony Blond, 1985).

11 Plato, *The Republic*, trans. with an introduction by Desmond Lee. 2nd edition (New York: Penguin, 1974), 432.

12 Seneca, *Moral Epistles*, trans. Richard M. Gummere. The Loeb Classical Library. 3 Vols. Vol. 1. (Cambridge, MA: Harvard University Press, 1917–25), I:295.

13 Alciphron, Aelian, and Philostratus, *The Letters*, trans. Allen Rogers Benner and Francis H. Fobes (London: William Heinemann Ltd., 1949), 111–12.

14 Plato, *Theaetetus; Sophist*, trans. Harold North Fowler (Cambridge, MA: Harvard University Press, 1921), 331.

15 Sextus Empiricus, *Outlines of Pyrrhonism*, edited by Julia Annas, Jonathon Barnes (New York: Cambridge University Press, 1994), 137.

16 Pierre Taillefer, "Conjurers Around the Mediterranean Basin," *Gibecière* 10, no. 1 (Winter 2015): 85.

17 Evans, "The mysteries of modern magic," 2; Frost, *Lives of the Conjurors*, 4.

18 Evans, "The mysteries of modern magic," 2.

19 Frost, *Lives of the Conjurors*, 59–60.

Chapter 2: False Accusations

1 Reginald Scot, *The Discoverie of Witchcraft,* with an introduction by Rev. Montague Summers (New York: Dover Publications Inc., 1972), 174–75. The book was originally published in London in 1584.

2 Ibid., 174.

3 Ibid., 174–75.

4 Brandon was the king's juggler until about 1540 (Philip Butterworth, *Magic on the Early English Stage* [Cambridge, UK: Cambridge University Press, 2005], 9), when Scot would have been two years old.

5 Scot, *Discoverie of Witchcraft*, 174–75.

6 *The Malleus Maleficarum of Heinrich Kramer and James Sprenger*, trans. Rev. Montague Summers (London: John Rodker, 1928), 59.

7   William Perkins, *A Discourse of the Damned So Farre Forth as It Is Revealed in the Scriptures, and Manifest by True Experience* (Cambridge, UK: 1608), 159.

8   Glanvill, *Saducismus Triumphatus*, 23.

9   For more on this, and on magic at this time, see the Philip Butterworth's excellent *Magic on the Early English Stage.*

10 Richard Kieckhefer, *Magic in the Middle Ages* (Cambridge, UK: Cambridge University Press, 2000), 91.

11 Scot, *Discoverie of Witchcraft*, 199.

12 P. G. Maxwell-Stuart, ed. and trans., *The Occult in Early Modern Europe: A Documentary History* (New York: St. Martin's Press, 1999), 161.

13 Francis Bacon, *Sylva Sylvarum: or, A Natural History in Ten Centuries* (London: 1670), 207.

14 Butterworth, *Magic on the Early English Stage*, 77–78, 83, 166.

15 Louis B. Wright, "Juggling Tricks and Conjury on the English Stage before 1642," *Modern Philology* 24, no. 3 (February 1927): 269–84.

16 According to Scot, he used the name of Feats as a juggler, and Hilles as a witch (*Discoverie of Witchcraft*, 82); a contemporary, George Peele, described him as "Feats" or "Cuts" (Butterworth, *Magic on the Early English Stage*, 14).

17 Butterworth, *Magic on the Early English Stage*, 17.

18 For more details, see Peter Lamont, "Modern Magic, the Illusion of Transformation, and How It Was Done," *Journal of Social History* shw126, https://doi.org/10.1093/jsh/shw126.

19 S[amuel] R[id], *The Art of Jugling, or Legerdemaine* (London: Printed for T. B., 1612), 4.

20 Ady, *A Candle in the Dark* (1655), 29; Webster, *Displaying of Supposed Witchcraft*, 12.

21 Philip Breslaw, *Breslaw's Last Legacy* (London: Printed for W. Lane, 1795), x.

22 Walter Scott, *Letters on Demonology and Witchcraft* (London: John Murray), 379–80. Scott, despite his fondness for folklore, shared the view that witchcraft was primarily a thing of the past and that this was a positive development (320).

23 Randall Styers, *Making Magic: Religion, Magic, & Science in the Modern World* (Oxford: Oxford University Press, 2004), 74ff.

24 Aprey Vere, *Ancient and Modern Magic, with Explanations of Some of the Best Known Tricks Performed by Messrs. Maskelyne and Cooke* (London: George Routledge and Sons, 1879), 81.

25 Henry Ridgely Evans, *The Old and the New Magic* (Chicago: The Open Court Publishing Co., 1906), xviii.

26 William Lecky, *History of the Rise and Influence of the Spirit of Rationalism in Europe* (London: Longmans, Green & Co., 1913), 104.

27 Clarke, *Annals*, 15.

28 Milbourne Christopher, *The Illustrated History of Magic* (New York: Thomas Y. Crowell Company, 1973), 16–17.

29 It seems clear from the content and form that his source was an essay published in 1823 by Richard Cumberland. According to both, the girl had torn the handkerchief "into pieces and immediately afterwards produced it whole and entire," and she had done this "in the presence of a great company of noble spectators." See Richard Cumberland, "Account of Magic from the ld Christian Writers, with Several Anecdotes of Magicians, &c," in Lionel Thomas Berguer, *The British Essayists, with Prefaces Biographical, Historical and Critical,* vol. 38 (London: T and J Allman, 1823), 197–206.

30 P. G. Maxwell-Stuart, *Witch Beliefs and Witch Trials in the Middle Ages: Documents and Readings* (London: Continuum International Publishing Group, 2011), 145–46.

31 Christopher, *Illustrated History*, 23.

32 Gerald Gardner, *The Meaning of Witchcraft* (London: Aquarian, 1959), 91.

33 James Charles Bouffard, *The Magician's Fight!* (Pomona: Lyn Paulo Foundation, 2008), 28.

34 At different points in the book, Bodin describes him variously as "Deseschelles" and "Trois-eschelles," but it is obvious from the context that this is the same individual.

35 Christopher, *Illustrated History*, 23.

36 Henry Charles Lea, *Materials Towards a History of Witchcraft: Volume II*, ed. A. C. Howland (New York: Thomas Yoseloff, 1957), 493.

37 Pietro Pomponazzi, *De Naturalium Effectuum Causis, Sive de Incantatibus* (Basel, 1520), 59–61. Pomponazzi mentions Reatius during a discussion of a case of the "moving sieve" (*cribrum moto*). This was a form of magical divination, in which a sieve was suspended on shears and would turn in response to questions being asked (cf. Scot *Discoverie of Witchcraft*, 149). Pomponazzi is considering that the sorcerer could use deception to move the sieve without being noticed, and Reatius is mentioned as an example of someone who practiced such deception and was punished for it. Our thanks to John Forrester for his assistance in translating, and discussing, the relevant passage.

38 J. M., *Sports and Pastimes, or, Sport for the City and Pastime for the Country* (London: Printed by H. B. for John Clark, 1676), 21.

39 Ibid., 26–27.

40 In what may have been an equally tongue-in-cheek remark, Samuel Pepys noted that when a juggler performed legerdemain, his wife thought it satanic.

41 The stories are ancient and can be found in many cultures, but it was not until the end of the nineteenth century that the modern legend of the Indian rope trick emerged. For the whole story, see Peter Lamont, *The Rise of the Indian Rope Trick* (New York: Thunder's Mouth Press, 2005).

42 Ibn Battuta, *The Travels of Ibn Battuta,* trans. Samuel Lee (London: Oriental Translation Committee, 1829), 162.

43 Henry Yule, *The Book of Ser Marco Polo*, vol. 1 (London: John Murray, 1871), 279–80.

44 Lamont, *Rise of the Indian Rope Trick*, 5ff.

45 Butterworth, *Magic on the Early English Stage*, 23.

CHAPTER 3: DISENCHANTMENT

1 Charles Gildon and Paul Dottin, *Robinson Crusoe Examin'd and Criticis'd, or a New Edition of Charles Gildon's Famous Pamphlet* (London: J. M. Dent and Sons Ltd., 1923).

2 Ricky Jay, *Jay's Journal of Anomalies* (New York: Farrar, Straus and Giroux, 2001), 59.

3 For examples of full advertisements, see: Clarke, *Annals*, 64; Jay, *Jay's Journal*, 57.

4 "Domestick occurrences," *Gentleman's Magazine*, February 1731, 79.

5 Clarke, *Annals*, 65.

6 The latter three quotes are from Ricky Jay's wonderful *Jay's Journal*, 57–58.

7 On this extraordinary individual, who deserves his own book, see Ricky Jay, *Matthias Buchinger: "The Greatest German Living"* (New York: Siglio Press, 2016).

8 *The Whole Art and Mystery of Modern Gaming Fully Expos'd and Detected* (London: J. Roberts and T. Cox, 1726), 46.

9 Jay, *Jay's Journal*, 61.

10 John Locke, *An Essay Concerning Human Understanding*. Abridged and edited with an introduction by A. D. Woozley, Professor of Philosophy, University of Virginia (Glasgow: William Collins Sons and Co. Ltd., 1980), 406. First published in 1690.

11 Thomas Woolston, *A Fifth Discourse on the Miracles of Our Saviour* (London: 1728), 49.

12 Thomas Woolston, *A Sixth Discourse on the Miracles of Our Saviour* (London: 1729), 27.

13 John Latham, *A General History of Birds*, vol. 10 (Winchester, UK: Jacob and Johnson, 1824), 224–25.

14 Palmira Fontes da Costa, "The Making of Extraordinary Facts: Authentication of Singularities of Nature at the Royal Society of London in the First Half of the Eighteenth Century," *Studies in History and Philosophy of Science* 33, no. 2 (June 2002), 265–88.

15 Clarke, *Annals*, 70.

16 Thomas Wright, *Caricature History of the Georges* (London: Chatto and Windus, 1876), 232.

17 William Clarke, *The Boy's Own Book* (London: Longman, Brown, 1844), 385.

18 Michael R. Lynn, *Popular Science and Public Opinion in Eighteenth-Century France* (Manchester, UK: Manchester University Press, 2006), 106–59.

19 Edwin A. Dawes, "The Card-playing Conjuring Jew," in *A Rich Cabinet of Magical Curiosities: Parts 1 & 2* (Surrey, UK: Peter Scarlett, 2010), 1051–55.

20 Edwin A. Dawes, "Wait Until the Sun Shines, Gustavus: Some Light on Katterfelto in Auld Reekie," in Dawes, *A Rich Cabinet*, 742–45.

21 Ibid. For more on Katterfelto, see David Paton-Williams, *Katterfelto: Prince of Puff* (Leicester, UK: Matador, 2008).

22 "Arts & Entertainment," *Whitehall Evening Post*, September 21, 1784.

23 James A. Smith, *Breslaw's Last Legacy* (self-pub, 2013), 21.

24 *Morning Chronicle and London Advertiser*, January 8, 1784.

25 See Smith, *Breslaw's Last Legacy* for an excellent summary, including additional primary sources.

26 "Theatrical Intelligence," *Morning Chronicle and London Advertiser*, September 28, 1784.

27 "Theatrical Intelligence," *London Morning Herald and Daily Advertiser*, September 30, 1784.

28 Letter to editor, *Parker's General Advertiser*, October 5, 1784.

29 "Theatrical Intelligence," *Morning Chronicle and London Advertiser*, October 28, 1784.

30 "Extract of a Letter from Dresden," *Morning Post and Daily Advertiser*, October 28, 1784.

31 "Extract of a Letter from Chatham," *Public Advertiser*, December 11, 1784.

32 Giuseppe Pinetti, *Physical Amusements and Diverting Experiments* (London: T. Moore, 1784), 6.

33 *Encyclopedia Britannica*, 11th ed. (1910), vii.

34 Frank A. Kafker, "The Achievement of Andrew Bell and Colin Macfarquhar as the First Publishers of the *Encyclopedia Britannica*," *Journal for Eighteenth-Century Studies* 18, no. 2 (September 1995), 142–43.

35 *Encyclopedia Britannica*, 2nd ed., vol. VI (1780), s.v. "legerdemain."

CHAPTER 4: SECOND SIGHT

1   "Scotch Balloon Intelligence," *London Magazine*, October 11, 1784.

2   "The English Theatre," *London Magazine*, September 22, 1784.

3   Scot, *Discoverie of Witchcraft*, 189; Jean Prévost, *Clever and Pleasant Inventions. Part one*. (Seattle: Hermetic Press, 1998), 166–68, first published in French in 1584.

4   This has sometimes been assumed to be a version of second sight, but a later advertisement reveals that it was one of Giuseppe Pinetti's "new magical card deceptions, particularly he will communicate his thoughts from one person to another" ("Classified Ads," *London Courant and Daily Advertiser*, January 25, 1783).

5   "Theatrical Intelligence," *Morning Chronicle and London Advertiser*, September 28, 1784.

6   "Haymarket Theatre," *Morning Herald and Daily Advertiser*, October 4, 1784.

7   Advertisement, *Public Advertiser*, November 29, 1784.

8   Ibid.

9   This is one of those remarkable little myths found in the history of magic. Henri Decremps had referred to how an "eloquent impostor" might pretend to be real and then mentioned "an Italian" who, he claimed, received letters from members of the public seeking advice. This was probably aimed at Giuseppe Pinetti and used to justify the exposure of his tricks, but no evidence was provided that Pinetti played it for real. In contrast, he made a very direct accusation that Pinetti used confederates, and this was the accusation to which Pinetti responded. In other words, there was nothing to suggest that Pinetti pretended that the blindfold act was real. When he performed in London, it was ignored. It is also clear that he was seen at the time as a conjuror who performed "tricks" and "deceptions" based on "dexterity" and "legerdemain." When he departed London in February 1785, he was hailed as the "first Conjuror of the age [for] his astonishing deceptions" ("London," *Morning Post and Daily Advertiser*, February 19, 1785). Nevertheless, the myth emerged. In his 1859 memoirs, French magician Jean-Eugène Robert-Houdin suggested that Pinetti was a charlatan, referring to the "pretensions to necromancy Pinetti affected" (Robert Shelton Mackenzie, *Robert-Houdin, the Great Wizard, Celebrated French Conjurer, Author, and Ambassador*, translated from the French [Minneapolis, MN: Carl W. Jones, 1944], 90). Robert-Houdin claimed that he had been told this by his mentor, Torrini. However, Torrini was a fictional character invented by Robert-Houdin. Later, Henry Ridgely Evans, who assumed that Torrini was real, claimed that "Pinetti pretended to the occult in

his exhibition of so-called "second-sight" (Evans, *The Old and the New Magic*, 18). And so the myth was born, which went on to gain a life of its own. Recently, it has been claimed that the "trick associated Pinetti with powers at the very limit of what was natural," and Pinetti has been described as "the first fully to exploit supernaturalism" as well as an exemplar of how magic "could fictionalize itself more and more thoroughly. An audience now existed which, at some level, did not care whether Pinetti really was the mysterious figure that he half pretended to be" (Simon During, *Modern Enchantments* [Cambridge, MA: Harvard University Press, 2004], 93–94). The irony is that the audience does not appear to have cared at all.

10 Advertisements from the December 6, 1784, issue onward do not mention the feat.

11 "Theatrical Intelligence," *Morning Herald and Daily Advertiser*, December 4, 1784.

12 Advertisement, *Gazetteer and New Daily Advertiser*, December 9, 1784.

13 It is hard to find any other mention of the blindfold act. Fellow historians of magic, James Smith and Pierre Taillefer, who have also tried to find accounts, have found only the same sources as we did. Another fine historian of magic, Pietro Micheli, has found a broadside from Mitau (now Jelgava, Latvia), at the end of the eighteenth century, which describes Signora Pinetti performing with a blindfold, but it is not clear that this is the same feat (per Peter Lamont's personal communications with Smith, Taillefer, and Micheli). Perhaps a source will appear at some point, but if this had been a successful act, then it presumably would have been easier to find references to it.

14 Experiments with mesmerized subjects who demonstrated "eyeless vision" were being conducted before 1808 and with blindfolds no later than 1814, per Eric Dingwall, ed., *Abnormal Hypnotic Phenomena*, vol. 1, *France* (London: J. & A. Churchill Ltd., 1967), 21ff.

15 Ètienne-Gaspard Robertson, *Mémoires récréatifs, scientifiqu et anecdotiques. Tome deuxième* (Paris: auteur,1833), 322ff.

16 From a playbill in Harry Houdini, *The Unmasking of Robert-Houdin* (New York: The Publishers Printing Company, 1908), 212.

17 The article was reprinted as "The Double-sighted Phenomenon," *Caledonian Mercury*, November 7, 1831.

18 The article was reprinted as "The Double-sighted Phenomenon," *Derby Mercury*, December 7, 1831.

19 From a playbill in Houdini, *The Unmasking of Robert-Houdin*, 221.

20 "Hertford Winter Assizes," *Jackson's Oxford Journal*, December 3, 1831; "London November 28," *Newcastle Courant*, December 3, 1831.

21 "Theatrical Chit-chat," *Morning Chronicle*, January 23, 1832.

22 "The Clarence Vase," *New Monthly Magazine* 36 (May 1, 1832), 210.

23 Newspaper clipping dated March 27, 1833 (Ricky Jay collection).

24 "Curious Case of Assault," *Morning Chronicle*, April 15, 1833.

25 J. C. Colquhoun, *Reports of the Experiments on Animal Magnetism* (Edinburgh: Robert Caddell, 1833), 245–46.

26 On the ongoing argument, see: Peter Lamont, *Extraordinary Beliefs: A Historical Approach to a Psychological Problem* (Cambridge, UK: Cambridge University Press, 2013).

27 The case of Goble is discussed in Lamont, *Extraordinary Beliefs*, 105ff.

28 Ibid.

29 W. B. Carpenter, "Spiritualism and Its Recent Converts," *Quarterly Review* 131, no. 262 (1871), 343.

30 "Mysterious Lady," *The Era*, March 30, 1845, 3; Geoffrey Lamb, *Victorian Magic* (London: Routledge & Kegan Paul, 1976), 66.

31 Christopher, *Illustrated History*, 63.

32 "Mysterious Lady," *Punch* 8 (January–June, 1845), 148; *The Court*, February 19, 1845, 6.

33 *Morning Chronicle*, March 12, 1845.

34 This was claimed around the time (John Ayrton Paris, *Philosophy in Sport Made Science in Earnest* [London: John Murray, 1853], 435) and later framed as genuine "thought-reading" (Edwin Lee, *Animal Magnetism and Magnetic Lucid Somnambulism* [London: Longmans, Green and Co., 1866], 122–23).

35 According to Max Maven's delightful red nose theory of mentalism: if a clown, complete with a red nose and giant shoes, in between the mouth coils and the balloon animals, performs a simple card trick in which he reveals the chosen card, at least one member of the audience will later ask if the clown does private readings (M. Maven, "I'll Build a Stairway to Paradox," *Magic* 5, no. 2 [October, 1995], 23).

36 Dawes, *Great Illusionists*, 110.

37 Biographical details have been taken from E. P. Hingston, *Biography of Professor Anderson: Sketches from His Note-book* (Birmingham, UK: John Tonks, 1858); Frost, *Lives of the Conjurors*; Anon., "The Wizard of the North: The Life Story of John Henry Anderson," *The People's Journal* (June 1, 1901); J. B. Findlay, *Anderson and His Theatre* (Shanklin, UK: 1967); and Dawes, *Great Illusionists*. Some of the quirkier elements were previously described in Peter Lamont, *The First Psychic: The Peculiar Mystery of a Notorious Victorian Wizard* (London: Little, Brown, 2005), 54ff.

38 J. H. Anderson, *The Magic of Spirit Rapping* (c. 1854), 92.

39 The earliest references to the trick seem to be in the 1830s. It is mentioned in A. B. Engstrom, *The Humorous Magician Unmasked* (Philadelphia: 1836), 88–90, and there is a print from around that time of Anderson performing the trick (Edwin A. Dawes, "Mary Toft, the rabbit breeder of Goldaming, and the origin of the rabbit in the hat trick: a critical assessment. Part two," in Dawes, *A Rich Cabinet of Magical Curiosities*, 651).

40 Dawes, *Great Illusionists*, 111.

41 Constance Pole Bayer, *The Great Wizard of the North* (Watertown, MA: Ray Goulet's Magic Art Book Co., 1990), 52.

42 Dawes, *Great Illusionists*, 112.

CHAPTER 5: SEPARATE SPHERES

1 Henry Mayhew, *London Labour and the London Poor*, vol. III (London: Griffin, Bohn, and Company, 1861), 107–13.

2 Dawes, *Great Illusionists*, 73–79.

3 Clarke, *Annals*, 152.

4 Lamb, *Victorian Magic*, 32.

5 "The Theatre," *Morning Post*, February 2, 1844.

6 John Forbes, "Illustrations of Modern Mesmerism from Personal Investigations," *Provincial Medical & Surgical Journal* 9, no. 49 (December 1845): 277–78.

7 David Brewster, *Letters on Natural Magic* (London: John Murray, 1832), 6.

8 Peter Lamont and Crispin Bates, "Conjuring Images of India in Nineteenth-Century Britain," *Social History* 32, no. 3 (August 2007): 309–25.

9 William Hazlitt, "The Indian Jugglers," in *Table Talk; or, Original Essays* (London: John Warren, 1821), 181.

10 Anonymous, "Hindoo Jugglers" (n.d.), 165; I. Platts, *Book of Curiosities* (London: Henry Fisher, 1822), 897. See also: "Indian Jugglers," *Chambers's Edinburgh Journal* (November 28, 1835): 351; "Jugglers of India," *Chambers's Edinburgh Journal* (March 16, 1839): 69.

11 "Chinese Jugglers," *Morning Post*, January 17, 1817.

12 Advertisement, *Caledonian Mercury*, January 19, 1822.

13 "Theatres and Music," *John Bull*, April 1, 1854.

14 Clarke, *Annals*, 286.

15 Ibid.

16 Dawes, *Great Illusionists*, 131.

17 Ibid., 170.

18 For a full account of Dickens and magic, see: Ian Keable, *Charles Dickens Magician: Conjuring in Life, Letters and Literature* (self-pub., 2014).

19 "The Japanese Jugglers," *Times (UK)*, February 14, 1867, 10.

20 Wilkie Collins, *The Moonstone* (New York: Harper and Brothers, 1868), 100.

21 "The Air Brahmin," *The Saturday Magazine*, July 28, 1832, 28.

22 "Indian Impostors and Jugglers," *Leisure Hour* no. 155 (December 14, 1854), 791–94.

23 Richard Davenport, *Sketches of Imposture, Deception and Credulity* (London: Thomas Tegg and Son, 1837), 287–88.

24 Hobart Caunter, *The Oriental Annual, or Scenes in India* (London: Edward Bull, 1834), 25–27.

25 "Juggling, Wizarding, and Similar Phenomena," *Family Herald* vol. 13 (1855), 349–59.

26 Edward William Lane, *An Account of the Manners and Customs of the Modern Egyptians. 5th edition* (London: John Murray, 1860), 385–86.

27 Justus Doolittle, *Social Life of the Chinese: a Daguerreotype of Daily Life in China* (London: Sampson Low, Son and Marston, 1868), 543–44.

28 "A Chinese Juggler," *Newcastle Daily Journal*, January 19, 1861, 3.

29 "Chinese Jugglers," *The Australian Journal*, December 19, 1868, 263. For a fuller discussion of Chinese and Japanese magic at home and abroad, see Chris Goto-Jones's recent book *Conjuring Asia: Magic, Orientalism, and the Making of the Modern World* (Cambridge, UK: Cambridge University Press, 2016).

30 Lamont and Bates, "Conjuring Images of India."

31 Charles Joseph Pecor, "The Magician on the American Stage, 1752–1874" (PhD thesis, 1976), 60–66.

32 Ibid., 103.

33 The first successful native-born American conjuror, Jacob Philadelphia, does not appear to have performed in America but had remarkable success in Europe.

34 Pecor, "Magician on the American Stage," 108ff, 161, 404.

35 Ibid., 173.

36 Ibid., 110.

37 D. Price, *Magic: A Pictorial History of Conjurers in the Theater* (New York: Cornwall Books, 1985), 52.

38 Christopher, *Illustrated History*, 65–68.

39 Pecor, "Magician on the American Stage," 131, 150.

40 P. T. Barnum, *The Life of P. T. Barnum* (London: Sampson Low, Son and Co., 1855), 193.

41 Antonio Blitz, *Fifty Years in the Magic Circle* (Hartford, CT: Belknap and Bliss, 1871), 139–40.

42 During, *Modern Enchantments*, 108.

43 For an example of the latter, see: Karen Beckman, *Vanishing Women: Magic, Film, and Feminism* (Durham, NC: Duke University Press, 2003). For an example of the former, just use your imagination.

44 Pecor, "Magician on the American Stage," 219–46.

45 Alex Owen, *The Darkened Room: Women, Power, and Spiritualism in Late Victorian England* (London: Virago Press, 1989).

46 Ibid., 10.

47 "Robert-Houdin's Soirées Fantastiques," *Morning Chronicle*, June 2, 1848.

48 "St James Theatre," *Morning Post*, May 3, 1848.

49 "St James," *Standard*, December 27, 1848.

50 Sam Sharpe, *Salutations to Robert-Houdin* (Calgary: M. Hades International, 1983), 28.

51 Pecor, "Magician on the American Stage," 285–86.

52 Ibid., 290.

53 Anderson, *The Magic of Spirit Rapping*, 68–74.

CHAPTER 6: THE CONFESSIONS

1 Robert Shelton Mackenzie, *Robert-Houdin, The Great Wizard, Celebrated French Conjurer, Author, and Ambassador,* translated from the French (Minneapolis: Carl W. Jones, 1944), xi-xii. This is one of many English language editions of Robert-Houdin's book, commonly called *The Memoirs of Robert-Houdin*, with a translation by Lascelles Wraxall.

2 "Robert Houdin," *Mahatma* Magazine 1, no. 1 (March 1895).

3 John Mulholland, *John Mulholland's Story of Magic* (New York: Loring & Mussey, 1935).

4 Christian Fechner, *The Magic of Robert-Houdin* (Boulogne: Editions F.C.F., 2002).

5 This recent construction by Stephen L. Macknik and Susana Martinez-Conde with Sandra Blakeslee, *Sleights of Mind* (New York: Henry Holt, 2011), included a remarkable leap of faith about Louis Napoleon.

6 Mackenzie, *Robert-Houdin, The Great Wizard*.

7 Ibid., 10. Curiously, although it isn't commented upon, Carlosbach reads like a fictional character. He entertained the audience and began to sell them an all-powerful balm; in other words, he was a typical mountebank, what would

later be called a snake oil salesman. But Carlosbach suddenly shifted gears, criticized the audience for being gullible, and instead sold them booklets on magic. Dramatically, Carlosbach predestined Robert-Houdin's own honest approach to his art. In other words, Carlosbach's lesson was that it takes a magician to understand credulity and expose it.

8 When later writing about this incident, Houdini stumbled over identifying this book, but Robert-Houdin's original copy still exists and was described in Fechner, *The Magic of Robert-Houdin*, vol. 1, 31.

9 Magicians' automata are often ignored in books on the subject of clockwork machinery, but the subject was addressed in Adolphe Blind, *Les Automats Truques* (Geneva, Paris: Edition Ch. Eggimann, Editions Bossard, 1927), and the Acrobat in the Box (sometimes the Harlequin in the Box) was described in a number of books, including Vere, *Ancient and Modern Magic*, which appears as the appendix in Louis Hoffmann, *Modern Magic* (New York: George Routledge and Sons, 1882). Author Jim Steinmeyer has worked with John Gaughan, who restored and demonstrated authentic Robert-Houdin automata (Antonio Diavolo, the trapeze artist) and reconstructed others, like the Orange Tree.

10 Jim Steinmeyer, *Hiding the Elephant* (New York: Caroll & Graf, 2003). Robert-Houdin's description of the Sawing in Half trick, attributed to Torrini, is one of the strangest elements of the tale.

11 Jean Chavigny, *Le Roman d'un Artiste, Robert-Houdin, Renovateur de la Magie Blanche* (Orleans, FR: Imprimerie Industrielle d'Orleans, 1969).

12 Fechner, *The Magic of Robert-Houdin*, vol. 1, 49.

13 This chapter was first translated into English by Philip Hayden of Columbia University and reproduced serially in *The Sphinx*, from October 1932 to February 1933. It was then incorporated into the Carl Jones edition of *The Memoirs of Robert-Houdin*. Christian Fechner discussed this chapter in Fechner, *The Magic of Robert-Houdin*, vol. 1, 50.

14 Fechner, *The Magic of Robert-Houdin*, vol. 1, 153.

15 I'm grateful for the insights of John Gaughan, who has had a chance to examine a number of intricate automata, including the Droz figures. These automata are described in Sam H. Sharpe, *Salutations to Robert-Houdin* (Calgary: Micky Hades International, 1983). The Maillardet figure was restored in 2007 and is exhibited at the Franklin Institute in Philadelphia. The Droz figures are exhibited at the Musée d'Art et d'Histoire in Neuchâtel, Switzerland. Christian Fechner's *The Magic of Robert-Houdin* discovered an inventory taken at the time of the death of Robert-Houdin's first wife and noticed

parts for multiple writing figures. He suspected that Robert-Houdin produced more than one of these figures and was cutting cams for the drawings into his retirement, though it seems highly unlikely that there had been multiple copies.

16 Mackenzie, *Robert-Houdin, The Great Wizard*, 223–25.

17 "Memoirs of Robert-Houdin," *The Saturday Review of Politics, Literature, Science, Art, and Finance*, January 14, 1860.

18 "King of Conjurers," *Harper's New Monthly Magazine*, November 1877. The article was written by actress Olive Logan.

19 Fechner, *The Magic of Robert-Houdin*, vol. 1, 249–53.

20 There are a number of mixed messages offered in Robert-Houdin's assessment of Philippe. "A gentleman dressed in black emerges from a side door and walks towards us. It is Philippe: I recognize him by the provincial twang of his accent. All the other spectators take him for the manager...." In other words, he's dressed in evening clothes. "Philippe was in great trouble about performing [the bowl trick], for he wanted a robe. He could not assume a Chinese costume, as his face had none of the distinguishing characteristics of a Mandarin, nor could he dream of a dressing gown, for however rich it might have been, the public would not have endured such a slight. Hence Philippe extricated himself from the difficulty by assuming the attire of a magician. It was a daring innovation, for till that period, no conjurer had ventured to take on himself the responsibility of such a costume." Yet later in the book, Robert-Houdin pretended that a wizard's robe was an old-fashioned, bizarre costume onstage. From Mackenzie, *Robert-Houdin, The Great Wizard*.

21 Sharpe, *Salutations to Robert-Houdin*, 124.

22 Fechner, *The Magic of Robert-Houdin*, vol. 1, 253.

23 The Pastry Cook had a person ingeniously concealed inside—in this case the magician's small son. It's an old-fashioned principle dating from one of the earliest trick automata, the Chess Player. In the Pastry Cook, there are several pieces of automata, spring-driven figures, that roll out dough or prepare the pastries and can be seen working through the windows. Today this beautiful piece of Robert-Houdin apparatus is in the collection of David Copperfield.

24 Sharpe, *Salutations to Robert-Houdin*, 27.

25 Mackenzie, *Robert-Houdin, The Great Wizard*, 393.

26 Jean-Eugène Robert-Houdin, *The Secrets of Conjuring and Magic, or How to Become a Wizard*, ed. and trans. Louis Hoffman (London: George Routeledge & Sons, 1878), 43.

Chapter 7: The Unmasking

1 There is no lack of Houdini biographies. The most recent, William Kalush and Larry Sloman, *The Secret Life of Houdini* (New York: Atria Books, 2006), addresses many of the genuine puzzles of his personality.

2 Houdini, *The Unmasking of Robert-Houdin*, 7. One of the silliest charges that Houdini made was that Robert-Houdin used a ghostwriter to write his book. It's evident that Houdini used ghostwriters throughout his career, as he did to refine the Robert-Houdin articles when they were turned into his finished book. The original articles feel quite different and certainly don't contain learned references to Blackstone, Hardee, or Bismarck. Recent examinations of the manuscripts of Robert-Houdin clearly indicate that he did not use a ghostwriter.

3 Mackenzie, *Robert-Houdin, The Great Wizard*, 53.

4 These accounts are from quotations found in Robert-Houdin, *The Memoirs of Robert-Houdin*; Henry Ridgely Evans's "Introduction: The Mysteries of Modern Magic," in Albert Allis Hopkins, ed., *Magic, Stage Illusions and Scientific Diversions* (London: Low, 1897); Henry Ridgely Evans, *Adventures in Magic* (New York: Leo Rullman, 1927); John Mulholland, *John Mulholland's Story of Magic* (New York: Loring & Mussey, 1935); Walter Gibson, *The Master Magicians* (Garden City, NY: Doubleday & Company, 1966); and Christopher, *Illustrated History*.

5 Mackenzie, *Robert-Houdin, The Great Wizard*, viii; this is from the editor's preface.

6 Evans, *Adventures in Magic*, 67.

7 Mulholland, *John Mulholland's Story of Magic*, 32.

8 Evans, *Adventures in Magic*, 67.

9 Mulholland, *John Mulholland's Story of Magic*, 34.

10 Christopher, *Illustrated History*, 148.

11 Ibid, 148.

12 These last three analogies to Robert-Houdin's tricks are suggested by Christopher, *Illustrated History*, 149.

13 Christopher, *Illustrated History*, 149.

14 Gibson, *Master Magicians*, 41.

15 Christopher, *Illustrated History*, 149.

16 Gibson, *Master Magicians*, 42.

17 Christopher, *Illustrated History*, 149.

18 Gibson, *Master Magicians*, 42.

19 Ibid.

20 Ibid.

21 Frost, *Lives of the Conjurors*, 290.

22 Gibson, *Master Magicians*, 42.

23 Christopher, *Illustrated History*, 149.

24 Ibid., 151.

25 Mulholland, *John Mulholland's Story of Magic*, 34.

26 Henry Ridgely Evans, "Introduction: The Mysteries of Modern Magic," in Hopkins, ed., *Magic, Stage Illusions and Scientific Diversions*, 18.

27 Frost, *Lives of the Conjurors*, 292.

28 "Robert Houdin," *Mahatma* Magazine 1, no. 1 (March 1895), 1.

29 Mackenzie, *Robert-Houdin, The Great Wizard*, 393.

30 Ibid., 394–95.

31 Ibid., 395.

32 *The Globe and Traveller*, September 20, 1856, 1. This is one of very few contemporary accounts that give evidence of the incident.

33 The account that follows is the magician's own, from Mackenzie, *Robert-Houdin, The Great Wizard*, 393–441, except where noted.

34 Jean-Eugène Robert-Houdin, *The Secrets of Stage Conjuring* (London: George Routledge & Sons, 1881). In his account of the trick in this book, Robert-Houdin described the Paris performance, which was a different presentation from Algeria.

35 The trick is described in Hoffmann, *Modern Magic*, 449; Christopher, *Illustrated History*, 149; as well as in Fechner, *The Magic of Robert-Houdin*.

36 This brief judgment of Robert-Houdin's performance appeared in *Le Moniteur Algerien*, November 5, 1856; the article was reproduced in Michel Seldow, *Vie et Secrets de Robert-Houdin* (Paris: Fayard, 1971).

37 The translation and comments are from Graham M. Jones, "Modern Magic and the War on Miracles in French Colonial Culture," *Comparative Studies in Society and History* 52, no. 1 (January 2010): 66–99.

38 Robert-Houdin explained the trick in his account; he had used a bullet mold to cast wax bullets, blackened with soot and filled with blood drawn from his own thumb.

39 Noted by Jones, "Modern Magic and the War on Miracles," 74.

40 J. Joseph-Renaud, "Contribution to the Establishment of a Biography of Robert-Houdin," *Journal de la Prestiditation* 106 (March–April 1939), quoted by Fechner, *The Magic of Robert-Houdin*.

41 The *Le Moniteur Universel* article was reproduced in Seldow, *Vie et Secrets de Robert-Houdin*. The text in the article suggests that it was first published in *Le Droit*, which was a law journal. English versions of the article appeared in

various English-language publications, including in *The London Observer*, October 11, 1857, and *The Brooklyn Evening Star*, October 29, 1857.

42 Quoted from *Le Moniteur Universel*, reproduced in Seldow, *Vie et Secrets de Robert-Houdin*; "New System of (French) Government Tactics in Algeria," *The London Observer*, October 11, 1857.

43 Houdini was quick to make judgments throughout his text: "I have spoken to quite a number of men who were in a position to understand magic, and saw Houdin perform quite a number of times in Paris and England. Henry Evanion witnessed every performance of Houdin during his entire first engagement [in London] . . . the combined opinion of these men was that Houdin was not original, and that he was only a little above average entertainer." And, "[My] letter was delivered . . . to Mrs. E. R. Houdin. She did not answer. . . . Personally, I think she should have shown a little common courtesy to the memory of Robert Houdin, especially as she is now living in her old age on the proceeds of his endeavors, as she received 35,000 francs several years ago for the Theatre R. Houdin." *Conjurer's Monthly Magazine*, September 15, 1906. Houdini's apparent rudeness with the family might be tempered by a recent revelation: when he was later introduced to Robert-Houdin's surviving daughter, he identified himself, through the interpreter, as "Monsieur Harry." He was evidently aware of the sensitivity of using the family name as his own. This is recounted in Fechner, *The Magic of Robert-Houdin*, vol. 3.

44 *Conjurer's Monthly Magazine*, September 1906–April 1908.

45 Houdini, *The Unmasking of Robert-Houdin*, 295.

46 Ibid., 318.

47 Milbourne Christopher, from articles that originally appeared in *Hugard's Magic Monthly*, compiled as Jean Hugard, *Houdini's "Unmasking": Fact vs. Fiction* (York, PA: Magicana for Collectors, 1989).

48 Originally published in *The Wizard*, July 1908; reproduced in Hugard, *Houdini's "Unmasking."*

49 As discussed in the previous chapter, Fechner, *The Magic of Robert-Houdin*.

50 Readers of the *Memoirs*, who had been introduced to Robert-Houdin's contemporaries as old-fashioned, would be surprised that Philippe was only three years older than Robert-Houdin. John Henry Anderson, who was represented as a relentless old "charlatan," was actually nine years younger than the French magician. Even P. T. Barnum was five years younger. By suggesting that Philippe was using old material and portraying Anderson's desperate advertising as a thing of the past, it gave the impression that Robert-Houdin was an innovator and a wellspring of good taste. Anderson's humbug advertising techniques were then a modern style.

51 The workings of the Orange Tree are very efficiently described in Hoffmann, *Modern Magic*. Our friend John Gaughan's modern re-creation has added finer touches to the mechanism, which must give a more delicate effect. For example, his choice was to push the blossoms through small tubes, so they open as they appear; the irises for the oranges are built in two parts, so that they split open like a vertical eyelid instead of one hemisphere that revolves around the orange. Our description here is a mixture of the original mechanism, from *Modern Magic*, and Gaughan's modern version.

52 Seldow, *Vie et Secrets de Robert-Houdin*, 98.

53 Jean-Eugène Robert-Houdin, *The Secrets of Stage Conjuring* (London: George Routledge & Sons, 1881), 62; Mackenzie, *Robert-Houdin, The Great Wizard*, 216.

54 Sharpe, *Salutations to Robert-Houdin*, 101.

55 Gibson, *The Master Magicians*, 28, 29.

56 Robert-Houdin, *The Secrets of Stage Conjuring*, 54–61.

57 Mackenzie, *Robert-Houdin, The Great Wizard*, 223–24.

CHAPTER 8: THE GOLDEN AGE

1 Theodore Bamberg and Robert Parrish, *Okito on Magic* (Chicago: Edward O. Drane and Company, 1952); and Peter Warlock, *Buatier de Kolta, Genius of Illusion* (Pasadena, CA: Magical Publications, 1993).

2 There is considerable controversy about the origin of Black Art. More than likely, the early principle was preceded in techniques during Pepper's Ghost, which, as will be discussed, was an illusion using a sheet of glass for reflection, but depended on the clever use of black velvet to visually isolate the reflected images. It was then used by Dr. Lynn, who performed at Egyptian Hall and who knew de Kolta when the French magician first came to London. At the same time that de Kolta introduced the effect in London, a German magician, Max Auzinger, performed as Ben Ali Bey and used the principle extensively in an elaborate act. The controversies are discussed in Steinmeyer, *Hiding the Elephant*, and Jim Steinmeyer, *The Science Behind the Ghost!* (Burbank, CA: Hahne, 1999).

3 *The Magician Monthly*, November 1913, 185.

4 Johann Hofzinser, *Non Plus Ultra*, 2 vols., Magic Christian, ed. (Seattle: Hermetic Press, Inc. and Conjuring Arts Research Center, 2013).

5 Ibid., 1:289.

6 Ibid., 1:253.

7 Steinmeyer, *The Science Behind the Ghost*, 26–7.

8 Ibid., 29.

9 Frikell's career is discussed in Houdini, *The Unmasking of Robert-Houdin*, and Clarke, *Annals*.

10 Verbeck is discussed in Clarke, *Annals*.

11 The Davenport brothers are discussed in Steinmeyer, *Hiding the Elephant*.

12 Maskelyne's career, theaters, and shows are discussed in ibid.

13 Devant's work is from ibid., and S. H. Sharpe, *Devant's Delightful Delusions* (Pasadena, CA: Magical Publications, 1990).

14 David Devant, *My Magic Life* (London: Hutchinson & Co., 1931).

15 Jean-Pierre Moynet, *L'Envers du Théâtre* (Paris: Librairie Hachette, 1875).

16 Percy Fitzgerald, *The World Behind the Scenes* (New York: Benjamin Blom, 1881).

17 Georges Moynet, *Trucs et Décor* (Paris: Librairie Illustrée, 1893).

18 Albert A. Hopkins, ed., *Magic, Stage Illusions and Scientific Diversions* (New York: Munn and Company, 1897).

19 According to the tradition of the Magic Circle, the famous London magic club, Maskelyne was involved in the production of the famous electrical duel between Faust and Valentine in Irving's famous 1885 production of *Faust*. The swords seemed to glow and spark with electric charges during the swordfight. Officially, Colonel Gouraud, one of Thomas Edison's associates, has been credited with the special effect.

20 Sharpe, *Devant's Delightful Delusions*.

21 Warlock, *Buatier de Kolta*.

22 Anne Davenport and John Salisse, *St. George's Hall* (Pasadena, CA: Mike Caveney's Magic Words, 2001).

23 Hoffmann, *Modern Magic*, 278.

24 Louis Hoffmann, *More Magic* (London: George Routledge and Sons, 1890).

25 Louis Hoffmann, *Later Magic* (London: George Routledge and Sons, 1904), 307. There was also a fourth book published, a lesser compilation titled *Latest Magic*.

26 Nevil Maskelyne and David Devant, *Our Magic* (London: George Routledge and Sons, 1911), v.

27 Devant, *My Magic Life*, 90.

28 Will Goldston, *Secrets of Famous Illusionists* (London: John Long Limited, 1933), 158.

29 Sharpe, *Devant's Delightful Delusions*.

30 David Devant, *Secrets of My Magic* (London: Hutchinson & Co., 1936).

31 Maskelyne and Devant, *Our Magic*, vi.

32 Ian Keable, *The Writings of David Devant* (privately printed by the author, 1997).

33 Davenport and Salisse, *St. George's Hall*.

34 Sharpe, *Devant's Delightful Delusions*.

35 Previous reports suggested that Devant's malady was a symptom of syphilis; it's now apparent that the symptoms of his illness suggest Parkinson's disease, often diagnosed at the time as "paralysis agitans." Paul Murray, *From the Shadow of Dracula* (London: Pimlico, 2005).

Chapter 9: Variety

1 Jim Steinmeyer, *The Glorious Deception* (New York: Carroll & Graf, 2005); Douglas Gilbert, *American Vaudeville: Its Life and Times* (New York: Dover Publications, 1940); Frank Cullen with Forence Hackman and Donald Mc-Neilly, *Vaudeville Old and New*, 2 vols. (New York: Routledge, 2007).

2 Steinmeyer, *The Glorious Deception*.

3 Ibid.

4 Margaret Steele, ed., *Adelaide Herrmann, Queen of Magic* (Wilton Manors, FL: Bramble Books, 2012).

5 Steinmeyer, *The Glorious Deception*.

6 Mike Caveney and Bill Miesel, *Kellar's Wonders* (Pasadena, CA: Mike Caveney's Magic Words, 2003).

7 Steinmeyer, *Hiding the Elephant*, 149.

8 Harold Kellock, *Houdini: His Life Story* (New York: Harcourt, Brace & Company, 1928), 125.

9 Jim Steinmeyer, *The Last Greatest Magician in the World* (New York: Tarcher, 2011).

10 Ibid.

11 Steinmeyer, *The Glorious Deception*; Eric Lewis and Peter Warlock, *P. T. Selbit: Magical Innovator* (Pasadena, CA: Magical Publications, 1989).

12 Steinmeyer, *Hiding the Elephant*.

13 George Jenness, *Maskelyne and Cooke: Egyptian Hall, London* (Enfield, Middlesex: self-pub., 1967).

14 Steele, *Adelaide Herrmann*.

15 Ibid., 208.

16 Ibid., 256.

17 Edwin Dawes, *Stodare: The Enigma Variations* (Washington, DC: Kaufman and Company, 1998).

18 Lewis and Warlock, *P. T. Selbit.*
19 Steinmeyer, *Hiding the Elephant.*
20 Steinmeyer, *Hiding the Elephant*; Jim Steinmeyer, *Art & Artifice* (New York: Avalon, 1998).
21 *The Sphinx Magazine*, December 1922.
22 Ibid., June 1921.
23 Kalush and Sloman, *The Secret Life of Houdini.*
24 Paolo Cherchi Usai, ed., *A Trip to the Movies* (Rochester: International Museum of Photography at George Eastman House, 1991).
25 Devant, *My Magic Life.*
26 Usai, *A Trip to the Movies.*
27 Guy E. Jarrett and Jim Steinmeyer, *The Complete Jarrett* (Burbank, CA: Hahne, 2001), 58.
28 Steinmeyer, *The Last Greatest Magician in the World.*
29 Ibid., 310–12.

CHAPTER 10: THOUGHT TRANSMISSIONS

1 Murray Leeder, *The Modern Supernatural and the Beginnings of Cinema* (London: Palgrave Macmillan, 2017), 88.
2 Barry H. Wiley, *The Thought Reader Craze* (Jefferson, NC: McFarland & Company, 2012), 45.
3 Ibid., 60.
4 Barry H. Wiley, *The Indescribable Phenomenon* (Seattle: Hermetic Press, 2005), 115.
5 Ibid., 129.
6 This experiment, which took place on February 19, 1875, was one of several experiments using a galvanometer, with different mediums.
7 Wiley, *Indescribable Phenomenon*, 200.
8 Ibid., 206.
9 W. B. Carpenter, "*Re* W. I. Bishop," *Nature* 24 (June 1881): 188–89.
10 George J. Romanes, "Thought-Reading," *Nature* 24 (June 1881): 171–72.
11 Ibid.
12 Carpenter, "*Re* W. I. Bishop," 188.
13 "The Exposure of Spiritism," *Scotsman*, January 17, 1879, 4.
14 For more on this and what it tells us about the nature of belief, see Lamont, *Extraordinary Beliefs.*
15 Wiley, *Thought Reader Craze*, 90.

16 Thomson Whyte, "*Re* W. I. Bishop," *Nature* 24 (July 1881): 211.

17 William Barrett, "Mind-reading versus Muscle-reading," *Nature* 24 (July 1881): 212.

18 For more on the relationship between physics and psychical research, see: Roger Luckhurst, *The Invention of Telepathy* (Oxford, UK: Oxford University Press, 2001), 75–92; Richard Noakes, "The "Bridge Which Is between Physical and Psychical Research": William Fletcher Barrett, Sensitive Flames, and Spiritualism," *History of Science* 42, no. 4 (December 2004): 419–64.

19 Wiley, *Thought Reader Craze*, 90.

20 "For the Bishop Autopsy," *New York Times*, June 29, 1892, 8.

21 Alfred Binet, "Psychology of Prestidigitation," *Annual Report of the Board of Regents of the Smithsonian Institution* 49 (1894): 555–71.

22 Joseph Jastrow, "Psychological Notes upon Sleight-of-Hand Experts," *Science* 3, no. 71 (May 1896): 686–89.

23 Norman Triplett, "The Psychology of Conjuring Deceptions," *American Journal of Psychology* 11, no. 4 (July 1900): 439–510.

24 Binet, "Psychology of Prestidigitation," 564.

25 Triplett, "The Psychology of Conjuring Deceptions," 453.

26 Thomas A. Sawyer, *S. S. Baldwin and the Press* (Santa Ana, CA: Thomas A. Sawyer, 1993), 45, 71.

27 Wiley, *Thought Reader Craze*, 135–37.

28 David Charvet, *Alexander: The Man Who Knows* (Pasadena, CA: Mike Caveney's Magic Words), 133.

29 Ibid., 143–48.

30 Ibid., 160, 221–25.

31 Lamont, *Extraordinary Beliefs*, 191–94.

32 Sungook Hong, "Syntony and Credibility: John Ambrose Fleming, Guglielmo Marconi, and the Maskelyne Affair," *Scientific Credibility and Technical Standards in 19th and Early 20th century Germany and Britain* (1996), 157–73.

33 Ibid., 167.

34 Bob Nelson was a performer, author, and businessman and one of the key figures in mentalism in the twentieth century.

35 Jeffrey Sconce, *Haunted Media: Electronic Presence from Telegraphy to Television* (Durham, NC: Duke University Press, 2000), 77.

36 Ibid., 116.

37 Lamont, *Extraordinary Beliefs*, 220.

38 Ibid., 221–23.

39 Seymour H. Mauskopf and Michael R. McVaugh, *The Elusive Science* (Baltimore: The Johns Hopkins University Press, 1980), 305.

40 Joseph Dunninger, *The Art of Thought Reading* (Evanston, IL: Clark Publishing Company, 1962), 4–6.

41 Joseph Dunninger, *Dunninger's Complete Encyclopedia of Magic* (London: The Hamlyn Group Limited, 1967), 288.

CHAPTER 11: BEFORE YOUR EYES

1 Jarrett and Steinmeyer, *The Complete Jarrett*, 58.

2 Steve Burton and Richard Kaufman, eds., *The Tarbell Course in Magic*, vol. 8 (Brooklyn, NY: D. Robbins & Co. Inc., 1993).

3 Author Jim Steinmeyer grew up just miles away from Tarbell's home in Elmhurst, Illinois, and was lucky to know friends of Tarbell, including Vic Torsberg, Robert Parrish, and Alton Sharpe.

4 Harlan Tarbell, *The Tarbell Course in Magic*, vol. 3 (New York: Louis Tannen Inc., 1943), 22.

5 Tarbell, *The Tarbell Course in Magic*, 3, 53.

6 *Thayer's Quality Magic, Catalog Number 8* (1936).

7 *Goldston's Magical Quarterly* 3, no. 1 (Summer 1936).

8 Al Baker Interview, typed transcript in the Conjuring Arts Research Center, June 7, 1941, 2.

9 James William Elliott, Clinton Burgess, Harry Houdini, *Elliott's Last Legacy* (New York: Adams Press Print, 1923).

10 David Ben, *Dai Vernon: A Biography* (Chicago: Squash Publishing, 2006).

11 Darwin Ortiz, ed., *The Annotated Erdnase* (Pasadena, CA: Magical Publications, 1991).

12 Ibid., 24.

13 Ibid., 146.

14 Ibid., 28.

15 Ibid. Candidates are also discussed in Marty Demarest, "Montana's Conjurers, Con Men, and Card Cheats: Wilbur E. Sanders, S. W. Erdnase, and 'The Expert at the Card Table,'" *Montana: The Magazine of Western History* 63, no. 4 (Winter 2013): 3–27, 88–93.

16 David Charvet, *Jarrow: The Humorist Trickster* (Lake Oswego, Oregon: Charvet Studios, 2013).

17 Max Holden, *Programmes of Famous Magicians* (Chicago: Magic Inc., 1968); and Christopher, *Illustrated History*.

18 Vernon's routine was described in Lewis Ganson, *The Dai Vernon Book of Magic* (London: Harry Stanley, 1957). Video of Vernon performing the trick is available online.

19 The Close-Up Room at the Magic Castle, a small room with less than twenty chairs arranged in front of a table, is probably the most famous purpose-built spaces for this sort of magic, and has hosted many famous magicians.

20 Ali Bongo, in a conversation with Jim Steinmeyer.

21 Christopher, *Illustrated History*, 427.

22 Hyla Clark, *The World's Greatest Magic* (New York: Crown Publishers, 1976), 110.

23 Jon Racherbaumer, *In a Class by Himself: The Legacy of Don Alan* (Tahoma, California: L&L Publishers, 1996).

24 "Doug Henning's World of Magic," broadcast on NBC television on NBC, December 26, 1975.

25 Jim Steinmeyer invented the idea of making the Statue of Liberty disappear, as well as the secret used to accomplish it; magician David Copperfield later made arrangements with him to perform it on his television special. T. A. Waters, "Jim Steinmeyer: Deviser of Illusions," *MAGIC Magazine*, September 1996.

26 Mark Wilson, in conversation with Jim Steinmeyer.

27 Mackenzie, *Robert-Houdin, The Great Wizard*, 129.

28 Jim Steinmeyer was a consultant for two of Ricky Jay's New York shows, *Ricky Jay and His 52 Assistants* and *Ricky Jay: On the Stem*.

29 Charles Fort, *The Book of the Damned: The Collected Works of Charles Fort* (New York: Jeremy Tarcher, 2008), 993.

30 Yif, the magician, waged a publicity campaign within the magic community to make the claim that he wasn't using trick photography in online videos. Richard Kaufman, editor of *Genii: The Conjurers' Magazine*, was sent videos and explanations from Yif.

31 Maskelyne and Devant, *Our Magic*, 200.

32 Mackenzie, *Robert-Houdin, The Great Wizard*, 64.

33 Ortiz, *The Annotated Erdnase*, 196.

34 Maskelyne and Devant, *Our Magic*, 201.

35 All quotations in this section from Will Houstoun, in interviews with the author, July 2017, unless noted otherwise.

36 All quotations in this section from Alba, in interviews with the author, July 2017, unless noted otherwise.

37 All quotations in this section from Alex Ramon, in interviews with the author, September 2017, unless noted otherwise.

38 All quotations in this section from Yann Frisch, in interviews with the author, August–September 2017, unless noted otherwise.

39 Henry Hay, *The Amateur Magician's Handbook* (New York: Thomas Y. Crowell Company, 1972), x.

CHAPTER 12: THE REAL SECRETS OF MAGIC

1 There is a version included in Hoffmann, *Modern Magic*, 313–15, but it is not described as a notable trick, and it is pointed out that one might use instead a guinea pig or a small kitten.

2 Harlan Tarbell, *The Tarbell Course in Magic*, vol. 5 (New York: Louis Tannen, 1948), 211; Devant, *Secrets of My Magic*, 72. In 1896, Devant was filmed performing the Mysterious Rabbit, using trick photography to pull a series of rabbits from a hat.

3 "Lord Curzon in Manchester," *Times (UK)*, January 5, 1910, 6.

4 "Tesreau Gives Two Hits in Brooklyn," *New York Times*, April 27, 1915.

5 "Confidence and Common Sense," *New York Times*, December 9, 1931. In 1938, a Clifford Berryman cartoon, entitled *Old Reliable*, showed FDR producing a rabbit (with the word "spending" written on it) from a hat.

6 "Modern Magicians Must Use Finesse," *Billboard*, December 1, 1928, 40.

7 Peter Lamont and Richard Wiseman, *Magic in Theory*, 169–75.

8 Edwin A. Dawes, "The Mystery (?) of 'She,'" in *A Rich Cabinet of Magical Curiosities*, 139–42.

9 George Alexander Stevens, *A Lecture on Heads* (Dublin: William Porter, 1788), 27.

10 When Robert-Houdin produced four military plumes, each a foot and a half in length, he had secretly "place[d] two of these plumes in each coat-sleeve."

11 Robert-Houdin, *The Secrets of Conjuring and Magic*, 72.

12 Edwin A. Dawes, "Dr. John Watkins Holden: The Wandering Wizard," in *A Rich Cabinet of Magical Curiosities*, 1434. De Kolta used to tuck up his sleeves before making a birdcage disappear from his hands.

13 John Northern Hilliard, *Greater Magic* (Minneapolis: Carl Waring Jones, 1938), 592; J. B. Bobo, *Modern Coin Magic* (Minneapolis, MN: Carl W. Jones, 1952), 50.

14 Peter Lamont, "A Particular Kind of Wonder: The Experience of Magic Past and Present," *Review of General Psychology* 21, no. 1 (March 2017): 1–8.

INDEX

Aaron, 3–5
Acrobat in the Box trick, 126
Adam and Eve, 7
Adams, John Quincy, 111
Ady, Thomas, 5
Aerial Treasury, 220
Aissawa, 170–171
Alan, Don, 284–285
Alba, 296–298
Alciphron, 13
Alexander, the Man Who Knows,
    261–263, 265
Algeria, 122–123, 146, 148, 152–176, 178,
    180, 183, 184
Ali Ben Bay, 217
Anderson, John Henry "Great Wizard of
    the North," 87–94, 102, 110,
    115–118, 138, 144, 179, 194
Andrews, E. S., 278–280
Andrews, Milton Franklin, 280
Animal magnetism, 73–74, 78–79
Aristotle, 207, 211
Artist's Dream trick, 198–199, 202, 210

Assistants, 111–113, 225–230
Augustine, 14

Bacon, Francis, 27
Baldwin, S. S. "The White Mahatma,"
    259–260, 265
Balfour, Arthur, 252
Ball and Vase trick, 295
Baltass, 299–300
Bamberg, David, 296
Banksy, 293
Barnum, P. T., 110, 136, 192
Barrett, William, 251–253
Basket trick, 103–104
Batavia (Jakarta), 51
Beard, George, 243–244
Beck, Martin, 220
Bell, Alexander Graham, 254
Bergmann, Wilhelmine, 188
Bertram, Charles, 204
Bertram, Ross, 281
Bible, the, 4–5, 7–8, 22–23, 51, 99, 100, 118

Binet, Alfred, 256, 258
Bird imitations, 108–109
Bishop, Washington Irving, 249–251,
    254–255
Black Art, 187, 202, 217
Blackburn, Douglas, 239–240, 252, 255
Blackstone, Harry Jr., 290
Blackton, J. Stuart, 234
Blaine, David, 290–291
Blanchard, Cecilia, 112
Blindfold acts, 72–74, 79, 81–82,
    125, 144
Blitz, Antonio, 110–111
Bodin, Jean, 35, 257
Bongo, Al, 283
Bosch, Hieronymus, 25, 26
Bosco, 134, 138, 140, 309
Bottle Conjuror, 53–54
Boucicault, Dion, 200
Boyle, Robert, 22
Brandon, Thomas, 19–22, 58
Brenon, Mrs., 112
Breslaw, Philip, 60–65, 71, 88, 102, 108
Breslaw's Last Legacy, 60, 61, 64, 65
Brewer, William Henry, 242, 248
Brewster, David, 100
Brookes, H., 81
Brown, J. Randall, 241–245, 248, 249, 255,
    260–261
Brummel, Beau, 138, 140
Buchinger, Matthew, 48, 295
Burns, Robert, 65
Butterfly trick, 103

Card tricks, 21, 24, 27, 35, 46–47, 67, 68,
    128, 184, 188, 220–221, 222, 274,
    276–278, 281–282
Cardano, Girolamo, 27
Cardini, 281
Carlyle, Francis, 281
Carpenter, W. B., 240, 249–251

Catalepsy, 81
Catching a Bullet trick, 174
Cautares, John, 26
Chaplin, Charlie, 235
Charles IX of France, 34, 35
Charlie, Bonnie Prince, 54
Chemistry, 22, 55
Chess Player figure, 136
Chevalier, Albert, 215
China, 10, 38, 41, 101–102, 104, 105
Christian Science, 114
Christopher, Milbourne, 34, 36, 284
Cinema (see Motion pictures)
Clairvoyant powers, 74, 80, 82, 86, 263
Clarke, Arthur C., 165
Clarke, Sidney, 1, 33–35
Close-up magic, 275–276, 281–283,
    285, 286, 290–291, 295, 297,
    300–302
Cobden, Richard, 91
Collins, Wilkie, 103
Colquhoun, J. C., 78
Coming Race, The (Lytton), 206–208, 288
Comte, 133, 134
Comus (Nicolas Ledru), 57, 60, 125, 127,
    130, 140
Conjurer, The (Bosch), 25, 26
Conjurer's Magazine, The (Houdini), 177
Context, 98–100, 106
Cooke, George A., 195, 197, 202, 203,
    206, 216
Copperfield, David, 286–290, 310
Cox, Edward, 82–84, 246, 248
Crookes, William, 246, 248, 249,
    254, 267
Crushing a Woman trick, 229
Culloden, Battle of, 54
Cumberland, Stuart, 261
Cumberland, William, Duke of, 54
Cups and balls (cup and dice) trick, 11, 13,
    17, 19, 24, 26, 43, 86, 126, 275, 282,
    295, 300, 305

Daley, Jacob, 281
Dancing Delft trick, 197
Davenport brothers (Ira and William
    Henry), 192–195, 217, 246, 248,
    249, 254, 259
Davis, Andrew Jackson "The Poughkeepsie
    Seer," 114
De Kolta, Joseph Buatier, 186–188, 198,
    202–205, 217, 221, 287, 308
De Neveu, Colonel, 156–157, 159, 166,
    170, 174, 176
Debailleul, Clément, 300
Decremps, Henri, 64, 281
Defoe, Daniel, 44
Demon Snapper trick, 275
Destroying a Girl trick, 229
Devant, David, 198–199, 202–214,
    217, 219, 222, 227, 232–236, 283,
    303, 306
Devaux, General, 172
Devil in Evening Clothes, 221
Dickens, Charles, 102, 103, 248
Diderot, Denis, 57
Didier, Adolphe, 80, 82, 86
Didier, Alexis, 79, 80, 82
Diminshing marginal utility, 62–63
Dircks, Henry, 190, 191
Discoverie of Witchcraft, The (Scot), 19–21,
    26, 29
Djedi, 1–3, 6, 13
DÖbler, Ludwig, 96–98, 145, 182
Dodgson, Charles (Lewis Carroll), 252
Downs, Thomas Nelson, 220, 230, 302
Draftsman figure, 135, 136
Dunninger, Joseph, 266–267, 270–271
Dyno, 209

Eagle, Barnardo, 87, 90
Ed Sullivan Show, The, 284–285
Edison, Thomas, 254, 263
Edmond, Count de Grisy, 125

Edward II, King of England, 25
Egypt, 1–6, 10, 104–105
Elastic Girl trick, 229
Electricity, 55, 57, 154, 182–184, 319
Electromagnetism, 122, 183, 254
Elizabeth I, Queen of England, 24
Elliott, James William, 276–278
Emerson, Ralph Waldo, 114
Encyclopedia Britannica, 65–69
Envers du Théâtre (The Theatre Inside Out)
    (J-P Moynet), 200, 202
Erasmus of Rotterdam, 205
Erdnase, S. W. (E. S. Andrews), 278–280,
    293, 296, 302
Escape tricks, 193–195, 219–222, 226,
    231, 234, 237, 286
Ethereal Suspension trick, 143–144,
    182, 226
Evans, Henry Ridgely, 4, 14, 33, 202
Everhart, Frank, 283
Exodus, book of, 3, 4, 6, 7
Expert at the Card Table, The (Erdnase),
    278–281
Extrasensory perception, 270

Fact and fiction, 44–45, 49, 53–54, 56–57
Fairbanks, Douglas, 235
Fakir of Ava, 217
Falconi, Signor, 106, 107
False automata, 127
Faraday, Michael, 240–241
Fawkes, Isaac, 46–51, 54, 88, 141
Fay, Annie Eva "Indescribable
    Phenomenon," 246–249, 254, 259
Fay, William, 194
Feats, Bornelio, 28–30
Ferdinand IV, King of Naples, 127–128
Ferguson, Adam, 66
Ferguson, J. B., 194
Fillmore, Millard, 111
Fire-eating, 48, 105, 112

Fitzgerald, Percy, 200–201
Flowers from the Cone trick, 205
Fogel, Maurice, 267–268
Forbes, Sir John, 82, 83, 98, 99, 258
Fort, Charles, 291
Fowler, Gus, 221
Fox, Charles James, 63
Fox, Kate, 113–115, 246
Fox, Maggie, 113–115, 246
Franklin, Benjamin, 55, 59, 74
Frenchman, 115–116, 118
Frikell, Wiljalba, 191
Frisch, Yann, 299–301
Frost, Thomas, 3–4, 14, 32
Fuller, Loie, 217

Galton, Francis, 248, 249
Gardner, Gerald, 35
Genesis, book of, 7–8, 23
George III, King of England, 58, 59, 62
Gerard, Jules, 172
Gladstone, William, 252
Glanvill, Joseph, 5
Goble, George, 80–84, 98, 99, 246
Goldin, Horace, 221, 229, 230, 234
Goldston, Will, 208–209
Gonin, 24
Greece, ancient, 10–16
Growing a Girl trick, 229
Guibal, Adolph, 192
Guillotin, Joseph-Ignace, 74
Gun tricks, 89, 107, 110, 111, 128–129,
    154–155, 165–167, 171, 173–174

Handcuff escape, 220
Harding, Warren, 263
"Haunted Man, The," 189–191
Hay, Henry, 302
Hazlitt, William, 101
Helvétius, 57

Henning, Doug, 285–286, 290
Henry, Mr., 96
Henry VIII, King of England, 19, 21
Herrmann, Adelaide "Queen of Magic,"
    216–217, 223–225, 230
Herrmann, Alexander, 216–217, 221, 223,
    230, 256–257, 274
Herrmann, Compars, 145, 216
Herrmann, Leon, 223
Hertz, Carl, 234
Heteb, Joab, 221
Hindu prayer cage, 236–237
Hocus Pocus (William Vincent), 24–25,
    41–42, 46
Hocus Pocus Junior, 42, 43
Hoffmann, Louis, 148, 179, 204–206, 258,
    273, 294–295
Hofzinser, Johann Nepomuk, 188–189
Hogarth, William, 46
Home, Daniel, 246
Hopkins, Albert A., 202
Horowitz, S. Leo, 283
Horsley, Samuel, 63
Hot air balloons, 69, 70, 75
Houdin, Jacques, 132, 134
Houdin, Josèphe Cecile Elegantine, 132,
    134–135
Houdini, Bess, 220, 226
Houdini, Harry, 149–152, 176–179,
    219–222, 226, 227, 231–232, 234,
    235, 237, 260, 271, 273, 275, 277,
    286, 291
Houstoun, Will, 294–296
Huggins, William, 248
Hume, David, 41, 51–52, 99
Hunter, G. W., 276
Hydrostatics, 16

Ibn Battuta, 38–41
Indestructible Girl trick, 229
India, 10, 38–41, 100–106, 195, 259

INDEX

Indian rope trick, 38
Industrial Revolution, 54–55
Inexhaustible Bottle trick, 143, 162, 179
Inner Secrets of Psychology, The, 263
Internet, 291–292
Invisible Girl trick, 96, 102
iPads, 181–182
Irving, Sir Henry, 203

Jack the Ripper, 261
Jahangir, Emperor, 41
Jamaica, 107
James, William, 256, 269
James I, King of England, 24
Japan, 102–103
Jaquet-Droz, Pierre, 126, 135
Jarrett, Guy, 272
Jarrow, Emil, 281
Jastrow, Joseph, 256–257
Jay, Ricky, 290
Jesus, miracles of, 51, 99
Joan of Arc, 34
Jonas (Conjuring Jew), 57–58, 60
Joseph II of Austria, 57
Juvenile Draftsman figure, 135, 136

Katterfelto, Gustavo, 58–59, 88
Kellar, Eva, 217, 225
Kellar, Harry, 217–218, 225, 230,
    256–257, 260
Kempelen, Wolfgang von, 136
Kia Khan Khruse, 101, 102, 110
Knife-juggling, 48, 105
Kowasky, Madame, 112

Lago, Madam de "The Magic Queen," 112
Lane, Edward William, 104–105
Later Magic (Hoffmann), 204, 205
Laughing gas, 96

Lavoisier, Antoine, 55–57, 74
Le Bon, Gustave, 253
Le Roy, Servais, 221
Lecky, William, 33
Lecture halls, 94, 95, 98–100
Legerdemain, 26–27, 31, 43, 66–67, 108
Leipzig, Nate, 281–282, 286, 295
Leitensdorfer, Eugene, 109–110
Levitation, 38–40, 103, 143–144, 182,
    217, 226, 230, 287, 299, 308, 311
Light and Heavy Chest trick, 153–154,
    162–165, 174, 182–183
Lives of the Conjurors, The (Frost),
    3–4, 32
Locke, John, 50
Lodge, Oliver, 252, 254
Losseau, Valentine, 300
Louis Napoleon, 123
Louis Philippe, King, 136, 145
Louis XVI, King of France, 57, 125
Lucid somnambulism, 79, 81, 98
Lumière brothers, 232, 233
Lunardi, Vincenzo, 70
Lyman, C. S., 243
Lytton, Lord Bulwer, 206

Macbeth (Shakespeare), 203
Mackenzie, Robert Shelton, 123
Maelzel, Johann Nepomuk, 140
*Magic, Stage Illusions and Scientific
    Diversions* (ed. Hopkins), 202
Magic Castle club, 283
Magic Circle, 213
Magic Land of Alakazam, The (television
    show), 284
Magic lantern shows, 232
Magic Show, The (Broadway show), 285
Magie Nouvelle, 300–301
Maillardet, Henri, 135, 136
Malleus Maleficarum, 22
Mamet, David, 290

Mango Trick, 41, 48, 104

Marabouts, 122, 153–155, 157, 158, 165–167, 170–176

Marco Polo, 38

Marconi, Guglielmo, 264–265

Maria Theresa, Empress, 136

Maskelyne, John Nevil, 195–199, 202–204, 206–212, 214, 216, 217, 219, 222, 225, 227, 232, 236, 254, 288, 300

Maskelyne, Nevil, 197, 198, 204, 206–212, 214, 222, 227, 229, 232–233, 236, 265, 288, 292, 294, 311

Maskelyne and Cooke Mysteries, 197–198

Master Mystery, The (movie), 234

Mayhew, Henry, 95

Mediums, 245–249, 254, 256, 259, 269

Méliès, Georges, 233–234, 239, 256, 283, 287–288

Memoirs of Robert-Houdin, The, 121–123, 129–132, 134–138, 140, 141, 144–146, 148–152, 156, 157, 163–164, 168–170, 172–175, 178–180, 183, 195, 227, 289

Mesmer, Franz Anton, 73–74

Mesmerism, 75, 78–86, 98, 99, 106, 114, 199, 318

Metamorphosis, 220

Mind-reading, 71–73, 86, 144, 188, 238, 240, 241, 249–270

Miracles, 14, 16, 51, 52, 99, 118

Miraculous Orange Tree trick, 141–142, 179, 180–181

Miser's Dream trick, 220

M'Kean, Louis, 75–79, 84, 88, 179, 196, 261

M'Kean Senior, 75, 77–78, 88

Modern Magic (Hoffmann), 179, 204–205, 273

Moonstone, The (Collins), 103

More, Henry, 22

More Magic (Hoffmann), 204, 205

Morritt, Charles, 188, 198

Moses, 3–5

Motion picture serials, 227–228, 256, 283

Motion pictures, 232–235, 239, 264, 287–288, 319

Moynet, Georges, 201–202

Moynet, Jean-Pierre, 200

Munn and Company, 202

Münsterberg, Hugo, 263–264, 270

Murdock, 223–224

Muscle-reading, 243, 250, 251, 261

Music halls, 214–215, 218, 220–222, 224, 226, 227, 230, 234–236

My Twin Spirit (N. Maskelyne), 222

Mysterious Lady, The (Georgiana Eagle), 84–87, 90, 108, 112, 196

Nashe, Thomas, 24

Native Americans, 107, 195

Navarro, Raphaël, 300

Neolithic Age, 10

Newton, Sir Isaac, 22

Nicholas, Tsar, 92

Nicholas Nickleby (Dickens), 102

Nider, Johannes, 34

Noriet family, 124

Old Curiosity Shop, The (Dickens), 102

Ouija boards, 241, 263

Our Magic (Devant and N. Maskelyne), 206–207, 210–213, 292, 300

Palming, 308

Pankhurst, Sylvia, 228

Paradoxes, 11, 12, 46

Paris, Comte de, 136

Paris Exhibition of 1844, 136

Pass, The, 281

Passion plays, 27

Pastor, Tony, 215
Pastry Cook of the Palais Royal trick, 142–143, 179
Paul, Robert, 232, 233
Peel, Sir Robert, 91
Penn and Teller, 312
Pepper, John Henry, 189–191, 192, 195, 202, 221
Pepper's Ghost, 189–191, 201, 202
Persecution, 23, 32–36
Phillipe, Monsieur, 97, 98, 102, 133, 134, 140, 145, 179, 182, 221
Pickford, Mary, 235
Piddington, Lesley, 268
Piddington, Sydney, 268
Pigeon trick, 19–21, 58
Pinchbeck, Christopher, 47, 141
Pinetti, Giuseppe, 59–60, 62–64, 71–73, 75, 88, 127–130, 140, 178
Pinetti, Signora, 72, 73
Pitt, William, 63
Plato, 10–11, 13, 14
Pliny, 257
Poetics (Aristotle), 207, 211
Pomponazzi, Pietro, 36
Potter, Richard, 108–109
Powers, Clyde, 277
Priestly, Joseph, 63
Priests, ancient, 16–17
Printing techniques, 56
Psychic phenomena, 6, 84, 239, 246, 255–256, 263–264, 269–270, 317
Psychics, 245, 256, 269
Psycho (automaton), 197, 209
Psychology, 241, 255–258, 263, 269–270, 313–314
Psychology Society of Great Britain, 84

Question and Answer act, 259, 261
Quimby, Phineas Parkhurst, 114

Rabbit from hat trick, 89, 306
Raboid, Rajah (Ray Boyd), 265
Radio, 254, 265–267, 269, 270, 271, 319
RaMayne, Korda (Bob), 265
Ramo Samee, 101, 102, 108
Ramon, Alex, 298–299
Randon, Jacques Louis, 161, 167
Rannie, John, 108, 109
Rational recreations, 56, 85, 94, 98
Rayleigh, Lord, 252
Reatius, 34, 36
Religion, 22, 23, 51, 99, 113, 118
Republic, The (Plato), 10–11
Resurrection, 51, 52
Rhine, J. B., 268
Ringling Brothers, Barnum & Bailey Circus, 298
Robert-Houdin, Emile, 139, 143–144, 148, 225, 226
Robert-Houdin, Jean-Eugène "The Father of Modern Magic," 92, 118–127, 129–185, 190–191, 194–196, 200, 202, 205, 207, 215, 216, 222, 225, 227, 233, 236, 258, 275, 281, 289, 291, 293, 298, 300–301, 308, 309
Robin, 202
Robinson, William, 217, 221
Robinson Crusoe (Defoe), 44–46, 50, 54
Rochester Knockings, 113–115
Roe, Sir Thomas, 40
Romanes, George, 249
Rudolf II, Emperor, 24
Rujol, 133
Rumball, J. C., 81
Rumsfeld, Donald, 303
Ruskin, John, 252

Sachs, Edwin, 281
Sanders, W. E., 280
Sawing in Half illusion, 128, 227, 228, 230
Schulien, Matt, 283

Science, 22, 53, 55–58, 88, 118, 122, 163, 190
Scot, Reginald, 19–21, 26, 28–31, 33, 41, 43, 46, 98, 115, 258, 275, 281, 291, 308
Scott, Sir Walter, 31, 88
Scotto, 24
Séances, 240–241, 246
Second Sight, 72–73, 76, 87, 115, 144, 178, 179, 182, 184, 215, 225–226, 239
Secrets, or Confessions, of a Magician (Robert-Houdin), 123
Secrets of Conjuring and Magic (Robert-Houdin), 147–148, 179
Secrets of Stage Conjuring (Robert-Houdin), 162, 183
Seguier, Baron, 147
Selbit, P. T., 221, 226–230, 234
Selbit Limited, 226, 227
Selim III, Emperor, 128
Seneca the Younger, 11, 13
Separate spheres, ideology of, 113
Sextus Empiricus, 13–14
Shadowgraphy, 232
Shakespeare, William, 27, 203
Shamans, 10, 107–108, 318
Siam, King of, 50–52
Siegfried and Roy, 290
Sleeves, 309–310
Sleight of Hand (Sachs), 281
Slydini, 286
Smith, Albert E., 234
Smith, George Albert, 239–240, 252, 255
Society for Psychical Research (SPR), 239–240, 252, 253, 268
Socrates, 11–12, 316
Soirées Fantastique, 137, 141, 142, 144
Somnambulism, 79, 81, 98
Son of William Tell trick, 128–129
Soo, Chung Ling, 221
Sophists, 11
Spirit Cabinet, 193–195, 230, 246–247

Spirit Paintings, 226
Spiritualism, 113–117, 231, 240, 245, 249, 250, 254, 317, 318, 197193
Sponge Ball trick, 275
Stagecraft, 27–28, 200–204
Stillwell, George, 221
Stodare, Colonel, 225
Street magic, 291
Suffragette movement, 228–229
Sullivan, Ed, 284–295
Supernatural phenomena, 6, 16, 21, 31, 122, 123, 153, 162, 240, 241, 243, 244, 246, 256, 263
Superstition, 88, 122, 163, 165
Suspension Chloroforeeme, 182
Suspension trick, 39–40
Swift, Jonathan, 49–50
Sword-swallowing, 105

Talma, 138
Tarbell, Harlan, 272–274
Tarbell Course in Magic, The, 273–274
Tarbell System, 273
Tearing a Woman Apart trick, 229
Telegraph, 264–265
Telepathy, 239–240, 252–255, 263, 266–269
Telephone, 253–254, 264
Television, 271, 283–291, 319
Tempest, The (Shakespeare), 27
Tennyson, Lord Alfred, 252
Thayer Magic Manufacturing Company, 275, 276
Theaetetus, 11
Thomson, J. J., 252
Through the Eye of a Needle trick, 229
Thurston, Howard, 220–221, 222, 230–231, 235–237, 260, 274, 277
Tilley, Vesta, 214
Tobin, Thomas, 190, 195
Tonight Show, The, 284

Torrini, 125–132, 136, 137, 149, 152, 166, 178, 293
Torrini, Antonia, 128, 129
Torrini, Antonio, 125, 128, 129, 132–134
Torrini, Giovanni, 128–129
Trapdoors, 308
Tree, Sir Herbert Beerbohm, 203
Triplett, Norman, 257, 258
Triscalinus, 34–36
Trois-eschelles, 35–36
Trucs et Décor (Tricks and Scenery) (G. Moynet), 201–202
Trunk trick, 220
Tytler, James, 65–66, 68–70, 73, 82

Underwater escapes, 221
Unmasking of Robert-Houdin, The (Houdini), 177–179, 222

Valdon, Paul, 217–218
Van Buren, Martin, 111
Vanishing Boy trick, 167–168, 174
Vanishing Lady trick, 203–205, 308
Variety shows, 215–217
Vaucanson, Jacques de, 140
Vaudeville, 215, 218, 220, 223–226, 229–231, 234–235, 272, 273, 281, 285, 286, 290, 291
Ventriloquism, 108, 199
Verbeck, 191–192, 205
Vere, Arprey, 32–33
Vernon, Dai (David Verner), 277–283, 286, 290

Vernon, W. J., 81, 86, 99
Victoria, Queen of England, 85, 145
Video, 283, 291–292

Walking through a Brick Wall trick, 226–227, 231, 286
Wallace, Alfred Russel, 252
War of the Worlds, 267
Water Torture Cell Escape, 237, 286
Webster, John, 5
Weiss, Erich (*see* Houdini, Harry)
Welles, Orson, 207, 267
Westcar Papyrus, 2–4
Weyer, Johannes, 36
Wheat, Zack, 306
Wilberforce, William, 113
Wilson, Mark, 284, 286
Wireless telegraphy, 264–265, 267, 270
Witchcraft, 4–6, 18–24, 27, 28, 31–37, 98, 112, 317
Women, as assistants, 111–113, 225–230
Women's suffrage, 228–229
Woolston, Thomas, 51, 99
World Behind the Scenes, The (Fitzgerald), 200–201
Wraxall, Lascelles, 123
Writer figure, 135
Wyndham, William, 71–72

Young Hollander, 107

Zancigs, the, 261

LIST OF
ILLUSTRATIONS

Illustrations are from the collections of the authors, with noted exceptions:

"An Indian Performer sits in the air," page 40, from the University of Edinburgh library.

"Breslaw reveals, in a letter," page 61, from the University of Edinburgh library.

"The second edition of *Encyclopedia Britannica*," page 67, used by permission of the National Library of Scotland.

"Louis M'Kean," page 76, from the Ricky Jay Collection.

"The Mysterious Lady," page 85, from the Ricky Jay Collection.

"An Anderson bill," page 91, from the Edwin Dawes Collection.

"Anderson debunks Spiritualism," page 117, from The Magic Circle Collection.

"David Devant, a Victorian conjuror," page 199, from The Magic Circle Collection.

"In the front row: from left, David Devant," page 210, from The Magic Circle Collection.

"Harry Kellar," page 218, from Mike Caveney's Egyptian Hall Museum.

"Adelaide Herrmann," page 223, from Mike Caveney's Egyptian Hall Museum.

"J. Randall Brown," page 242, from Barry Wiley, the William Rauscher Collection.

"Annie Eva Fay," page 247, from Barry Wiley, the William Rauscher Collection.

"Washington Irving Bishop," page 251, from Barry Wiley, the William Rauscher Collection.

"Alexander, the Man Who Knows," page 262, from Mike Caveney's Egyptian Hall Museum.

ABOUT THE AUTHORS

DR. PETER LAMONT is a senior lecturer at the School of Philosophy, Psychology, and Language Sciences at the University of Edinburgh. He is a past winner of the Jeremiah Dalziel Prize for British history, a former Arts and Humanities Research Council fellow in the creative and performing arts, and a past secretary of the British Psychological Society (history and philosophy of psychology section). He is also a former professional magician, an associate of the Inner Magic Circle, and a past president of the Edinburgh Magic Circle. He has been publishing books and articles on the history and psychology of magic (for both academics and normal people) for more than twenty years.

JIM STEINMEYER has been called "the celebrated invisible man, inventor, designer, and creative brain behind many of the great stage magicians of the last quarter century" by the *New York Times*. He is the author of numerous books on magic and magic history, including the *Los Angeles Times* bestseller *Hiding the Elephant*, as well as *The Glorious Deception* and *The Last Greatest Magician in the World*. He has designed the special deceptions used by many professional magicians and illusion effects featured in many popular Broadway shows. He is the current president of the Academy of Magical Arts in Los Angeles, the private club associated with The Magic Castle.

357